The 6 Husbands Every Wife Should Have

How Couples Who Change Together Stay Together

DR. STEVEN CRAIG

Simon & Schuster
New York London Toronto Sydney New Delhi

Simon & Schuster
1230 Avenue of the Americas
New York, NY 10020

The individuals and individual cases described in this book have been created to illustrate common themes and situations that arise in the author's practice.

First Simon & Schuster hardcover edition February 2012

Designed by Jill Putorti

Manufactured in the United States of America

10 9 8 7 6 5 4 3 2

Library of Congress Cataloging-in-Publication Data

Craig, Steven.
The 6 husbands every wife should have : how couples who change together stay together / Steven Craig.
p. cm.
Includes bibliographical references and index.
1. Married people—Psychology. 2. Marriage—Psychological aspects.
I. Title.
HQ734.C882 2010
646.7'8—dc22 2009051666

ISBN 978-1-4391-6798-4
ISBN 978-1-4391-6805-9 (ebook)

We are not the same persons this year as last; nor are those we love. It is a happy chance if we, changing, continue to love a changed person.

—*ANONYMOUS*

CONTENTS

This book is dedicated to Ronna, my wife and best friend. Through her I've learned that the more we each commit to growing and changing as a couple, the deeper our love becomes. For her, I would gladly change anything about me in any way I could. I consider it an honor, and I love her more than I can possibly explain.

The 6 Husbands Every Wife Should Have

AUTHOR'S NOTE

As both a clinical psychologist who specializes in couples therapy and the author of a book on relationships, I find that people often expect that I am, or should be, an extraordinary husband. Well, let me set the record straight: I'm not. At any given time, I'm just as flawed, selfish, and ornery as the next guy. Sure, my knowledge of relationship dynamics and my training and professional experience working within those dynamics provide me with a specialized set of skills, but those skills and experiences only go so far. Unfortunately, they can't magically transform me into a person who is above or beyond the basic human flaws we all have.

I make this point for two reasons. The first is that it concerns me when people elevate me or anyone else in that manner. Elevating people separates us from one another and implies that others have skills or abilities we can't possibly match. That just isn't true. I've worked with more couples than I can count, and I've seen people from all walks of life accomplish amazing things. I don't want anyone to read this book and assume that the concepts and behaviors outlined here are only accessible to individuals who possess a unique set of skills, insights, or experiences. To assume that would be to sell yourself short, and I don't want you to do that. Everything I describe in this book is attainable by anyone who puts his or her mind to it. *Everything*.

The second reason I make this point is because I want people to understand that, as humans, we are *all* flawed, even those of us who guide others. No one is superhuman. A case in point: While my marriage is the most meaningful and important relationship in my life, it is often the relationship I mishandle the most. And even though I have a wonderful wife and an outstanding marriage, both of us still struggle with our own baggage, poor coping skills, and occasional selfishness. We struggle not because we don't love each other, but because, no matter how hard we try, we sometimes cannot help but pour our own flaws into our relationship.

But that's par for the course, and we're not alone in this. No one can be close—truly intimate and vulnerable—to another person without feeling hurt by him or her from time to time and occasionally hurting their partner as well.

The simple truth is that no marriage exists over any significant length of time without the spouses facing one (and often all) of what I call the Three Big Hurts of Marriage:

1. Occasional painful periods of emotional distance (sometimes minor, sometimes severe)
2. Occasional feelings of discontent, resentment, regret, anger, and/or hurt (sometimes minor, sometimes severe)
3. Occasional threats of emotional or physical infidelity (sometimes minor, sometimes severe)

Whether you're soon to be married or have been married for a number of years, it's important to understand that all marriages at one time or another contend with some or all of these issues. The good news is that these problems don't have to be deal breakers. When handled well, they often make relationships stronger. In healthy marriages, it's the process of working through life's issues that brings the couple together, not the absence of problems.

My wife and I have had to deal with each of the Three Big Hurts of Marriage in one way or another through the years and, as much as I don't want to admit it, sometimes I'm the cause of the problems. At other times, the issues were on her end. Sadly, despite how much we love each other, there are times when we have both taken each other for granted, behaved selfishly, and been verbally hurtful to each other. The two of us have even been, to some degree, on both the giving and receiving ends of breaches in intimacy that were potential (and direct) threats to our marriage.

But, as a team, we've learned not to blame, point fingers, or hold grudges, no matter what happens. Instead, we've come to accept that no marriage is perfect and that problems only remain problems when we're unable to solve them. As a result, our marriage thrives and remains healthy because of our ability to work continually through the hurts and pains caused by our issues—and fix them so they don't keep causing problems.

In other words, our marriage is successful not because it's devoid of problems, but because of all the terrific things our relationship provides to us and all the wonderful things we each bring to the party. This frees us up to see that for every difficult moment, there are hundreds of beautiful ones. Our positive experiences always manage to outweigh our occasional unhealthy behaviors, and this allows us to move forward even in tough times. We've learned that as long as we focus on handling things maturely and growing and changing whenever possible, we're always rewarded with a deeper, more meaningful relationship.

So while my marriage (and I) aren't without flaws, I wouldn't want it any other way. Learning how to handle those flaws more and more successfully has allowed me to grow, and those changes always lead to my becoming a better partner and parent. This book is about how change makes us better. I should know, because I've been there; I've changed in all the ways depicted in this book and will likely change some more as time goes on.

My promise to you is that, if you focus on growth rather than stagnation, maturity rather than denial, and change rather than finding fault, you will discover new ways to love, greater depth in your feelings, and a life and marriage you never imagined.

Have faith in yourself. I do.

Steve

PART I

Change:
The Only Constant

Introduction:

My Wife's Six Husbands

In a way, I'm my wife's third husband. And if we keep doing everything correctly, I'll be her fourth husband sometime very soon. After that, as long as I keep working on it, I will have the opportunity to be a couple more husbands in the years to come. In fact, if I try really hard, by the time she's in her sixties, she will have had at least six husbands—and I will have been each one of them.

This may seem a surprising (if not disturbing) way to begin a book about marriage. But it's really quite simple when you think about it. As people grow, they invariably change. And as they change, the things they need from life and from their relationships change as well. That means the person most spouses need their partner to be when they're in their twenties is considerably different from the person they need their spouse to be when in their thirties, forties, fifties, and beyond.

That's why my wife will need a new husband soon.

Sixteen years ago, when we got married, my wife needed me to be a certain kind of husband. I was fun, carefree, headstrong, and full of dreams and potential. I made her laugh and helped her feel good about herself and her future. She did the same for me. We loved each other and loved how we felt together. That's why we got married.

Then life changed.

Time went by and we grew up. And what was important to us in the beginning was replaced by entirely different priorities. In our thirties, my wife no longer wanted me to be fun, carefree, and the life of the party. She now wanted a guy who was settling down to build a life together with her. She was looking for me to focus on establishing a stable career and to begin preparing for a family. In short, she needed me to grow up.

Then, when we had kids, I had to evolve once more. The husband she needed during the baby years was almost completely different from the husband she first married. This husband had tremendous humility and patience, whereas the one she married was cocky and in a hurry. This guy agreeably changed diapers, watched cartoons, and engaged in long conversations about the virtues of breast pumps. The husband she married couldn't be bothered with those things. The new husband made it a point to be home as much as possible and scaled back on almost all his extracurricular activities. The guy she married spent most of his free time away from home.

As our sons grew, I changed even more. Eventually, I became the kind of husband who enjoyed staying at home on Saturday nights wrestling with the kids and doing horribly messy and pointless kindergarten art projects. I also began to look forward to spending Sunday afternoons (time previously reserved for watching hours of football on television) chasing children through germ-infested habitrails at our local Chuck E. Cheese. During those years, my wife needed me to be more focused on the kids than I was on her because she longed for a guy who loved them just as much as she loved them and who thought of them first—just like she did. Those were years when she needed me to be "daddy" more than she needed me to be "honey." The husband I was at that stage of our marriage believed his family came first, *no matter what*. The one she married put himself first.

It was a lot of work, but I was up to the challenge. Of course, by the time I had this husband mastered, our lives changed again and she needed me to be somebody else. As the years went by and our relationship continued to mature and our children continued to grow, I needed to keep pace. When our children were very young, I needed to be a hovering dad who kept an extremely close eye on the kids. Eventually, as they continued to grow up, I needed to morph into a dad who trusted them to make good decisions and supported them as they ventured further into the world of school, friends, and gradual independence.

As our marriage and our family grew, my relationship with my wife grew as well. Through the years, she became a more confident, assertive woman who had progressively less need for a strong-but-silent man she could lean on. Instead, she wanted a vulnerable and sensitive man who could lean on her at times and value her as an equal.

As she matured, I did the same.

I also began to realize, much to my chagrin, that many of the characteristics she initially loved about me—things of which I was very proud—were slowly becoming the very things she no longer liked! In other words, as we were growing and changing, the reasons she loved me were changing as well. When we first met, she used to look warmly and lovingly at me whenever I said or did something she thought was funny or smart. In those days I knew I could always win her over with a smile, a joke, or a thoughtful gesture. But after a few years of marriage, I started getting those same looks for different reasons. Whenever I would connect with her parents or grandparents, or when I demonstrated how responsible and trustworthy I could be with her feelings and our marriage, I could feel her beaming at me. Then, when we had children, I would catch her looking lovingly at me when I was playing with the kids or changing diapers. Eventually it became clear to me that

that's what turned her on in those days, not that I was cool, fun, or smart!

That's why I like to think of myself as a stock on the stock market. When my wife said, "I do," she wasn't really marrying me; she was marrying my *potential.* She bought low and counted on me to mature through the years (and to pay a handsome dividend). She was investing in my future gains, not in who I was at that particular moment. And who would keep a stock around that didn't improve, mature, and grow through the years?

Of course, I'm not a stock and this isn't about financial paybacks. It is about *interpersonal* paybacks. Marriage is about forming a lifelong relationship that continues to feed your emotional needs as your needs change. The hard part of relationships isn't all the arguments about dirty socks and unbalanced checkbooks; it's having the courage and maturity to change yourself as your marriage dictates.

Soon, my wife will need me to be a husband completely different from the one I am today, and I am eagerly looking forward to it. By the time we're in our sixties, if I'm lucky, I will have been all the different people she needed me to be, when she needed me to be them.

My job as a partner is to constantly reinvent myself, maturely and without resentment or regret. Doing so not only makes my marriage better, it makes my life fuller and it makes me a better person as well as a better husband. If I didn't face and make these transitions, my wife wouldn't want me. Not because I wasn't a good guy, but because I didn't grow up.

I LOVE YOU, YOU'RE PERFECT, NOW CHANGE

When they marry, most people say things like, "I love you just the way you are; don't ever change!"—and they really mean it. The notion that their spouse might change is scary and nonsensical to most newlyweds. Furthermore, popular opinion supports this idea, dictating that marriages fail because people change. But of course people change! All healthy people grow and change as they mature. It's those who *don't* change who find themselves trapped in unhealthy marriages. The truth is, most marriages don't fail because people change, they fail because people *don't* change.

Couples need to change and grow in order to invigorate and rejuvenate their relationship. Despite all we've been told about the power of love to surmount all odds, successful marriages don't happen because two people fall in love; they happen when two people fall in love over and over again with each other. That can only happen when two people change together in whatever ways their lives and their marriage require.

If you accept this basic premise, a lot of the seemingly contradictory pressures of modern marriage make a lot more sense. As a marriage counselor and psychologist with more than fifteen years of experience, I often see men and women who feel like they just can't win. It's as if they're living a life filled with relentless pressure: pressure to stay home with the kids and, at the same time, pressure to go to work and make more money; pressure to drop some of their old friends and old habits and develop new friends and new habits. They also feel pressure to be tough and in charge, but also to be sensitive and vulnerable. They think that if they could just eliminate these pressures, their life and their marriage would be okay again.

Women often say things like, "He knew what I was like when he married me, and now he wants me to be different. He knew that I had a lot of hobbies and interests and that I didn't like spending weekends at home being a couch potato."

"It sounds like he wants a different wife," I usually comment.

"Absolutely!" is the common response.

Men often say things like, "She knew what I was like when she married me, and now she wants me to be different. She knew that I liked to drink and hang out with my buddies and that I wasn't particularly interested in talking about my feelings and stuff like that."

To this, I usually respond, "It sounds like she wants a different husband."

"Absolutely!" is the common response.

"So what am I supposed to do?" they both want to know.

My advice is usually the same. "It sounds like it's time for a change," I say. "It's time for you to become the new spouse he (or she) is looking for—the one you both deserve."

PUTTING IT ALL TOGETHER

This book is based upon a simple but extremely important fact of life: since healthy people's needs are always growing and changing, the things spouses need from each other repeatedly grow and change as well. With that in mind, in the pages that follow, you'll learn something that usually seems both fundamental and fascinating to people once they've heard it: over time, most marriages actually need both spouses to become six different people in order for their relationship to survive and grow.

First we need to prepare you a bit for making whatever changes you decide you need to make. Therefore, in part 1 we will look at why many men and women either resist change, fail to change altogether, or believe that change has a negative effect on relationships. Explaining these misconceptions—and how to overcome them—will help prepare you for developing a productive way of thinking about your own marital evolution.

In part 2, we'll describe how most marriages go through six different major stages and outline each of the six different spouses most successful partners become as they transition through these stages. I will include specific guidelines for how effective spouses can modify their communication, transform their identities, change their activities, and produce new ways of achieving intimacy through the years. By the end of this section, both spouses will understand what it takes to become a great partner and enjoy a long and healthy marriage.

In part 3, you'll learn specific tips for dealing with reluctant spouses, and you'll learn how to customize the information covered in the six stages to fit your unique situation. I'll provide a short quiz to help you identify your readiness for making these changes yourself. Then you'll learn step by step how to create a climate in your home and your relationship that is conducive to healthy change by learning exactly what steps to take. In the appendix, you'll find a Change Worksheet to help you and your spouse work together to identify the specific change(s) you want to make and make the process as smooth as possible.

Throughout, here's my promise to you: I promise not to provide you with superficial platitudes like "communicate better" or "treat each other better," nor will I provide trendy quick fix tools like the "Top Ten Romantic Things to Say to Your Spouse" or the "Five Ways to Get What You Want in Your Marriage."

We all know that tools are only as effective as the person using them. That's precisely why my expensive new golf clubs continue to produce the same dreadful shots as my previous set. It's also why, even when I spend top dollar on paint and brushes, every picture I paint still looks like it was done by a seven-year-old. Tools don't fix problems; people do, and life's most successful people are the ones who best know how to use the tools they're given. I want you to be the best when it comes to using your relationship tools.

I've found that when couples learn better ways to communicate, it's kind of like having a brand-new tool: at first they feel better equipped and newly energized to work on their relationship. But if they have no idea what to do about the underlying problems in their relationship, many end up using their newfound communication skills to express their dislike for each other in a more sophisticated manner than before, ultimately giving up on the new technique altogether.

I don't want that to happen to you. I will show you how mature spouses approach their marriage, and, with some specific tried-and-true methods, how they (and you) can keep love interesting, active, and alive even after many years of marriage.

To achieve these goals, only one thing is needed, but it's an important thing. You will have to be prepared to change yourself, sometimes even when you don't want to.

So open your mind to gaining some insight. When you do that, every tool you use will produce a miracle.

EMBRACING CHANGE:

Growing Together Instead of Growing Apart

Day after day clients come into my office and insist that the reason their marriage is failing is because their spouse changed. From men, it usually sounds something like this: "She's the one to blame for all this. She's the one who's changed, not me. She's completely different from the woman I married, and now she wants me to be someone I'm not. It's bullshit! I am who I am, and that's not going to change. She should know that you can't change people, and you shouldn't try."

From women, it usually sounds something like this: "He's changed from the guy I married. We don't talk anymore, we don't hang out anymore, and we just don't seem to have anything in common. I hate to say it, but I don't look forward to him coming home. Sometimes I wonder why I even married him. I'm not sure why I need him other than for the income he provides."

These men and women are demonstrating two crucial misconceptions. First, they fail to see that everyone changes—at least, we all *should* change. Every healthy person grows and matures over time. Earlier this year I counseled a man who hated the fact that his wife was advancing in her career because it meant she was out entertaining clients several times a month instead of being home with him. For the first ten years of their marriage, she'd been home every night, cooking meals and taking care of his needs and their children's. But over the past few years, she'd taken advantage of an opportunity to pursue professional achievements she had always dreamed of. So, in exchange for only a few extra hours a month, she accepted a promotion and started taking care of herself a little more (and her husband a little less). This change, he asserted, was "destroying their marriage." She was, he said, "becoming a completely different person," someone who "didn't care about the rest of her family" and who "cared more about having dinner with other people than she cared about having dinner with me." Instead of applauding his wife's decision to challenge herself, he treated her as if her desire to grow her talents was catastrophic. You can imagine the emotionally damaging effects that this perspective would have on their marriage and their family.

Men with this attitude fail to see that their own lack of growth is part of the problem. Typically, they become chronically disconnected from their partner and feel increasingly disrespected by the rest of the world. In most cases, unless they learn to view change as a necessary part of relationships, their marriage is destined either to end in divorce or to exist in a perpetual state of conflict and despair.

Women have just as much responsibility to grow and change as men. Many women focus so much on trying to get their husband to change that they fail to see the areas in which they need to evolve. I counseled a woman once who freely admitted to being something of a control freak. Still, the only areas she felt needed to be addressed in her marriage centered on her husband's failings. In her mind, her controlling behaviors were actually virtues that helped her be extremely productive; therefore, they didn't need fixing. It wasn't until her husband filed for divorce that she realized how truly difficult she was to live with, but by that time it was too late.

But, if the secret to a happy marriage is embracing change, why do so many people resist it? The answer is that society fosters many misconceptions about change that encourage people to resist or refuse it altogether, inhibiting many couples' ability to mature and evolve.

Although both genders share the seven common misconceptions about change, as you'll see below, some tend to be more prevalent in one gender or the other.

THE SEVEN COMMON MISCONCEPTIONS ABOUT CHANGE

Misconception 1: Adults don't need to change.

Many people operate from the assumption that they're already grown up by the time they get married. The thought pattern goes like this: you grow up, get married, and raise a family—in that order (well, mostly).

But growing up is a continuous process. People who seem to have magically stopped maturing at age twenty-two tend to be pretty boring. They're the folks who effectively stifle every meaningful conversation among friends by rehashing the same tired stories and plot lines from the past. Sometimes it's a thirty- or forty-something guy who always seems to turn lively discussions about current events into rambling reminiscences of his college days when he and his buddies drank too much and did inappropriate things. At other times it's the perpetually stuck woman who agonizes over the same hopeless dating issues in every conversation.

These people are difficult to have a relationship with because they rarely contribute new ideas that might give the relationship life.

Emotional maturity is closely tied to one's ability to navigate the important developmental changes of life. For example, many experienced substance abuse counselors can determine the age at which a patient started frequently abusing drugs or alcohol because that person remains stuck at that particular emotional age, regardless of their chronological age. When these people turned to substances as their method for coping, they stopped maturing along a normal, healthy path. When emotional growth is impeded, whether by mind-altering substances or any other successful avoidance technique, the result is a failure to mature. And it's no fun to be in a relationship with an immature person.

When people stop growing, their relationships do the same. It's pretty safe to say that if you or your spouse are basically the same person you were ten years ago, or when you got married, then something is not going well.

REALITY: Those who recognize the need to continue developing at every stage of life are the ones who build successful marriages.

Misconception 2:
A spouse who makes changes now won't need to make changes in the future in order to still be a good partner.

On the outskirts of Detroit there's a company that's been an award-winning manufacturer of automotive fuel pumps for more than twenty years. Its fuel pump design consistently receives the highest rating in the automotive world, and its success has historically been phenomenal. These fuel pumps have operated in vehicles made by almost every major automotive company in the world. But over the last five years something happened. Customers started returning vehicles by the thousands to their dealerships because the pump was too loud. In response to the complaints, all the major automotive companies demanded that this company completely reengineer its pump or risk losing their contracts.

So, in a very short period of time, without doing anything other than continuing to produce a fantastic product, this company found itself in highly conflictual relationships with all its major clients. Today, this company is on the verge of losing most of its business.

How did an award-winning design that received accolades and operated successfully for twenty years suddenly become undesirable?

The problem is not that the award-winning product changed. The problem is that the rest of the world changed. Through the years, the other engine-parts manufacturers developed quieter products. As a result, the previously subtle noise of this company's pump now stands out—and that means, despite its excellence over time, this company's product is no longer desirable.

In the business world, this phenomenon is known as "legacy disease," the commonly held belief that what made a company great in the past is what will make it great in the future. Unfortunately in business, in relationships, and in marriages, this just isn't true. Businesses must constantly reinvent themselves in order to remain relevant, and so must people. It's not how good we were in the past that predicts our future success; it's how well we adapt to the present to fit the changing needs of those who matter to us most.

REALITY: Don't assume that the strategies that were successful yesterday will be successful today.

Misconception 3:
Change weakens a couple's bond.

Strong marriages are built on the loving things people do in the present, not on the memories of the things they did in the past.

That doesn't mean you should stop being the wonderful person your spouse married; it means you should focus on continually changing and growing in order to make sure you are someone your spouse would still choose today. That's what you're doing when you make it a point to meet your partner's needs at every stage of life.

And that's where the magic comes in. The biggest difference between happy couples and unhappy ones is that healthy spouses are always creating new bonds and experiences that help the couple stay in love, whereas unhealthy spouses spend most of their time clinging to outmoded identities and behaviors that no longer serve the relationship well.

Most of us have seen adorable elderly couples who still seem madly in love after many years together. Many people think those couples got to that wonderful place because they were somehow lucky enough to avoid having to endure great change. But that's not the case. It couldn't be. No one gets through life without facing significant problems from time to time. Whether it's the challenges of raising children, the pressures of work, or even unexpected calamities like illness and death, no couple can live a long and fulfilling life together without experiencing some degree of turmoil from time to time.

Research bears this out: While one might assume that life traumas such as deaths and severe illnesses would often lead to divorce, most research shows the opposite is true. In the majority of cases, couples who experience a traumatic event report that, while the event itself was awful, its impact on their marriage was ultimately positive. Not coincidentally, they also report a heightened sensitivity to others, closer relationships with friends and family, and a commitment to living life more fully following their tragedy. In fact, happy couples who experience a trauma actually fare better than unhappy couples who are in marital therapy. This phenomenon is likely due to the fact that these couples have developed the ability to cope with change, maturely addressing the problems life throws at them.

In my many years as a therapist and in my personal life, I've polled countless couples about this issue. When pressed, they all say the same thing: they faced numerous crisis periods in their relationship, but the problems they faced, and how they dealt with them, made them stronger. They didn't survive and thrive because they were able to avoid change; they got there precisely because they did change.

Change enables a relationship to refuel itself, whereas love, without a certain amount of tension to keep it interesting, eventually burns out or fades away.

REALITY: Successful couples don't escape difficult times; they change and adapt, forging a stronger relationship.

Misconception 4:
A couple won't need to change because their love will surmount all difficulties.

As a marriage counselor, when I meet young people who are planning to get married, I always politely ask them how they reached their decision. Invariably, the answer is, "Because we're in love." When I ask how they plan to handle all the difficulties that are inevitable, they look at me as if I'm an idiot and simply reassert that they're getting married "because we're in love."

Their response demonstrates an important misconception: many people think that as long as they're in love, everything will work out fine. That's simply not true, and here's why: although being in love is a wonderful thing, it's actually the easiest part of the relationship because it's the piece that occurs on its own—it's beyond anyone's control. Emotions are like that; they just happen whether people like it or not, hence the expression "falling in love." The truth is that our emotions are usually in charge and our rational mind is just along for the ride.

So, falling in love is easy. *Staying* in love is hard. As the years pass and your mate does stupid or selfish things, parents the kids differently from you, or becomes glued to the chair in front of the television set, how do you stay in love with him then? When you have new babies and he sees you, like it or not, as someone who looks haggard, makes no money, and complains incessantly about diapers and sleepless nights, how does he stay in love with you? That's when the going gets tough, and that's the stuff most of us, despite loving each other, never seem to know how to handle.

That's why couples who have spent many years together will tell you the secret isn't being in love, it's figuring out how to handle everything that happens *after* you fall in love. I always tell young couples that being in love is like being on second base: when you're in love, you're only halfway home. Sure, finding love is hard—you have to find a good person, get to know him or her, and reveal your dark little secrets—but marriage is much more than that. A marriage is a lifelong commitment. And isn't the goal not just falling in love, but having a lifelong love affair?

So once you get married, you can't stop there. You have to plan for the fact that your relationship will continually evolve. That means some of your best traits—even attributes that were initially appealing and useful in your marriage—may ultimately become annoying or even detrimental as years go by. In other words, in order to keep your love alive, you will have to reinvent yourself continually.

That's why those who rely on the power of love rather than the power of change to fuel their relationship risk becoming a burden in their marriage.

REALITY: Being in love isn't enough. *Staying* in love happens when you and your spouse work out how to embrace change, solve problems, and treat each other when the going gets tough.

Misconception 5:
Most marriages fail for much more serious reasons than failing to change.

Many people believe marriages fail mainly because of infidelity, emotional abuse, incessant arguing, and irreconcilable differences. As long as they're not experiencing any of those, they figure they're doing fine. I thought this very thing myself for many years, but after fifteen years as a marriage counselor, I've learned that none of those seemingly more serious issues are the primary reasons marriages fail.

Although most couples have a variety of trouble spots (some big, some small) when they marry, often these seem tolerable to people basking in the glow of newlywed love. However, as couples travel along, they face hurdle after hurdle, each of which requires them to adapt, adjust, and compromise. Making these changes takes maturity, respect, and willingness on the part of both spouses. While all of us are slow to change from time to time, repeatedly failing to do so breeds a lack of trust, a decline in respect, and an erosion of intimacy that threatens the core of any relationship. Both spouses start to feel resentful, bitter, and hopeless—which ultimately leads to the more outwardly obvious problems of constant arguing, disrespect, infidelity, and worse.

REALITY: Most of the commonly accepted causes of marital problems are typically symptoms of a greater problem: a couple's inability to grow and change.

Misconception 6 (predominantly female): Expecting your spouse to change is selfish—and besides, it's impossible for men to change.

The most common misconceptions women hold about change in marriage stem from one of two core beliefs: that it is *their* job to change (since men won't—and can't), or that women who attempt to change their mates are being foolish and selfish.

Before women's liberation really took hold in the 1970s, women were taught in many high school home economics classes (and in other ways throughout society) that it was their duty to cater to all the needs of their husband when he got home from work. In fact, to burden him with anything other than his slippers and a cool drink was both selfish and inconsiderate. After all, he'd had a hard day, and a wife shouldn't tax him with her problems, her needs, or even the irritant of conversation.

Although this sort of poison is no longer formally taught, there are still mutant remnants of this rubbish floating around in our culture, and thus in the minds of many women. Women end up tolerating outlandish and immature behavior from their spouse because they feel that requesting almost anything from their spouse is selfish—so imagine how they feel about asking him to change!

That is completely absurd. Marriages are a fifty-fifty proposition, which means each spouse's needs must be equally addressed. If you ask me, men's common arguments refuting this position (such as "I make more money," "I have a stressful job," or "That's how I was raised") are really what ought to be evaluated for selfishness. Amazingly, many women accept these arguments unchallenged!

Our society still expects women to play many different roles and teaches them that the more changes they make, the better things will be. As a result, many women embrace and incorporate changes so well that they risk losing themselves in their many roles. However, as they work tirelessly over the years to change from student to businesswoman, to sex kitten, to wife, to mother, to soccer mom, and then sometimes back to businesswoman, many women devote so much energy to meeting others' needs that they lose focus on who *they* are and what *they* want from life. When this happens, they also lose focus on feeding their marriage—and marriages need just as much food and attention as children.

If you or your spouse feel that one person's feelings and needs should take a backseat in your marriage, I urge you to reevaluate your relationship (and your self-esteem). When there is a significant power imbalance within the relationship, the powerless person inevitably feels left out, depressed, and lonely. *That* is where the marital problems come from.

Often when I'm discussing this point I'm asked if I am really saying that a woman should try to change her spouse. And, actually, I am. I realize that goes against conventional wisdom, but I believe we have to look at that notion from a different perspective. Both people in a marriage will change (or should change) throughout their years together, and each should expect that he or she will have some influence on the changes that occur in the other. The problem comes when we expect our spouse to make a fundamental personality shift. It's highly unlikely that the meek, introverted guy will become the life of the party, or that the unfeeling boor will develop a heart. One shouldn't expect great change in those people, and those who expect those traits to change usually end up supremely disappointed. But the immature guy who wants to go fishing every weekend or the workaholic who spends every evening working instead of hanging out with his family are both in need of, and capable of, a little change. Unfortunately, it's usually his wife who has to nudge him in the direction of growing up if he doesn't do it himself. In a perfect world, we would change by ourselves, but in reality, many of us need a little coaxing. That's often where therapy plays an important role. Skilled therapists not only help couples resolve conflicts, they help them build reasonable expectations regarding change.

I should mention here that a few women use this misconception in an unhealthy and manipulative manner. These women use this predicament to passively get attention and comfort from their friends by positioning themselves as the trapped and helpless victim of a selfish and ignorant spouse. While it appears on the surface that these women resent their husbands for getting everything their way, they actually derive a benefit out of the situation through their continued stories of woe. This game can be painfully limiting for women. Whereas they should be seeking a more mutually respectful relationship with their husband and working to fix things, find common ground, or move on, these women find solace in martyrdom and remain stuck in their ways, continually believing that misery is a cross women have to bear.

REALITY: You can and should seek to change many things about your spouse. Each spouse can be instrumental in helping the other grow and change in a variety of ways.

Misconception 7 (predominantly male): Change is selling out.

Men in general resist change, believing they shouldn't be expected to grow and change because their wife married them for the many good traits they already possess. The idea that they should drop some of their old traits and behaviors feels like an insult to their identity and makes changing seem both unhealthy and unwarranted. To these men, changing means giving in (selling out) or turning themselves into a completely different and subservient person (like a gutless wimp who is "whipped" and can't make a decision on his own). But that just isn't the case. The majority of people who make mature, responsible changes in their lives remain at their core the same people they always were. They keep many of their interests, maintain many of the same beliefs—and even make decisions on their own! All that really changes is how maturely they approach problems and how defensive they become when life thrusts changes upon them.

These men need to understand that changing isn't about giving up old traits; it's about developing new ones. Just because someone settles down doesn't mean he has to give up all the things he used to enjoy.

It's not that men are inherently afraid of or incapable of change; it's that throughout most of their lives, most men endure an unbelievable amount of peer pressure and receive bad advice (presented as sage wisdom), all encouraging them to avoid change. For example:

- **She's trying to control you.** "Whatever you do, man, don't give in to your wife. If you do, it's all downhill from there. She's just trying to control you."
- **Women are nags.** "Women just like to complain. There's nothing you can do about it, and it'll never change so just ignore it."
- **Real men do whatever they want.** When a friend is calling to check in with his wife: "Cut it out, man! I thought you ran your own life. Does she tell you when to go to the bathroom, too?"
- **Don't be a wimp.** "Look at you! You're turning into a woman! You don't have to change; you're better than that!"
- **It's better to ask for forgiveness than to ask for permission.** "Just do what you want and then ask for forgiveness later. That's what I do, and it's working just fine."
- **She'll never be satisfied, so you might as well do what you want.** "Women are impossible to please. There's nothing you can do to make them happy, so just do whatever you want. If you're going to be in the doghouse anyway, you might as well have done what you wanted to do in the first place."

Virtually none of this "wisdom" is true or wise. Nonetheless, these immature and destructive messages abound, constantly discouraging men from growing up and building mutually respectful relationships.

Many of my male clients have told me that even agreeing to see a marriage counselor felt like selling out or was a sign of weakness and incompetence. However, after spending a little time in a therapist's office, they typically come away with the opposite impression; the skills they learn with me actually make them stronger and more capable of dealing with problems on their own.

Those who think change is selling out often secretly believe that their best days are behind them. Operating out of the hidden fear that they won't measure up to the challenges ahead, they hang on to the old times, insisting that change will somehow strip them of their identity.

I sometimes suggest to my male clients that they think of change as branching out. Literally. And just as growing new branches doesn't destroy a tree, but makes it bigger, stronger, and more enduring, so growing and changing makes us stronger, more capable, and more balanced.

REALITY: Change is a normal part of maturing, and it certainly doesn't mean one has to become an entirely different person.

GETTING PAST THE MISCONCEPTIONS

The take-home lesson from all this is that purposeful, continual change by both spouses is vital to marital success. While love, respect, and shared interests and values are important components of an excellent relationship, those traits only go so far. So how can we assess our own and our partner's potential for change?

When I counsel couples who are contemplating marriage, I

suggest each partner take the following quiz to determine how strong the core attributes of openness, maturity, and a willingness to change are in their relationship, themselves, and their partner. Usually I instruct each partner to take the quiz on his or her own and then get together to discuss the answers. That conversation should include more than just a review of the results; it should include a discussion about how and why each person's perceptions of his or her partner may be different from that partner's perception of self.

Change Readiness Quiz

1. How good are your and your partner's coping skills?

You:

a. Very good b. Above average c. Below average d. Poor

Your partner:

a. Very good b. Above average c. Below average d. Poor

2. How flexible are you and your partner in new situations, especially when those situations are beyond your control or preference?

You:

a. Very good b. Somewhat good c. Not good d. Terrible

Your partner:

a. Very good b. Somewhat good c. Not good d. Terrible

3. How well does your relationship tolerate the stress that occurs as a result of these new situations?

a. Wonderfully, with little conflict
b. Good, but some small conflicts occur
c. Difficult, with a lot of resistance and conflict
d. Poorly, with anger and avoidance

4. List examples of times when you or your partner *were not* flexible in a new situation and how that inflexibility affected your relationship, both emotionally and behaviorally:

____

____

____

____

____

____

5. List examples of times when you or your partner *were* flexible in a new situation and how that flexibility affected your relationship, both emotionally and behaviorally:

____

____

____

____

____

____

6. How likely are you and your partner to become more flexible in the future?

You:

a. Very likely   b. Somewhat likely   c. Not very likely   d. Not at all

Your partner:

a. Very likely   b. Somewhat likely   c. Not very likely   d. Not at all

7. How would your friends and family answer the same question about you and your partner?

You:

a. Very likely b. Somewhat likely c. Not very likely d. Not at all

Your partner:

a. Very likely b. Somewhat likely c. Not very likely d. Not at all

8. Overall, how do you rate the ability of you/your partner/your relationship to handle change maturely?

You:

a. Very well b. Somewhat well c. Not very well d. Not at all

Your partner:

a. Very well b. Somewhat well c. Not very well d. Not at all

Your relationship:

a. Very well b. Somewhat well c. Not very well d. Not at all

9. As a general rule, do you and your partner tend to address problems or avoid them?

You:

a. Address them immediately and maturely
b. Put them off for a little while
c. Avoid them as much as I can until they blow up
d. Avoid them even when they start to cause conflicts

Your partner:

a. Addresses them immediately and maturely
b. Puts them off for a little while
c. Avoids them as much as he/she can until they blow up
d. Avoids them even when they start to cause conflicts

10. When problems do arise, what do you and your partner typically do to address them?
    a. We talk about them maturely and usually find a healthy resolution that works for both of us.
    b. We argue about them but do so maturely and respectfully and eventually find a solution.
    c. We avoid the problem and hope it goes away.
    d. We argue repeatedly without gaining resolution.

11. How do you and your partner talk about problems?
    a. We talk rationally and respectfully, acknowledging and appreciating each other's point of view.
    b. We acknowledge each other's point of view but still hold our own opinion as more right.
    c. We yell at each other, call each other names, and shut out, disparage, and dismiss the other's perspective.
    d. We don't talk about problems.

12. When an issue is finally resolved, what typically occurs?
    a. We reach a mutual and respectful accord, with each of us making some degree of sacrifice.
    b. We agree to disagree, but do so with respect and without resentment or attitude.
    c. One or the other eventually gives up in order to avoid further conflict.
    d. We never seem to resolve conflicts.

13. When a problem is eventually resolved, do you typically feel upbeat or beat up?

There is no scoring key for this quiz, as it's intended as a tool to elicit reflection and discussion, not a way to precisely measure the likelihood of success in your relationship. However, your results should be self-explanatory. People who have poor coping skills and are inflexible, resistant to change, and difficult to communicate with make poor long-term partners. Make sure you understand that before you go any farther in your relationship.

You should be brutally honest with yourself regarding the answers to these questions. All of them matter. If you don't like your answers to any of the questions, here are some other things to consider:

- Do you think you will somehow manage to just get past this stuff? (Most people can't.)
- Do you realize that, no matter how good it feels, love is not strong enough to carry a relationship through the long haul? Do you realize that relationships built solely on love are usually doomed?
- Are you prepared and eager to change, sometimes drastically, when your marriage needs you to do so?
- Will you make those changes on your own, or will your spouse have to coerce you?
- Will you be happy about these changes, or will you become bitter and resentful that you "had to" change?

THE DECATHLON THEORY OF MARITAL SUCCESS

It seems to me that many people view their marriage as a marathon that begins when they marry and continues for many years. They see themselves slogging through the difficult periods, never knowing if they'll reach the finish line. I believe it's a mistake to view marriage that way. A marriage isn't a marathon; it's a decathlon. It's a series of many uniquely different races, all linked together, each of which requires different strategies and skills in order to perform well. Thus success in a marriage, as in a decathlon, is determined by how well one achieves in each individual event, not simply by getting to the finish line.

If you view marriage from this perspective, it's easy to see many opportunities for victory along the way. And clearly, the skills that serve us well in one event may be a hindrance in another, just as the attributes in a spouse that are appealing in the early years of marriage often need to change dramatically by the time he or she reaches middle or old age. With this in mind, it becomes easier to switch things up, change things around, and get suited up to meet the challenges of the new stage. Flexibility and awareness become the watchwords. And I promise you, you'll never get bored.

ON YOUR MARK . . .

I hope you'll keep this metaphor fresh in your mind while we explore the stages most couples experience during their marriage in the chapters that follow. You'll learn the goal of each stage, what skills are required of each spouse to perform well during that stage, and specific ways to cultivate those skills.

When things go well in a particular stage, you'll likely be able to see a direct connection between your behavior and attitudes and the specific goals of that stage. When that happens, you should be proud of yourself. When things aren't going well, don't get stuck in blame. Instead, look for clues. Often when things aren't going well in one stage, it's because some things also didn't go well in the previous stage—remember, these stages are interconnected. That's why I recommend you read through all of the stages of marriage, not just the one you're in right now. Many people discover issues they overlooked or ignored in previous stages that are undermining them in their current stage.

Also keep in mind that, as in a decathlon, doing poorly in one stage does not necessarily mean you won't do well in those that follow—or that things aren't going to work out overall. There's always a new stage (a new event) just around the corner and a new opportunity to demonstrate a new expertise. So don't give up! Keep at it; you'll always have more chances to improve.

PART II

The Six Stages of Marriage: *A Road Map for Success*

STAGE 1:

Getting Started

A man can be a fool and not know it, but not if he is married.

—H. L. MENCKEN

As a marriage counselor, I work with clients who are soon to be married, newly married, and long married. However, regardless of what stage of marriage they're in, I find that the majority don't just want to repair their relationship—they're consumed with figuring out whether their marriage (or potential marriage) is viable in the first place. That makes good sense. It takes a lot of effort to make a marriage work, and whether they're just getting started or trying to salvage what they already have, they want to feel sure that their relationship, at its core, is fundamentally sound and capable of positive change.

That's why the first stage of marriage begins long before a couple's wedding day. It starts months and years ahead of the big day when people become mature, responsible individuals who are willing—without resentment, selfishness, or attitude—to put the interests of the relationship above their individual pursuits, without losing themselves in the process. Healthy spouses must be capable of strength when a situation needs them to be strong, flexibility when a situation requires compromise, change when their relationship needs them to adapt, and growth when life requires more from them. Without those traits, a marriage cannot thrive, even if both spouses have other redeeming qualities.

Did you notice that attributes like attractiveness, compatibility, sense of humor, financial stability, and sex appeal—the traits many people seek in a mate—are not included on this list? That's because each of those traits are characteristics found in *another* person. Many people believe that the secret to a successful marriage lies in finding the right person, but this couldn't be farther from the truth. The secret to a successful marriage is in *becoming* the right person.

If you explore the profiles of people on some of the popular dating websites, you'll find ample evidence to support this point. If you read closely, you'll see that "single—never married" people almost always answer the "Biggest fear about getting married" question completely differently than the "single—but previously married" folks do. One would think that, since both groups are single, their answers would be similar, but they're not. People who've been married before tend to report that their biggest fear is growing apart, whereas the people who have never been married report that they fear they won't find the right person.

From this it seems clear that before people get married, the majority of them think that the secret to a happy marriage is finding the right person, but after enduring a failed marriage, they realize that the real secret to marital happiness is finding someone who is committed to growing together as a couple.

THE GOAL OF THIS STAGE

The goal of the first stage of marriage is one of personhood. Whether you're single and anticipating getting married or married already and seeking to improve your relationship, evaluating your and your partner's ability to perform maturely in a relationship is vital to determining the future success of the relationship. Thus, the Getting Started stage involves some careful self-exploration. Are you and your partner (or potential partner) good marriage material? Even if you're madly in love and even if you've been married for many years, if certain specific character traits aren't in place, you'll find it difficult to have a marriage that's meaningful and fulfilling. After all, even the most talented couples counselor on the planet cannot help a client who is unwilling or unable to change.

In my business, I usually find two types of people: those who have never been married who want to know how to choose a good partner, and those who have previously been married (or are currently in unhappy relationships) who want to know how to keep themselves from falling into the same painful relationship patterns over and over. I usually tell both groups the same thing. The best way to choose a mate and the best antidote for making poor choices is to be brutally honest with yourself, even if it hurts. That usually requires people to look closely at their emotional makeup and their relationship habits. Here are some errors couples commonly make that prevent them from getting off to a great start in their marriage.

Denying the Obvious

Many people realize that they overlooked obvious signs of immaturity and selfishness in their spouses. Most either figured they could handle those undesirable traits or assumed they would somehow work themselves out. Not so.

If this is your situation, be honest with yourself and even ask a few very trusted others what they think of the person you're married to (or considering marrying)—and tell them to be straight with you. Then listen seriously to what they have to say. You needn't take everyone's opinion into account or do what they say, but do give the feedback some honest thought. Don't let denial get its hooks into you, or you can easily end up in a bad relationship or, for those who've already been there, right back where you started. Love and emotion are vital in relationships, but make sure your decisions are also based on logic, experience, honesty, and integrity. Decisions based mostly upon emotion, hope, denial, or wishful thinking are almost always decisions that people regret later.

Letting Shame, Embarrassment, or Fear of Failure Influence Relationship Decisions

Many clients tell me that they had a gut feeling that their relationship wasn't going to work, but they dreaded the sadness or the embarrassment of ending the relationship. The way to avoid this mistake is to remember that you are, or will be, married to a person, not an ideal. Chances are, the way that person acts today will likely be the way he or she acts tomorrow and in the future. That means how he solves (or avoids solving) problems today will likely be the same way he'll deal with them in the future. If she bulldozes others today, she'll bulldoze others in the future, and eventually she will bulldoze you. If he lies to others, he will lie to you. And if she resists change now, she likely will resist it in the future.

So don't kid yourself: if you don't like something today, you will continue to not like it tomorrow. Watch how your partner deals with others—family, colleagues, friends, and even strangers. Make sure your evaluations of your future together are based on what your gut tells you about his or her ability to handle relationships maturely, not on your fear of failure or making a change.

Valuing the External over the Internal

Many people (or their families) believe that marrying someone with the same religious, political, socioeconomic, or cultural background automatically gives the couple shared values that will carry them through tough times. This is only true in the most extreme of circumstances. Still, many people place those criteria above their own internal beliefs. With our divorce rate as high as it is (and our marital dissatisfaction rate even higher), one would think that we would make our relationship decisions based on more proven criteria. I believe we must insist on using our own internal compass for choosing a mate. This doesn't mean we shouldn't seek a mate within our chosen religious or cultural domain. It just means that we should use our own criteria of maturity, selflessness, and character as the cornerstone of our decision-making process, not solely the fact that this person fits the requirement of being part of our group. Staying this course can be difficult, as family pressures can be intense, but you owe it to yourself to make decisions based upon the characteristics that are most important for *you* in a mate.

Placing Emotional Needs Above the Merits of the Relationship

Many people marry or stay married because it would be scary, difficult, or painful to end the relationship. But marriages are not a cure for personal dysfunction or loneliness—they are not for people who long for someone to complete them, save them, or fix them, or for those unable or unwilling to grow, change, and compromise. No major decisions born of avoidance ever turn out well. Couples should always evaluate whether they're making decisions in an attempt to avoid bad feelings or in an attempt to grow and mature. Obviously, the latter is greatly preferable.

Assuming They'll Learn to Love Each Other

This old wives' tale is directly responsible for countless failed or miserable marriages. If you don't love the person before you marry, it is highly unlikely that you will magically learn to love him or her once the two of you are tethered together. True love comes when we have the freedom to make other choices in mates yet would still choose this person any day. It rarely, if ever, comes when we are forced to make a relationship work. Some arranged marriages are happy, but it's usually a very difficult situation that only works out when one of the spouses abdicates power to the other.

Learning the Hard Way

Brad and Robin were both thirty-one years old when they came to see me and had been married for five years. Robin was carefree, fun loving, and avoided confrontations at all costs. She prided herself on being "accommodating" and "amazingly flexible," not realizing that these traits are usually most appealing to someone who wants everything his way.

Not surprisingly, Brad was that guy. He prided himself on "not letting anything or anyone get in my way." When they married, he'd been driven and focused. As he saw it, he had a lot of things to accomplish now that he'd finished college, and he was eager to get on with it. Robin interpreted Brad's powerful ambition and inflexibility as signs of strength and stability. She picked Brad in part because she was sure he would handle everything.

Brad and Robin are a great example of people who got married because it seemed like the right thing to do. They had dated for five years, and marriage seemed like the next logical step in their relationship. However, after a few years both of them realized that something wasn't right. They just weren't sure what it was.

When I asked each to speculate on what he or she believed the problem to be, they both struggled to find any answers other than that they fought all the time because of something the *other* person was doing. They did, however, have answers for how they were attempting to solve the problem: each was desperately trying to become more grounded in who they already were.

Brad felt that his strengths were his intelligence, his work ethic, and his ability to take charge of situations. Therefore, every time they had a disagreement, he would explain to Robin exactly what it was that she was doing wrong and craft a solution plan outlining the steps she should take to improve the situation. His plans rarely detailed any changes *he* needed to make other than condescending things like "have more patience with her" and "explain things more clearly." He felt hurt and bewildered that Robin refused to follow his plans and didn't appreciate his efforts.

Brad couldn't see that he wasn't working things out with Robin in a mutually respectful and complementary manner. Moreover, his self-righteous style made it difficult for him to have any mature and meaningful relationships—and the few friends he did have were as self-centered as he was.

While being strong, domineering, and uncompromising are useful life skills on certain occasions, they're extremely detrimental when wielded in a marriage. A marriage is a partnership requiring kindness, maturity, flexibility, vulnerability, humility, and the willingness and ability to compromise and grow. Brad wasn't interested in any of those traits.

Robin was stuck in some immature behaviors of her own. She originally perceived Brad's rigidity as a sign that he was powerful; she would be protected and wouldn't have to make tough decisions on her own. She'd been aware that he had few friends and that she didn't much care for them but figured their relationship would be able to handle it.

Robin felt that her strengths were in her ability to get along with people. Every time she and Brad had an argument, she'd go out of her way to avoid the confrontation, turn the other cheek, and focus on happier moments. "After all," she surmised, "couples are always going to fight, so as long as we don't go to bed angry, everything will eventually just work itself out." Robin, like Brad, was proud of her problem-solving skills and was equally hurt that Brad seemed unimpressed with her approach and her ability to forgive and forget.

What Robin didn't realize was that, although her mate's inability to compromise felt warm and comforting at first, a relationship that shelters people from change is not very good for them. Inflexible and static by nature, those relationships quickly tend to become breeding grounds for conflict, anger, and blame.

Far too often women like Robin are encouraged and rewarded throughout their lives for "getting along" behavior and are socialized to believe that as long as they accommodate and smooth things over, everything will work out fine. Unfortunately, going along to get along usually isn't the best recipe for success in a marriage. Take another woman I once counseled named Kelly. Kelly came to me filled with anger and confusion. Her main vexation was that she had no idea why her husband of only six months had lost all trust in her. He was extremely jealous and would become angry and accusatory whenever she wanted to go out with her friends. She described it this way: "For the entire time we've been together, I've gone out of my way to do almost everything *his* way instead of mine, specifically to avoid a huge argument—things like having our wedding the way *he* wanted it, living in the town *he* wanted to live in, agreeing to raise the children in *his* religion. I've given in on most everything we fight about, and now I just want to go out to Chili's once a month or so with my girlfriends on a Friday night, and he has a problem with it! I've given him everything and he can't do even this for me!"

While there was no excuse for her husband's controlling behavior, Kelly had unwittingly taught him that she was incapable of standing her ground on issues that were important to her. Since she had completely acquiesced on every major decision in their short but tumultuous relationship, she had lost credibility. How was he to believe that she'd stay true to her marital vows when faced with a smooth-talking, pushy man at the bar? Sure, she'd promised him that she would never cheat, but it was his experience that all one needed to do was be persuasive and persistent enough and Kelly would eventually acquiesce.

This revelation was shocking to Kelly because she believed that her actions were actually helping to strengthen the marriage and keep it together, when in reality they were having the opposite effect. Someone who cannot stand up for her convictions is hard to trust, and trust is the cornerstone of a relationship. What both Robin and Kelly did not understand was that mature, trustworthy people stand firmly for what they believe in, especially in matters important to them. Those who are unable to do this simply don't make very good mates. Since they aren't strong enough to stick up for themselves, it's highly unlikely that they'll be able to do so for their spouse or for their relationship—at least, that's what their spouse generally concludes, consciously or subconsciously.

Both Robin and Kelly were operating under the dangerous assumption that if they surrendered their personal opinions and subjugated themselves to their husband, he would love and respect them more. This, however, never happens. Most women in relationships like these find their husbands becoming progressively less connected to, less interested in, and less respectful of them over time.

As you might have guessed, both Robin and Kelly ended up divorced. However, we must remember that not all divorces are tragic. In these cases, both of their relationships were damaging to the women's emotional and physical health and involved spouses who were incapable of (or uninterested in) changing. While as a general rule I am not in favor of divorce, there are times like these when it is the only viable option.

Making It Happen: Assessing the Long-Term Viability of Your Relationship

THE FIVE RELATIONSHIP CORNERSTONES

To help couples determine whether their current relationship is likely to achieve long-term success, I've compiled a list of what I call the Five Relationship Cornerstones. These five traits are the most important attributes to look for in both yourself and your spouse. The presence of these characteristics is what separates good marriages from bad ones, even from the very beginning. You'll notice that common axioms like "we enjoy each other's company," "we have a lot in common," or "we never fight" are not included in the list. These platitudes all sound good, but they offer very little in terms of producing long-range success. Note that while these traits are obviously important at any stage of marriage, they are particularly useful when contemplating major decisions like "Should we marry?" or "Are my partner and I really capable of and invested in change?"

1. **Maturity.** Maturity is not defined by things like "has a full-time job," or "can discuss politics," or "says he wants to have kids." Maturity is a healthy state of mind that can be demonstrated in the following ways, all of which are important in a relationship:
   a. **The ability to view multiple sides of an argument.** Mature people recognize that there are many correct points of view in every argument, and they take the time to discover, understand, and respect alternate perspectives. Partners who insist that their opinion, and only their opinion, is correct fail to display a level of maturity that is essential for healthy relationships. People who can't

maturely explore contrary opinions are difficult to have meaningful relationships with over time.

b. **The ability to problem-solve carefully and respectfully.** Successful relationships are made by people who devise mature solutions to difficult problems. Partners who refuse to find workable solutions for resolving disputes produce relationships mired in stalemates and turmoil.

c. **The ability to give oneself to another person openly and honestly.** Healthy relationships require both partners to be vulnerable. Mature spouses share their insecurities, fears, and personal oddities with their partner and respectfully accept their mate's embarrassing collection of the same. Partners who are unable or unwilling to engage in this level of vulnerability typically are also reluctant to grow and change in their marriage.

2. **Flexibility.** Flexibility is not defined by the absence of opinions or the willingness to agree to anything. Flexibility is an assertive choice people make to bend and adapt in an attempt to learn and grow. Some examples:

a. **The ability to compromise from time to time and to do things differently than one would like without complaining about it or keeping score.** Healthy spouses are open to new ideas and embrace learning new ways to think or behave. Partners who rigidly cling to their way of doing things typically become even more rigid as the years go by.

b. **The ability to change one's plans, goals, and even aspects of one's personality if a relationship or situation dictates.** Life is unpredictable.

Flexible people roll with the punches and adapt to life as it comes along without sacrificing their own values in the process. Partners who struggle with the many unpredictable and uncontrollable annoyances of daily life usually experience even greater growing pains when faced with the larger changes life invariably throws at them.

3. **Commitment.** Commitment in healthy relationships is not demonstrated through controlling behaviors or jealousy ("I only get angry because I care so much") or through an unhealthy dependency that involves a complete abandonment of one's own identity, opinions, and goals. Commitment is demonstrated by:
   a. **A concerted effort on the part of a partner to make the relationship a priority, even when it cramps his style or forces her to make unpopular or uncomfortable decisions.** Commitments invariably lead to choices. Mature spouses understand the inevitability of this and embrace it as a positive change in their life. Immature spouses get angry when they have to make these choices and blame others for how these decisions negatively impact their life.
   b. **A pattern of following through on promises and fulfilling responsibilities to the relationship even when doing so is not enjoyable or self-gratifying.** Mature spouses take pride in these decisions, whereas immature ones sulk, complain, argue, or negotiate endlessly.

4. **Trustworthiness.** Trustworthiness is essential in a relationship, but it's not achieved simply by avoiding infidelities and always telling the truth. It is much more than that and includes:

a. **The ability to respect others' feelings, failings, and secrets even when you disagree with that person's values and behaviors.** Trustworthy people are nonjudgmental and refuse to place their own opinions above the feelings and privacy of others. Spouses who place their own values above the values of your friends, family, co-workers, and so on often quickly become untrustworthy because they can't be trusted to treat these people with respect and dignity. It becomes increasingly hard for such couples to discuss issues involving these people because of the other person's lack of respect for them. Eventually, these issues become off-limits, which breeds separation.

b. **The ability to forgive and forget.** We all make mistakes. Partners who hold grudges and continually use their partner's past against him or her are difficult to trust and hard to establish a comfortable intimacy with for any length of time.

5. **The ability to understand and achieve intimacy.** The concept of intimacy is misunderstood by many people; it's not found through sex, shared secrets, or even emotional conversations. Intimacy is found through vulnerability. It's the special emotional bond that occurs when two people are willing and able to open themselves up completely to each other, to share their lives, their feelings, and their peccadilloes without fearing judgment, mockery, or rejection. For a relationship to have long-term success, both partners must be able to operate in this space. Without it, the relationship struggles to ever become something more than two people with shared interests who happen to like each other.

Below I've listed four examples of great ways to achieve

intimacy in your relationship. I suggest you adopt these ideas for yourself and incorporate them into your relationship. Notice how your spouse responds and whether he or she is able to be effectively and appropriately vulnerable in return. How well your spouse or partner embraces these experiences will tell you a great deal about the level of intimacy you will be able to achieve in your relationship. Notice that none of these techniques include the common go-tos like flowers, candy, backrubs, dinner, and so on.

a. **The gift of intimate time together.** Whenever my wife and I are at a formal function like a wedding or party, I make a point at some time during the event of whisking her away to share a little time together, just the two of us. At a friend's outdoor wedding, there was a popular band playing in an open-air auditorium nearby, and my wife and I walked together at the perimeter of the crowd, just listening to the music and talking about how much we cared for each other. At another event, we snuck out and sat in our car in the parking lot (it was winter) and talked about all the things we enjoyed about each other. At a reception in San Francisco, we sat on an outdoor ledge overlooking the city and talked about our dreams for the next ten years. I always make it a point to share these intimate moments with my wife because I know they mean far more to her than flowers, slow dances, or jewelry. Every time we have a special event like this planned, I make sure I use that time to tell her all of the things I love about her and why my life wouldn't be the same without her.

b. **The gift of empathy.** Empathy is one of the most powerful gifts we can give, and it's one we can offer at a moment's notice. People are desperate to be understood, and when you give them the gift of your understanding—honestly and lovingly—they feel intimately connected to you in a warm and special way. For men, showing empathy to their wife sometimes means taking the time to truly understand who she is, how she feels, and what her dreams are. It's also doing things like spending quality time with people in her life (like her grandmother, whom she dearly loves, or her best friend). Note that quality time means actually interacting with a person, not surfing the Internet in one room of the house while she's in another. Sometimes empathy just means enthusiastically supporting her in whatever endeavors she wants to take on, even if you personally think the endeavor is silly. I once counseled a couple who were having numerous arguments about the wife's new foray into a work-from-home business. The husband brought into therapy long lists of documentation to prove that her venture was netting absolutely no income, thereby proving his point that she was wasting her time. What he failed to see was that this activity made her feel hopeful, exuberant, and interesting. He was operating logically in an area that called for empathy. Women, despite their generally better ability to empathize with others, often miss these opportunities as well. The ubiquitous fantasy sports world is a good example. To the casual observer or to the non-sports-minded, the entire exercise is absurd. Still, many men devote countless hours to poring over stats, desperately trying to gain some edge over their imaginary opponents. Well, this silly, time-wasting activity is in many ways no different than the work-at-home venture I just mentioned. It gives the participant energy, excitement, and something interesting (at least to him) to think and talk about. A woman who expects her spouse to sit and listen intently to the nuance of choosing makeup colors for her clients needs to show the same enthusiasm for listening to him choose fantasy football players.

c. **The gift of common ground.** Have you ever had the experience of coming home after a hard day at work and feeling as if you're talking at instead of with your spouse as you try to share the ups and downs of your respective days? Many people spend hours each evening struggling to connect with each other. The struggle is almost always one of finding a common denominator in their experiences. One of the best gifts a spouse can give is a way to find that common ground. For example, a man who is describing a long business day of meetings and unappreciative clients is not really talking about business; he's talking about the frustration of feeling as if he's spinning his wheels. Well, any woman, whether she works or is a stay-at-home mom, knows exactly what it's like to feel as if she's spinning her wheels and dealing with unappreciative people. Spouses who give the gift of shared experiences find a way to relate to each other's daily dilemmas without shifting the focus to their own reactions, opinions, or ideas of what the other person should do to fix the problem. A spouse who only hears the business part of his story (or the housework part of hers) misses a great opportunity to bond over the story's deeper level—and the virtually identical feelings both are experiencing.

d. The gift of integrity. When a spouse clearly puts his own ego aside, or makes significant changes in her character simply because it's the right thing to do for the relationship, it's often perceived as a powerful gift by his or her spouse. We all have strong opinions, emotional baggage, and bad habits. Typically, these are the traits we have the most difficulty changing through the years. When people take it upon themselves to make these changes, either for themselves or for the good of the relationship, they demonstrate a level of integrity and maturity that is hard not to admire. Far too many people spend many years of their life saying either "I can't change it" or "Everyone else does it, so what's the big deal?" when they could be stepping up to the plate and improving themselves on a daily basis.

THE IDEAL MATE IN THIS STAGE

Husband #1: The Good Catch

In order to become good husband material, men have to be both strong and flexible. They must have outgrown many of their self-centered ways and be willing to maturely and respectfully share their lives with another person.

The ideal husband at this stage of life is a young-at-heart guy who is fun and full of potential but also mature enough to be vulnerable, insightful, and comfortable in his own skin. This guy is kind, caring, and easy to talk to, but he's also mentally strong and psychologically sound. He's protective of those he loves without being domineering. One gets the idea this guy could do anything if he put his mind to it.

Wife #1: The Girl of My Dreams

The ideal wife at this stage of life is a vibrant woman who is loving, fun, full of life, and maybe even a little wild or adventurous. She's overflowing with energy and dreams, but she's also very grounded in who she is and who she wants to be in life. She believes firmly in her convictions yet is also eager to learn and grow. She's easy to be with and secure enough to not become overwhelmed or overwrought when things don't go her way. She makes her guy feel that she loves him even when he makes stupid mistakes or acts inappropriately. Her mate feels that he can be himself with her and that she doesn't cramp his style or expect him to take care of her.

SUCCESS STORIES: HOW YOU KNOW WHEN IT'S WORKING

As a marriage counselor, I am constantly asked to provide people with one simple concept to take with them as they start on their marital journey. I usually tell them the following story.

The Story of Two Trains

I like to view two people in a marriage as two high-functioning, high-powered trains speeding along next to each other on two separate tracks. When they first pull up next to each other and look across, they each see a fine-looking train, full of energy and potential, speeding along toward a million possible fascinating destinations. When the couple decide to date, they begin traveling along next to each other, sharing their lives and discussing all the places they want to go and how they want to get there. This is the best part of a new relationship as the two trains explore the world together, side by side. Often, this is when the couple decide to get married. However, it is also at this juncture that many make a fatal mistake. As their relationship moves along, the difficulty of traveling on two separate tracks begins to strain the relationship. Both spouses have plans, goals, and places to go, but the more they pursue those activities, the more anxious they become that their spouse is going to grow apart from them. In time, to alleviate their fear and insecurity, they decide that it would be best to travel along on one track together. So they decide to join their trains, with the woman (typically) jumping on board the man's train, leaving her train behind.

This works wonderfully for a while, but unfortunately, it eventually falls apart in an awful way. As the husband labors to pull this train along, he no longer looks out his window to see a sleek, fast-moving, fascinating train speeding along next to him. In fact, he rarely sees many of the things that initially attracted him to her train in the first place, because her train is long gone and all her dreams and interests are packed up in boxes in the last few cars. That means that all of the wonderful places she was going to go and all of the wonderful adventures she initially presented are now memories buried in their past.

What he does see are all sorts of other trains speeding around, full of dreams and energy and fascinating things to talk about, just like she used be. And that's awfully dangerous . . .

Meanwhile, with all her stuff packed up and stored away, the wife is slowly forgetting who she was and where she was going when her train left the station. At the end of the day, she and her husband meet up to talk but slowly find that they have increasingly less to talk about and even fewer moments of excitement. Eventually, they become more roommates than lovers—and we all know what happens from there.

But it doesn't have to be that way. The secret to a long and happy marriage is this: neither spouse should ever—and I mean ever—give up his or her train. While it is true that, for a relationship to work, both spouses must embrace a certain amount of sacrifice and compromise, it's imperative that those gestures be made in a healthy and mature way that allows for each spouse to remain whole in the process. Compromise is tricky, and few people do it well. Most of the time one spouse gives up his or her train much more than the other, and this typically leads to resentment, discontent, depression, and a variety of other problems. I will discuss more about healthy compromises later, but, at this juncture the point is that relationships require a give and take that is bound to cause conflicts. The goal is to make sure your conflicts are healthy conflicts, not unhealthy ones. Healthy conflicts occur when each spouse has to bend and adapt to keep up with the continued growth of his or her partner—in our story, the strain of making sure their tracks continue to run parallel and close together, despite the many twists and turns they each make in life. Unhealthy conflicts occur when there is stagnation, when one train is speeding along while the other has stopped or dramatically slowed. Unless they're both moving with their own energy, the spouses will lose a vital connection and come to find they barely know each other anymore.

In general, men don't typically tend to be the ones who give up their trains, but they mess up relationships in another way. It's usually guys who come up with the idea that their spouse should just jump aboard their train. Why? Because when there are two tracks, men have to compromise and adapt—they have to change their ways and curve their tracks in a (sometimes drastically) different direction than the one they'd intended to travel. That's a lot of reengineering. Also, to men, it's much simpler to have one driver than two. As the sole drivers, they decide to take the easy route and pursue whichever course they feel is best (of course, without asking for directions or input). In doing so, they fail to create a life that feeds their spouse's needs as much as it feeds theirs.

Even in the closest relationships, both spouses can and must travel along separate tracks. Both people must always have individual goals that they plan to accomplish in life or they slowly become uninteresting. Relationships must bend their tracks in such a way that each train speeds along with purpose and ideally, with joy.

STAGE 2:

We're in This Together— The Young Married Couple

Marriage is like pantyhose.
It all depends on what you put into it.
—PHYLLIS SCHLAFLY

Even though the story goes that people meet, fall in love, get married, and live happily ever after, it rarely goes that smoothly. Many relationships begin to show signs of strain after just a few months of marriage simply because the couple find it extremely difficult to function effectively as a team. Most couples quickly discover that the process of combining two lives into one involves a lot of work and usually requires people to change in ways they hadn't imagined.

Most of us falter in our relationships simply because we weren't taught that we needed to change in our marriages, let alone given the tools we really needed to do so. It's not that we don't try, or that we're incompetent or incapable people; it's that when you get down to it, a marriage is more than just the joining of two people—it's the blending of two *worlds*. And when you consider that those worlds contain all of the beliefs, habits, quirks, attitudes, and expectations not only of each spouse, but also of their friends and families, it's easy to see why most people enter into relationships with very divergent—even opposing—expectations and misconceptions about how to conduct themselves and what the roles of a husband and wife should be, even in the simplest of situations. It usually goes something like this:

Tim's family never had meals together when he was growing up, so he just eats when he's hungry. This habit continued throughout his college years and into his bachelor life, when he was either working long hours and catching meals on the fly or hanging out with his buddies eating takeout and watching sports. To him, this is just what's normal, and he's never thought much about it.

Tim's wife, Nicole, believes that couples and families should eat together. Her parents divorced when she was in grade school, and she believes that families who want to stay together spend time together—including meals. She is hurt when Tim is not available or hungry for the meals she takes time and effort to prepare. When this happens, Nicole expresses her hurt by ignoring Tim for the next hour (based on how anger was handled in her family: "Ignore each other until the other person apologizes or the anger dissipates"). Tim finds her cold shoulder equally hurtful, so he leaves the house and heads to the bar (based on how his family handled anger: "Go away until she cools off").

Nicole experiences Tim's departure as further rejection and even abandonment, which hurts her significantly more than the initial incident. She then withdraws even farther (based on her belief system for handling hurt: "Lick your wounds") and begins remembering all the other times Tim has let her down.

Moping depresses her more, so (again, based on her beliefs about how to handle hurt: "Turn to others who can help you feel better") she begins calling her girlfriends and telling them about what an uncaring husband Tim is. Her girlfriends' sympathy makes her feel vindicated and justified in her actions. In the end (based on Nicole's beliefs about what spouses should do: that her husband should understand how she feels and take care of these feelings), she sits at home sulking and waiting for Tim to come home and apologize.

When Tim gets home a few hours later, he is oblivious to her hurt and the painful emotional spinning she has been going through, because the only thing he experienced was her anger and cold shoulder from several hours before. He (based upon his conflict-resolution beliefs: "Wait it out and things will blow over") expects the situation to be resolved by now. In fact, he is actually expecting an apology from her—not a long, tear-filled conversation. Consequently, he feels blindsided by her tears and falsely blamed for the entire fight. He gets angry and (based on his beliefs about women and relationships: "Women are moody and impossible to deal with") begins criticizing her and saying things like, "You're too sensitive" and "You just don't get it." These just add to the gulf she feels between them.

You can see how this conflict has grown well beyond the events that led to it, as well as the danger that it will color future interactions. This is how couples set precedents that become entrenched habits with a long and convoluted history. Once this momentum gets going, it's easy to see how otherwise intelligent and well-intentioned spouses inflict emotional wounds on each other that take their toll, making it more and more difficult to communicate. Eventually, each spouse retreats to his or her corner, and they begin to grow apart. In time, their disconnection can become so severe that they start wondering why they married their spouse in the first place—all because the interpersonal tools they bring to their marriage didn't equip them to deal with the problems they face.

THE GOAL OF THIS STAGE

The ultimate goal of this stage, therefore, is to build a team: a team that lives together, thinks together, and solves problems together. The couple, above all else, must put their relationship first and focus on strengthening and solidifying their partnership, making sure that everything they do serves the ideals and goals they've established for their family. That means they decide upon their very own set of rules for how their relationship will operate, rules that are uniquely theirs—not those of their parents, their friends, or even their fantasies. It's a tall order to smoothly blend two individual beings into one cohesive, happy, respectful whole, but it is vital to the ultimate success of any relationship, and it is the main challenge in the early years of a marriage.

The Joining of Two Worlds

Once, during my first year of marriage, my wife and I spent almost thirty minutes arguing about whether or not, after finishing a shower, one should leave the valve turned up—so the water comes out the showerhead for the next user—or whether one should turn it down so that the water pours down into the tub. (As you might expect, my opinion regarding the proper way to do this was apparently completely wrong.) Like everyone else, my wife and I also argued about whether the toilet seat should be left up or down, whether the dishes go in the dishwasher this way or that way, and whether the new roll of toilet paper should be installed so as to distribute new sheets over or under.

Even people who have dated for many years and share many of the same general family, religious, and socioeconomic values still bring to a marriage a widely varying set of ideas about married life and everyday interactions and activities that they fully believe in and are willing to defend, from the pivotal ("how to deal with my mother") to the puny (how to load a dishwasher correctly).

It's in these seemingly banal arguments that the problems in this stage really begin. Couples must find a way to live together in harmony while negotiating the many widely different opinions they (and their extended family and friends) have regarding how to behave in all areas of life.

When Kurt and Jackie first came to see me, they had been married just under two years, yet they were already arguing constantly. Jackie was irritated on almost a daily basis with Kurt. As she explained it, she felt that he only thought about himself. He worked all day, played pickup hockey several evenings a week, and spent most of the rest of his free time either on the computer, in front of the television, or working on the house or on his car. Jackie wondered where she fit into his life. She wanted him to spend time with her, to have dinners together, to not spend every night doing things with other people or involved in other interests.

Kurt found these expectations to be suffocating: "When I got married, I didn't think I had to give up my life and my interests. She didn't have a problem with it before we got married. Why is it a problem now?" To Kurt, all that had really changed in his life was that he now had a wife to come home to. He wasn't interested in having dinner together each night and was agitated by the whole idea of it: "Why does she need me to be around so much? If I'm gone for a few hours, she starts calling and asking when I'm coming home. It's like she forgets that I love her. I love her, but I can't take this. The other stuff I do has nothing to do with how I feel about her. Why is she making such a big deal out of it?"

Jackie was also upset with the way Kurt was handling his job. Things at work weren't going well. He hated his boss, felt mistreated by the company, and often remarked that the company was going nowhere fast. Jackie was sympathetic to these problems (she had a difficult job as well) but was distressed that Kurt wasn't doing anything about it other than complain. Kurt's usual response was, "What can I do? It's not my fault things aren't going well." When she asked him about finding a new job, he said there was no use looking for one because "no one's hiring." To Jackie, these responses were incredibly frustrating, and she leaned on him frequently to get a new job or find a way to fix his current situation. That only led to him choosing to stay away from home more often.

Kurt's main complaint about Jackie (other than that she constantly nagged him about his job and his hobbies) was "she checks with her mother about *everything*." In fact, he said, Jackie "can't make a single decision without first checking with her mother." He felt shut out, saying that she never took his feelings into account: "If her mother or grandmother invites us over for dinner, she automatically accepts—even if we were at their house two days earlier."

Jackie's family had historically operated with a very open interpersonal style that contained few boundaries. Jackie's mother had a key to the couple's home, and she often stopped by when Kurt and Jackie were at work just "to help out," straightening up a few things or doing some laundry. She was also eager to offer her uninvited opinion on a wide variety of subjects.

Jackie viewed these behaviors as bothersome but also as a great help. She would remark that her mother was "only trying to help" and that "that's just how my mother is; you're going to have to learn to accept that." Kurt viewed these behaviors as both a violation of their privacy and as proof that his mother-in-law was hopelessly entangled in their lives.

Jackie's response to these criticisms was, "That's just how my family is. My mother and I have always been very close; we discuss everything. And if Mom or Grandma wants us to come over for dinner, what's wrong with that? It saves us money and it's nice that they want to see us. If Kurt actually spent a little time with my mom, he might like her better. I know she can be controlling, but she means well, and I can't just blow her off. If we don't have any plans anyway, what's the problem?"

Jackie and Kurt were dealing with the classic issues many couples confront in this stage of a marriage. Most of the time this has to do with the fact that, almost immediately after marrying, couples move into a new stage of their relationship—one that requires them to reexamine some of their core beliefs and long-standing behavior patterns. This can be difficult for a new couple because it forces each of them to gain a great deal of insight into themselves and to make a commitment to putting the needs of the relationship above their individual needs.

DIFFERENT GOALS, DIFFERENT ROLES

Usually when things go awry in a marriage, each partner has some degree of responsibility. Jackie and Kurt were able to work through their issues once each of them realized that they had to change some of their attitudes and beliefs about how to behave in a marriage. It began with an understanding of what exactly was wrong with the positions each was taking.

Kurt was clearly dropping the ball in his responsibilities to the marriage. Sure, he was taking care of his responsibilities to himself, but he was failing to see that the goal of this stage of marriage is to start working on strengthening the bond of the couple. That doesn't mean he couldn't play hockey, see his friends, or do most of the things he was doing, but it does mean he had to start devoting a lot more time and energy to understanding the needs of his wife and the expectations she had of a husband.

In this phase of marriage, women quickly tire of the fun but somewhat self-centered guy they dated. Now that they've become a team, their goals have changed. During this stage, both spouses need a partner who's working just as hard as they are to make sure that they go places *together*—as a unit. This doesn't mean they have to physically go everywhere together; it means they need a mate who's a team player, who constantly strives to make sure that they make decisions together, and who considers the other in every decision he or she makes (this doesn't mean they have to *do* everything the other says, just genuinely *consider* it).

Kurt needed to understand that every decision he made now affected two people. By not dealing effectively with his subpar job situation, he was dragging Jackie down as well. It didn't matter whether or not he, personally, could tolerate the bad job; the question was whether or not the relationship could tolerate it. Did Jackie want a husband who settled for a dead-end job and just accepted this as his fate? Absolutely not. She wanted a guy who did the right thing for the family, regardless of how difficult the challenge was personally. Jackie was heading toward the baby years and was beginning to evaluate how committed Kurt was to doing whatever it took to make their life (and the lives of their children) as fulfilling as possible. When he adopted an "I can't do anything about it; that's just the way things are" stance, it felt like a mortal wound to her. She couldn't figure out why Kurt wouldn't do whatever it took to ensure the family's safety and prosperity. It seemed to her as though she was the only one thinking about "them" and working toward becoming a team.

As a marriage counselor, I usually find two types of men at this stage. There are the guys who argue their points in a way that starts with "But that's how I've always done it . . ." and the guys who start out saying something like "Well, let's discuss this . . ." The guys who figure out early that they have to start considering what's best for the marriage do much better in their relationships than those who insistently hold on to all of the things they used to feel were important, all the while wondering why the magic is slowly fading.

Jackie was doing some damage of her own. By allowing her family to live inside the boundaries of her marriage, she too wasn't working toward building a cohesive team, and Kurt was picking up on it. In this phase, most men are looking for a stable, confident woman focused on solidifying her relationship with her husband and making *their* home and *their* way of life her main priority.

When Jackie failed to see (and correct) how her mother was invading their marital life, it created a serious rift in her marriage. Despite Jackie's beliefs to the contrary, Kurt's reaction had little to do with whether or not he liked his mother-in-law; in fact, to Kurt, his mother-in-law was "fine." It was his wife who bothered him. Although he wasn't able to articulate it smoothly, Kurt felt betrayed by his wife. To him, what they (the couple) decided should be what mattered, not what her mother said—even if she had a valid point, and even if she knew a great deal about the situation at hand.

To men, feeling competent and capable is a major psychological necessity. They work extremely hard to attain these goals (or at least the illusion of them) and feel hypersensitive and insecure when they feel they've lost them. Having Jackie's mother intimately involved in their daily life reduced Kurt's desire to be home with her and undermined his self-esteem—which, in turn negatively affected his job search by depressing him and disempowering him. He wanted his wife to discuss questions with him, or at least take into consideration the needs of the relationship and not just acquiesce to her mother. When she failed to do this, Kurt felt hurt and withdrew from her.

So, we had a wounded duo here: both felt wounded by the other's refusal to make the couple a priority. Recognizing this was their first step in healing as a couple. Then they had to learn how to take action based on their new insights.

Working Out New Rules with Families

Typically, families don't expect their rules to be compromised simply because one of the family members got married. It's not uncommon for a family to expect that the new spouse will adopt all their rules and traditions and seamlessly integrate into their way of life. So how is a couple to formulate new rules for how "they" are going to operate that are different (sometimes drastically) from the rules of their extended families?

In the case of Kurt and Jackie, this was a big issue. As we worked on the situation in couples therapy, we were able to identify the core problem underlying their disagreements. It turned out that all of their arguments centered on what was "right," instead of what was *right for them*—for the team. Jackie had been raised with this particular family style and assumed it was right. Kurt had been raised with a completely different style that he, naturally, also assumed was right. They were getting nowhere with this issue because each was heavily dug in to their own opinion of what was right. But when two people marry, they have to realize that many of the assumptions with which they were raised either are not "right" or, at least, are not right for the new couple. A couple must create their *own* set of rules that work for the two of them.

Now, here's where things can get tricky: once a couple agrees on their own new set of rules, it's time to start sharing them and enforcing them with their families and friends. Jackie's mother found their request that she call before coming over to the house insulting and demeaning. She added that she felt as if she were being treated like a stranger rather than a mother and that Kurt was brainwashing her precious daughter.

Although it seems extreme, this reaction of betrayal is actually a common one when couples establish new rules with their families. Resentment and push-back are frequently strong. In some ways, Jackie's mother couldn't be blamed for her brainwashing accusation, because even though Jackie and Kurt had both agreed it was best for Jackie's mom to back off a bit, Jackie wasn't strong enough to tell her mother how she felt. Instead, when speaking with her, she would sympathize with her mother's position, saying things like, "Well, Kurt isn't comfortable with it" or "Kurt likes his privacy." Instead of making it clear that the rules of their marriage superseded the rules of their extended family by saying, "Well, Mom, both Kurt and I agree that we would like to run our lives this way . . ." she threw Kurt under the proverbial bus. While doing so enabled her to avoid a conflict with her mother, it put a wedge in her relationship with Kurt. Jackie had to learn how to stand up to her mother without making it be "because Kurt made me." It had to be because she, not Kurt, had decided that she wanted things to be different now.

Balancing family with marriage is a major dilemma for many couples in this stage because navigating that balance almost always creates conflict. While most people will tell you that their marriage comes first, when faced with a situation where they have to put their marital relationship above their relationship with their family, they usually sell out the marital relationship. Then, in order to avoid dealing with the turmoil of going against their family, they try to make their spouse acquiesce to the situation or just ignore it altogether. Sometimes they even blame their spouse for creating these problems ("If he would just cooperate, everything would be fine!").

The greater the dysfunction in a person's family, the more pronounced this struggle can be in the marriage. Most people expect their spouse to adapt to the dysfunction like everyone else in the family does. When the spouse refuses to play along, the tension builds, with each spouse continually pressing the other to just give in. In the end, most couples end up avoiding these sorts of confrontations at all costs, all the while telling themselves that things are worked out. But avoidance only prolongs the tension and keeps the couple from moving forward together in this important early phase.

Essential to building a strong and resilient marriage is that each spouse feels that the other has his or her back and will vigorously defend what they've agreed between themselves. When this doesn't happen, it not only creates problems at this stage of marriage, but it also creates serious, sometimes insurmountable problems in future stages.

Consider the example of Troy and Kim. Troy's family was extremely controlling and openly critical of almost everything Troy and Kim did. In their Young Married Couple stage, both of them learned to just give in to Troy's family and tolerate the behavior, which both of them despised. It never went well when they tried to confront Troy's family, so they figured they could just live with it.

Well, once Troy and Kim entered the Then Comes Baby stage, things got exponentially worse. Troy's mother, accustomed to dictating how Troy and Kim should behave, became increasingly more controlling and critical and would leave long lists of what each of them needed to do to improve their parenting (and their relationship). She would even intervene and supersede their authority when they disciplined their children. Eventually, the situation got so bad that Kim threatened to leave. That's when the two of them showed up in my office.

As we worked together, it became clear that they needed to go back to the challenges and goals of the Young Married Couple stage and make some decisions about their priorities. Importantly, they had to decide whose rules they were going to follow—theirs or his family's—and how they were going to discuss this with each other and his family (and, should the need arise, hers). They also had to acknowledge that not making their own rules paramount in every situation was resulting in each of them feeling angry and disenchanted with the other.

So they sat down and made a list of decisions regarding their family (like bedtime for the children, disciplinary actions, family visitation rules, eating guidelines, and so on). Then they had the tough conversations with his family regarding these rules. In those conversations they laid out their decisions clearly, assertively, and without bitterness or judgment. Some examples of the things they said:

- "Mom and Dad, we very much respect your opinions and your experience, so don't think we haven't heard what you've said, but we have decided that we want to do the following with our family."

- "We would like you guys to respect our rules. We realize that you may not agree with them, but we need to make sure as a family that we create our own rules, ones that we are comfortable with."
- "We are afraid you will feel offended by some of our decisions, but that is not our intention. We, again, feel that we have to make some rules of our own, that work for us."
- "We do not want you commenting on our parenting. As much as we appreciate all the wisdom you have to offer (and how often you are correct), we need to learn these things ourselves. It's our job to parent our kids and to learn along the way, just as you did."
- "Don't think we don't want to hear your opinions or that we are stripping you of your ability to have a relationship with your grandchildren; we want you to have very meaningful relationships with them. We just need to do it in a different manner. The way we are doing it now isn't working for us, and that affects the children."

I wish I could say that this process went smoothly, but it didn't. As expected, Troy's family wasn't pleased. However, even though it caused a difficult confrontation with Troy's family, Troy and Kim came through it together and are more solid and happy in their relationship today then ever before. Interestingly, Troy's family is slowly coming around. The more they see the solidarity and happiness in Troy and Kim's relationship, the harder it is for them to argue with the changes that have occurred.

DEVELOPING A NEW IDENTITY

With each new stage of marriage comes a new identity. In the Young Married Couple stage, the new identity is that this duo is now a "we." This means that every decision they make—yes, *every* decision—now affects two or more people. Although it sounds simple enough, it's an identity that many people find difficult to accept and remember, even after many years of marriage. There's a forty-eight-year-old woman I work with now who has been happily married for many years, yet she still forgets to call and check in with her husband when she's out having a good time and is going to be home later than expected. While her intentions are always good, she frequently gets caught up in the moment and forgets that her husband has no idea where she is or what she's doing. Even after years of marriage, she still struggles to remember that she is a "we."

While many people are simply forgetful, others feel uncomfortable and even resentful about adjusting their independence for the benefit of their relationship. These folks usually feel that standing their ground on most issues is vital to their self-esteem and individuality. Unfortunately, many also end up divorced. In fact, a great number of people get divorced after only a few years (or less) of marriage simply because they have trouble integrating their life with the life of another person. Sometimes it's a function of the couple being unable to work together; sometimes it's the result of a spouse who refuses to compromise; and sometimes it's the result of an individual who truly feels that putting others first is a betrayal of their self.

Many men, for example, have great difficulty integrating their life with another's because they insist on keeping a strong hold of their premarriage individuality and independence. At the root of this issue is often that they feel very vulnerable giving up the power and autonomy that comes with being an "I." Unfortunately, since these men are unable to be appropriately vulnerable, they never experience the even greater power and intimacy of being a unified team. Men who operate this way often have marriages containing long periods of loneliness and discontentment on the part of both spouses.

Women, too, can have difficulty fully adopting this new identity, though usually for different reasons. Many women have problems taking on the new "we" of marriage because they're unable to let go of the "we" they experienced with their extended family. For them, adopting a new identity that primarily serves their new marriage feels disloyal and cruel. In situations where they're forced to choose between their new attachment and their old one, they experience tremendous guilt and fear. The guilt comes from feeling that they have sold out their family. Their fear comes from a deep sense of vulnerability born of the realization that "they can't go home again." To adopt this new identity is to shed the old one. That's both a scary and rewarding experience all at the same time.

Don't get me wrong: it's not that the qualities that initially attracted our spouse become unimportant—in fact, they may be very helpful—it's that those who don't also develop additional tools fail to pull their own weight. When the "we" transition is done well, many couples find that they have a stronger and more fulfilling relationship than the one they had with their families while growing up. Those who do it poorly often find themselves constantly straddling the line between the needs of their marriage and the needs of their original family, an exhausting place filled with conflicts. Usually these people find themselves overwhelmed and feeling very alone in the later stages of their marriage.

Here are the four most common conflicts I see when a couple is not transitioning well into their new identity:

1. **Planning and purchasing problems.** These typically occur when one spouse or the other makes major plans or purchases without consulting the other, usually a clear indication that that spouse is not thinking of the "we" first.

2. **Disentanglement dilemmas.** These typically occur when one spouse or the other has great difficulty making any decisions without first checking with parents or friends. It

also occurs when one spouse or the other is unable to appropriately put the new family ahead of the old one.

3. **Power ploys.** These typically occur when one spouse or the other engages in controlling or selfish acts for the sole purpose of meeting his or her own needs: "Hey, it's my money; I can do with it whatever I want" or "I did it because I wanted to; you're my husband, not my boss."

4. **Identity ignorance.** Some people operate in their marriage with no clue as to the importance of developing a new identity and working as a team: "She can do whatever she wants, and I'll do whatever I want; what's the big deal?" or "Let's keep our money separate. I don't want to have to discuss all my purchases with you, and this way we won't fight about money all the time."

When a couple disagrees, they have to resolve their conflicts in a way that feeds the relationship instead of the individual (the "we" as opposed to the "I"). Why? Because happy, fulfilling relationships create happy, fulfilled people. Two people in a good marriage tend to have an endless supply of energy and satisfaction, whereas two individually happy people in an unhappy marriage tend to end up miserable. After fully considering the input from both sides, spouses have to decide to do what is right for "us."

And then they need to embrace it. That means that couples can't gripe endlessly or act the martyr about decisions that were made for the good of the couple, and it means that they have to assume their new role enthusiastically, including making compromises, communicating differently, and engaging in new interests and new activities on an ongoing basis.

With these goals in mind, I've outlined below the fundamental characteristics of ideal mates at this stage.

THE IDEAL MATE IN THIS STAGE

Husband #2: The Team Player

The ideal husband in this stage recognizes that his sense of fun and adventure, while still enjoyable to his wife, are no longer his main assets. Now his stability and his sense of commitment count the most. Therefore, in order to ensure a comfortable, enjoyable future together, he often puts the needs of his wife and his relationship above his own, or at the very least on par with his own. When he makes plans, he considers her schedule as much as his own. When he spends time with his in-laws, he treats them as if they're part of his own family. If he hates his job, he doesn't just sit around and complain about it, he gets a new and better one. If he doesn't have enough education, he goes back to school. He no longer leaves the office early every Friday and he no longer drags himself in to his 9:00 a.m. job at 9:15 every morning. Nowadays he often shows up to work at 8:30 and occasionally even misses important social events either because he has to work or because he just wants to spend time with his wife. If he and his wife live in inadequate housing, he finds a way to get them into an appropriate home—and it's a home well equipped for a family, not an upgraded bachelor pad or postcollege dump.

This guy realizes how much effort is required to make a relationship work and how devastating it is to a marriage over the long haul when a couple fails to work as a team. Thus he strives to find ways to discuss the important issues in their life and respectfully find agreement in the areas where they differ—as opposed to ignoring them or resorting to power moves or emotional outbursts.

Wife #2: The Relationship Builder

The ideal woman at this stage of marriage is still very connected to her family, but the mature way she handles things without becoming frazzled, overwhelmed, or running to her mother, her friends, or her family is what makes her special and what her partner is looking for.

In the premarriage stage, how she looked, how much fun she was, and how much she excited him is what made him desire her, but in this stage it's something more. A wife who not only looks good but who also competently and reliably handles all the things life throws at her is irresistible. The woman he first met was a woman he wanted to date and to marry. A woman who stands up for herself when she needs to and does the same for him and their family is someone with whom he wants to make a life. A woman who can't separate herself from her family, can't make decisions that respect the needs of their relationship first, or can't take a stand to defend him when he needs to be defended quickly becomes undesirable.

This woman is also an efficient and assertive problem solver. As she becomes more confident in herself and her priorities, she no longer insecurely defers her decisions to others or acquiesces to others simply because she fears that she will make a mistake or hurt other people's feelings.

Making It Happen: Mastering the Young Married Couple Stage

Although most people recognize that they need to learn how to begin working as a team during the first few years of their marriage, often they miss the real-life opportunities to do so. That can be disastrous in many cases because there are certain skills that, while important in all stages of marriage, are vitally important in this stage. The remainder of this chapter will outline the specific skills couples need to develop in this stage and provide real-life examples of how to employ these in daily life.

COMMUNICATION SKILLS FOR THE YOUNG MARRIED COUPLE STAGE

Despite managing to find a mate, get married, and function reasonably well in life, most people still enter the early years of their marriage with relatively poor communication skills. Improving these skills is an essential part of succeeding in a marriage and, because it's always a work in progress, requires perseverance, patience, and a bit of humility. Some communication skills, however, are more important at this stage than others because these particular skills play a crucial role in helping the couple effectively build a cohesive, mutually respectful partnership. The following illustrates this point well.

Once, during the early years of my marriage, I crawled into bed late on a violently stormy night only to have my wife innocently ask me if I had remembered to take the trash out to the curb. Well, of course I had forgotten—for probably the fifth time in ten weeks! So, being the stubborn, newly married man I was at the time, I grumbled something about not forgetting it next week and then rolled over and tried to go to sleep.

As you might expect, that didn't go over well. Before long, we were in a heated argument regarding both my negligence with the garbage and my apparent lack of interest in correcting this egregious flaw in my character.

My response to all this was to leap out of bed and stomp downstairs to take out the garbage—in the pouring rain. After getting thoroughly and satisfyingly soaked, I returned to the room, leapt back into bed with dripping wet hair, and declared, "There! Are you happy now?"

Well, of course she wasn't happy, and neither was I. After all, my solution to the problem wasn't really a solution; it was an immature and angry way of dealing with my absentmindedness. It also missed the point. The problem wasn't really whether or not the garbage was put out; it was whether we were going to find a constructive way to talk about what this argument was really all about. My wife didn't really need me to take out the garbage at that moment; she needed me to understand why my repeated forgetting bothered her so much. It was important for her to know that I was a team player, aware of all the things I needed to do around the house and responsible enough to take care of them without a reminder. This mattered to her not because she was a control freak about the garbage, but because she was trying to figure out how much she could trust me to pull my weight. We were in the beginning stages of a lifelong journey together, and everything—even small, stupid things like taking out the garbage—added up to an impression of how responsible and proactive I was going to be in our life together. If I couldn't be responsible enough to remember to take out the garbage once a week, how was I ever going to be responsible enough to handle her, the children, and everything else that comes along with having a family?

In hindsight, it all seems ridiculous now, but I realize today that during that period we were both putting each other through mini trust exercises all the time. Our marriage was still new and, whether we were fully aware of it or not, we were both very insecure in our relationship. Despite the commitments we'd made on our wedding day, and all the time we'd spent together before and afterward, we were both still testing each other in our own separate, sometimes obscure ways.

Unfortunately, this type of behavior is both common and necessary. As couples move through the Young Married Couple stage, they're establishing lifelong patterns and precedents for how they're going to discuss and handle most issues. That's why everything—even something as pedestrian as not taking out the garbage—seems so important: because it is.

That's why mastering certain communication skills is of paramount importance during this stage. The following are some specific communication skills couples in this stage of marriage need to become proficient in so these minitests don't become flashpoints for fights—or worse, entrenched signs of deeper problems.

Understand First, React Second

Some of the most common communication errors spouses make at this stage are errors of certainty. Often spouses feel certain they know exactly what their spouse said, exactly what their spouse *really* meant, and exactly what their spouse is feeling, thinking, and intending. Usually, they're correct only a fraction of the time.

As I've mentioned, the great challenge for Young Marrieds is finding a way to blend two separate people into one productive, smoothly functioning team. When spouses make significant errors in communication, compounded by fundamentally different interpretations of what's being said, you can imagine how quickly the team can become derailed. Couples can avoid that by remembering two things. First, you're not alone: everyone makes these types of errors—everyone! The sooner you accept this and try to do something about it, the better. Second, make sure you listen carefully and patiently to your spouse with the specific intent of attempting to grasp your partner's feelings and experiences rather than trying to change his or her opinion, "fix" his or her incorrect thinking, or ignore his or her input altogether. In other words, you seek to *understand first, react second.*

Often this skill is referred to as "active listening," a process in which the sole intent of the listener is to understand what is truly being said and to reflect that point back before responding with his or her own thought—but it is actually much more than that. It's also "active caring": a process of connecting with and respecting each other in a way that few take the time to do. When spouses feel that their partner truly cares about them, understands them, and takes the time to *really* get them, the relationship flourishes.

You can see the positive results in couples who do this well. They clearly respect each other and go out of their way to identify and appreciate their spouse's point of view. If I had asked my wife why my taking out the garbage was important to her and tried to understand her feelings from her point of view rather than repeatedly justifying my own inaction, it's quite possible that we might have spent that time doing other, more enjoyable things in the bedroom that night than fighting.

Active listening grounds conversations in a well-defined feedback loop: after one spouse speaks, the other spouse agrees to first ask questions without getting defensive or clearly restate what he believes he heard his spouse say, what he believes his spouse meant, and what he feels he is supposed to do with the information. The first speaker must concur with that feedback before the second spouse can respond with his own point of view.

Although it seems as though it would be cumbersome and time-consuming, the process actually doesn't take all that much time—and compared to the several hours of fighting that can ensue when things don't go well, taking a little more time is certainly worthwhile.

Let's look at three examples of interactions without and with active listening.

Example 1:
"I Forgot to Take out the Garbage Again"—Without Active Listening

Step One	*Spouse 1* "Honey, did you remember to take the garbage out?"
Step Two	*Spouse 2* "No, I forgot. I'll do it next week. Good night."
Step Three	*Spouse 1* "What do you mean, 'I'll do it next week'! You forget it all the time. It needs to be done! Apparently you just don't care."

Step Four	*Spouse 2* "I said I'll do it next week. Get off my back; I just forgot. I'm not perfect. Why are you always on me about these things? Geez, calm down. It's only garbage."
Step Five	*Spouse 1* "It's not just about the garbage, it's about how you don't do what you say you're going to do."
Step Six	*Spouse 2* "Fine, I won't forget next week. But this is ridiculous! Why can't you just drop it? It's not like *you* never forget things! Do you want me harp on every little thing *you* forget?"
Step Seven	*Spouse 1* "What do I forget? Don't make this about me! I don't blow off nearly as many things as you do! At least I try to do something about it. You just roll over and go to sleep. Now the garbage will be overflowing all week!"
Step Eight	*Spouse 2* "All right, all right, already! I'll do it! [getting out of bed] I'm never going to get any sleep this way anyway. Sometimes you are such a pain in the ass!"

Example 1:
"I Forgot to Take out the Garbage Again"—With Active Listening

Step One	*Spouse 1* "Honey, did you remember to take the garbage out?"
Step Two	*Spouse 2* "No, I forgot. I'll do it next week. Good night."
Step Three	*Spouse 1* "I need to talk to you about this. It bothers me that you forget these things so often."
Step Four	*Spouse 2* "It bothers you? What do you mean? Why does it bother you? It's only garbage."

Step Five	*Spouse 1* "Call me crazy, but I really need to know that you're going to be responsible about these things. I worry that you'll just leave all these things to me."
Step Six	*Spouse 2* "Wow, I'm sorry, I don't mean to dump that on you. I get that you don't want to be responsible for everything. I need to do a better job at remembering these things. I don't want you to worry."
Step Seven	*Spouse 1* "Thanks. I know you're not perfect, but I just need to know that these things are on your mind. Is there something I can do to help you remember?"
Step Eight	*Spouse 2* "Well, I need to remember on my own, but if it makes you feel better, write me a little note to remind me."

Example 2:
"Did You Go Grocery Shopping Today?"—Without Active Listening

Step One	*Spouse 1* (calling from the office) "Honey, I'm hungry. Did you go grocery shopping today?"
Step Two	*Spouse 2* "No, of course not. I told you I was going to be very busy today. Didn't you listen to me? I can't get to everything, you know—I can't just run around taking care of your hunger all the time. I have a life, too, you know."
Step Three	*Spouse 1* "Why do you always have to talk to me that way? I just wanted to know if you went shopping!"
Step Four	*Spouse 2* "No, you didn't. You wanted to see if I was productive today. All I ever hear you say is that I get nothing done while you get everything done. I'm sick of it. Why don't you do your own grocery shopping from now on!"

Step Five	*Spouse 1* "What the hell is going on? This is exactly what I'm talking about: why can't we just have a normal conversation without you turning it into an attack on me?"
Step Six	*Spouse 2* "What I'm talking about is your selfishness. It's always about you being perfect and me screwing something up—and here we go again, you're even making this my fault!"
Step Seven	*Spouse 1* "You know what? I'm just going to call Dave and see if he wants to stop on the way home and get something to eat and watch the game. I'll see you later."
Step Eight	*Spouse 2* "Yeah, why don't you do that. I wouldn't expect you to actually come home and apologize anyway."

Example 2:
"Did You Go Grocery Shopping Today?"—With Active Listening

Step One	*Spouse 1* (calling from the office) "Honey, I'm hungry. Did you go grocery shopping today?"
Step Two	*Spouse 2* "No, of course not. I told you I was going to be very busy today. Didn't you listen to me? I can't get to everything, you know—I can't just run around taking care of your hunger all the time. I have a life, too, you know."
Step Three	*Spouse 1* "Whoa, whoa, slow down. You sound so angry with me. I wasn't saying that you screwed something up. I just figured that if you didn't get to the shopping, I would stop and pick something up for us."
Step Four	*Spouse 2* "Oh thanks, that would be great. I'm sorry I jumped to the wrong conclusion and snapped at you. How about some Chinese?"

Example 3:
"Sunday at My Parents' House"—Without Active Listening

Step One	*Spouse 1* "Honey, we need to see my mother this weekend for her birthday, so I told them we'd come over on Sunday afternoon; is that all right with you?"
Step Two	*Spouse 2* "Great—there goes my whole day. Now I'll have to cancel all my plans. This really pisses me off."
Step Three	*Spouse 1* "What are you talking about? I just said we'd go over there on Sunday afternoon."
Step Four	*Spouse 2* "No, that's not what you said; you said Sunday, and besides, I know we'll be there all day anyway—that's what always happens."
Step Five	*Spouse 1* "That's not true! Why do you hate going to my parents' so much? You're so selfish. Why can't you think of anyone other than yourself?"
Step Six	*Spouse 2* "*I'm* selfish! Look who's talking! We always do whatever you want! Did you stop to think about what I might be doing on Sunday?"
Step Seven	*Spouse 1* "Sure I did—that's why I was checking with you. I specifically said, 'Is that all right with you?' "
Step Eight	*Spouse 2* "No, you didn't. You said, 'We're going to my parents' on Sunday,' just like that! Just like you always do. Now you're just lying to get out of it!"

Example 3:
"Sunday at My Parents' House"—With Active Listening

Step One	*Spouse 1* "Honey, we need to see my mother this weekend for her birthday, so I told them we'd come over on Sunday afternoon; is that all right with you?"
Step Two	*Spouse 2* "Did you say Sun*day*, or Sunday *afternoon*?"
Step Three	*Spouse 1* "I said Sunday afternoon. I don't want to spend all day there. Besides, weren't you thinking of going golfing?"
Step Four	*Spouse 2* "Yes, but I can do it early in the morning if you want to go over there in the afternoon."
Step Five	*Spouse 1* "That would be great. How about we leave around two o'clock?"
Step Six	*Spouse 2* "That sounds good. I'll tell the guys we need to reserve an early tee time."

As these examples clearly demonstrate, things go much better when people take the time to slow down and ask a couple of neutral, clarifying questions before making an independent statement of their own. Those who master this technique tend to progress through this stage of marriage very smoothly.

Master the Ability to Communicate Your Feelings Respectfully, Clearly, and Deliberately

In order to become a productive and cohesive team, each spouse has to be intimately aware of how the other feels in a wide range of situations. Key to that is learning how to reveal our feelings in a productive way. Although it sounds easy enough, the reality is that, when attempting to do this, most people engage in any or all of the following unhealthy behaviors:

- **Being vague, obtuse, indirect, or confusing.** Some people have trouble telling their spouse (or anyone else, for that matter) when their feelings are hurt. Instead of simply stating how they feel, they withdraw, lash out, or become critical, making it almost impossible for the people around them to recognize and address their hurt feelings. Men in particular tend to engage in this type of communication, but whether men or women do it, it significantly hinders the couple's ability to fully understand each other.

  Many women expect their husbands to read their mind and know how they're feeling. Sometimes a woman will ask her spouse a question about *him,* expecting him to recognize that she's really talking about herself. A conversation might go something like this: "Tom, we've been driving for a while; do you need to stop to go to the bathroom?" "No," Tom replies. After about thirty minutes, she starts berating him about how inconsiderate he is for not pulling over for her to go to the bathroom. She expected him to understand that since *she* was asking him that question, *she* must be feeling that way. Unfortunately, most people just don't think that way, especially men. They think, "If you want me to pull over to go to the bathroom, just say so."
- **Becoming overly emotional.** Often when trying to communicate how they feel, people become overcome with emotion and then, through either tears or anger, continue to attempt to make their point. Unfortunately, it becomes very difficult for the listener to hear anything other than the strong emotion being expressed,

so although the listener is able to identify the emotion attached to the subject, he or she misses the deeper content. As a result, half of the communication is lost.

For example, when their wife breaks down while trying to explain how she felt about a particular event, many men come away thinking, "I'm not sure what the big deal is, but I know not to go near that subject again." The marital terrain becomes marked by these no-trespassing areas. Sometimes the husbands even feel proud of their sensitivity in avoiding the subjects their wives find so difficult. Meanwhile, wives are waiting for their husbands to address the deeper issue(s) lying at the heart of their tears.

By no means am I saying that spouses should not get emotional or that they shouldn't express their feelings. It's healthy and productive for all couples to have highly emotional interactions from time to time. The point here is to recognize that when you are highly emotional, it's unlikely that your partner will fully understand your point, so when that particular subject rolls around again (as it always does), you should not feel angry at your spouse for not getting it the first time. During highly emotive situations it's usually best for the couple to step back and take a break, reconvening later to try again in a more levelheaded manner.

- **Being critical, accusatory, or demanding.** Some people rarely talk about their feelings. When they do, they often express themselves in a way that either blames others for causing them to feel as they do, or they criticize others for not fixing the situation. It's very difficult to understand and appreciate another person's feelings when we feel attacked or held responsible for their feelings. Here again, the spouse quickly learns not to explore how the other feels, which leads to further separation.

More than at any other stage in their married life, Young Marrieds must learn how to truly walk in each other's shoes. Some of the best ways to do this are listed below:

1. **Use "I" statements.** Your feelings are yours, not anyone else's. That means that you and only you are responsible for them. Statements like "You did that to piss me off" are not "I" statements. They're "you" statements that blame others for your emotions. Conversations go much more smoothly when people take responsibility for their own feelings. That means saying things like:
   - "I get angry (or hurt) when you do that" instead of "You're a selfish jerk!"
   - "I feel lonely when you're gone" instead of "You're blowing me off, you don't care about me." Note that "I feel lonely when *you* blow me off like a selfish jerk" doesn't qualify as an "I" statement. That's still blaming someone else.
   - "I feel like you think I'm stupid when you say that" instead of "You're acting superior."

2. **Don't beat around the bush.** Identify and express your feelings in a clear and cogent manner. People can't read your mind, and they certainly don't have time to play games. If you want your spouse to understand how you feel, you have to tell him or her. That means making clear statements such as:
   - "I feel hurt by the way you treat me because it makes me feel like you don't take my feelings into account."
   - "I am very angry at this situation, but I am not angry at you."
   - "I can't listen to you well when you are yelling at

me. I need you to talk to me in a respectful way if you want me to understand you better."

3. **Assert yourself.** In addition to stating your feelings, you also need to tell people what you expect from them. So say what you want in a particular situation. Say it kindly, yet deliberately. Here again, people can't read each other's minds. Your spouse isn't likely to know exactly what you want if you don't tell him or her (politely). That means saying things like:
   - "I need you to be a person who thinks of me (or us) first when making plans with others or when speaking about our lives. So, when you do X or Y, it makes me feel like you aren't thinking that way."
   - "I need you to be a person who talks respectfully to others, because you are now a reflection of me. When you act selfishly or rudely by doing X or Y, it makes me look bad."
   - "I need you to behave in a way that is respectful of my feelings. When you do X or Y, I don't feel respected."

4. **Own your feelings and defend your spouse's.** You are now part of a team. That means that all the decisions you make are for the team. If you selectively remove yourself by blaming your spouse in order to avoid conflicts or hurt feelings with others, you're actually undermining your relationship. Your spouse will know when you do this because others will react differently to him or her. Think about how you'd feel if he or she did that to you. So instead, say things like:
   - To your family: "Tom and I have talked about it and this is how we want to do things now" in-

stead of "I disagree with it, but Tom wants it this way."

- To your spouse: "I understand that my family does X or Y and I realize that it's aggravating, so let's agree on how we're going to handle it" instead of "That's just how my family operates. You're just going to have to get used to it."
- To your friends: "I've decided to do things differently now" instead of "Scott won't let me do X or Y" or "If I do that, she'll go crazy!"

5. **Respect your spouse's feelings.** Most spouses aren't unreasonable people who make outrageous demands on their partner's time or lifestyle. If your spouse is unreasonable, you have to determine together what's at the root of it. In most cases, however, if your spouse requests reasonable actions of you, do them. If he wants you to call if you're going to be late, do it. Really, what's it going to cost you? If she wants a phone call during the day to check in, do that. If he wants you to spend a little time with him rather than mindlessly chatting on the phone, make it happen. If she wants you to speak your mind in an argument, assert yourself. Your spouse is telling you how you can make it work. Why not oblige your partner? You'll never interact effectively in a marriage if you're rebelling against each other.

TOOLS FOR BUILDING INTIMACY IN THE YOUNG MARRIED COUPLE STAGE

When couples are young, engaged to be married, or very newly married, sex is their primary form of intimacy. Before they have a common history and shared experiences, all they have that is uniquely theirs is the wonderful feeling that comes from being extremely close to each other. Sex, during these years, is the ultimate expression of that closeness.

However, as they enter into the Young Married Couple stage, healthy couples develop new levels of intimacy in two significant ways. First, the more familiar they become with each other, the better they are at truly empathizing with each other in a variety of situations. This in itself can forge a powerful and unique bond, leading to deepened feelings of intimacy. In addition, as their list of shared experiences continues to grow, they begin to feel an increasingly stronger emotional attachment.

That's what intimacy is all about in the Young Married Couple stage of marriage. To tell you the truth, it's why people get married in the first place. When we fall in love, we believe we're falling in love with a person, but we really fall in love with the sense of security, oneness, and deep connection that we hope this person will bring us someday.

I remember once, about three years into our marriage, my wife gave me a look from far across the room at a family gathering that made me feel absolutely wonderful—so wonderful that I can still remember it today. For the longest time, I had been struggling to describe to her how disrespected and awful I regularly felt when interacting with one of her family members. In response, she usually either defended this person or implored that I just ignore it, neither of which made me feel any better. That day, when she shot me a look that said, "Ouch. I get it now. I get how awful this must feel for you," everything changed. In that moment, I understood that we'd reached a new level of intimacy and I realized that I loved her in a way I hadn't felt before. It didn't matter that she couldn't fix the problem or that it was sure to happen again the next time we were in the same room with this person. What mattered was that *she got it*. She understood. I was no longer alone in my misery. She was letting me know that we were in this together. And that made all the difference. From that moment on, I knew I really had a partner. I knew she would defend me when I needed defending and comfort me when I needed comforting.

Couples who achieve this level of intimacy thrive in their relationship and find themselves comfortable being vulnerable with each other, enthusiastic and embracing of change, and tightly bonded no matter what life throws at them. When I work with couples in this stage, I find that the best way for them to achieve this level of intimacy is to sit down and make a list of the ten most important behaviors, statements, or actions they feel their spouse wants from them. At first, this task seems difficult, but those who take some time and really think about what their spouse feels most strongly about and what, specifically, they seek from their partner to meet those needs eventually come up with a pretty insightful list.

Some couples assist each other in developing these lists. Sometimes they make a date out of it and devote an evening to discussing one spouse's needs, then doing the same the following week for the other spouse. The key is to remember that you don't have to agree with your spouse's feelings in order to support him or her (in the example I shared earlier from my own marriage, I knew my wife didn't agree with what made me so upset, but by the look she gave me across the room at that family gathering, she let me know that she did understand and support how I felt—and that made all the difference). Many people experience long, happy marriages despite having wildly differing opinions on many different subjects. They accomplish this not because they avoid those subjects, but because they support each other and appreciate their differences.

When making your lists, make it a point to drill down deeply into each item and discuss:

- Why each item is so important to you
- How having your partner support you makes you feel
- What specific things you want to see your spouse do or say in the act of supporting you

- How you want to talk about the item when it comes up in your life as a couple.

In the box on this page is a worksheet for you to use with your spouse to complete this task. The idea here is, after a disagreement (or ideally before, if you can anticipate well), write down your answers to the following questions before you discuss the situation. This will allow you to outline your answers to the above bullet points before the conversation gets emotional, and possibly unproductive.

What's Important to Me

1. What specific action, event, comment, etc. was (or is) important to you and why?

____

____

____

2. What specifically do you need your spouse to do or say when this situation occurs?

____

____

____

3. Why is that action so important to you?

____

____

____

4. What sacrifices, changes, modifications, etc., will that require your spouse to make in order to accommodate your request? Why, if at all, will this be difficult for your spouse?

____

____

____

5. What will you say to your spouse after he or she has accomplished this and what will you say when your spouse has completed his or her end of the bargain?

____

____

____

Sometimes emotions heat up just talking about these issues. If that happens, take it as a sign that you've correctly identified the hot spots in your relationship that need some work. Then take a few moments to reaffirm your mutual agreement to engage in this process without anger, resentment, judgment, or criticism. Couples who form the best teams make no room in their marriages for any of these energy sappers.

Next, I ask couples to make a list of the specific changes they want to make in themselves. These can be simple day-to-day activities like drinking less, being on time, spending more time together, or calling each other more often to check in. But they can also be global, interactive changes like becoming more patient, allowing oneself to be more vulnerable, sharing more feelings, or being more supportive.

You might then home in on some specific actions like "I will make it a point to spend at least an hour together each evening" or "I will stop criticizing your family" that would put these global goals into real-world practice. In the end, you should come away with a road map for how each of you plans to change.

Having these discussions and making these lists doesn't guarantee intimacy, but it sure makes for a fertile breeding ground for it. Couples who create these lists and then make it a point to review, add, and remove items every few months or years often find themselves talking more intimately about their changing goals in life and discovering new ways to understand and meet each other's needs.

TROUBLESHOOTING IN THE YOUNG MARRIED COUPLE STAGE

"To Whom Do We Listen?"

One of the biggest challenges at this stage is fending off the influence of outside forces as the couple work to create their own policies and procedures. Almost every family has very specific rules and expectations regarding holidays, religious practices and traditions, time commitments, signs of respect and courtesy, communication styles, financial practices, vacation preferences, and more. Sometimes we aren't even aware of these rules until we bump into them—in the form of repeated conflicts with our spouse.

Recognize that both families will likely expect that you adopt their particular rules and traditions and that they may take offense if this doesn't happen. They may exert a great deal of pressure (overt or subtle) to get you as a couple to adopt their beliefs and habits. Together, you and your spouse will have to address this issue head-on and deal with it maturely, confidently, and clearly.

It's best to think these things through in advance and have a clear, mutually agreed plan in mind rather than wait until the situation comes up. That way, you won't be blindsided if, for example, your mother calls and says, "Now, when are the two of you planning to be here for Thanksgiving?" The difficulty in this question is not the "what time" part of it. It's the presumption that you're coming in the first place. If you and your spouse have not previously decided whether or not you're going to your mother's for Thanksgiving, you immediately have a sensitive situation on your hands. If you answer the question by giving her a specific time, you're agreeing to go without first checking with your spouse. If you say, "Well, let me check with Paul first and see what he says," it's possible that you'll let your mother down and, worse, create the impression that you merely acquiesced to your husband—especially if you end up deciding not to go to her house. But if you and your spouse have predetermined your plan, you can quickly bring things to closure with your answer: "Mom, Paul and I have talked about this and we've decided that we're going to alternate years to be fair to both families. We were with you last year, so we'll be with Paul's family this year." Your mother may be disappointed, but it's far more damaging to waffle and appear vulnerable to pressure and persuasion, leave her hanging while you hash things out with your spouse, or make your spouse the bad guy.

Here's one that happened to me. Once, early in our marriage, I was playing softball in a Sunday morning league. Right before the start of the game my wife called me to tell me that her sister-in-law was on the way to the hospital to deliver her second child. "Great!" I said, "thanks for letting me know." Well, about two hours later I got a call from my very angry wife wondering where I was. It seems that, in her family, everyone who is even remotely related to a person going into labor goes to the hospital and sits around in the waiting room anticipating the big news. I was stunned. It never even occurred to me to go to the hospital, let alone to sit there all day fretting and eating deli sandwiches. But interestingly, I was the only one in all of the extended family who didn't show up. That meant my wife was forced to sit there in a small, crowded room and answer pointed questions about my lack of consideration and apparent uninterest in her family. The problem wasn't that it was either right or wrong to go to the hospital (their traditions are their traditions); it was that, since we never anticipated this situation, we had no idea how to handle it in the heat of the moment.

So, sit down together and decide how you plan to handle things in each and every situation you can think of, keeping in mind that whatever decision you make is likely to ruffle someone's feathers. Given that, also decide how you plan to respond to that person and, always, how you plan to ensure that your response protects the needs of the couple. Once the decision is made, commit to it and support it as a team, never allowing yourselves to get drawn into blaming the other for this new behavior.

Here are a few common situations where couples run into problems:

- **Holidays.** Whom do you spend them with? How long do you stay? What traditions are important to you and your family? Are you going to alternate years between families or split the time? Who is going to communicate your decision to the rest of the family and when?
- **Religious practices.** If the two of you are of different religious beliefs, how are you each going to practice your faith, and what are your expectations of how your spouse should handle this? How will your family practice differently from you and what do you expect your spouse to do about it? How are you going to explain this to the members of your extended family? If you are from the same religion, how do your beliefs and practices differ? How are you going to address that?
- **Vacation preferences.** When do you go? How often? Alone or together? Where do you go? How long do you like to stay? What do you do? Who else goes? How do you communicate with others when you are on vacation?

- **Sickness rules.** When one of you is sick, what are the expectations for caretaking?
- **Weekend activities.** How do each of you spend weekends and what are your expectations of each other and others?
- **Daily communication.** How often do you check in with each other and others during the day and how detailed should those communications be?
- **Financial decisions.** Do you make individual decisions or joint ones? What are the criteria?

Make sure that these decisions are truly decisions you reach *together*. If one spouse strong-arms the other or one spouse gives in because he or she dislikes conflict, the agreement isn't really an agreement, and it will eventually fall apart. Remember that these decisions, and how you reach them, form the foundation for the rest of the decisions and behaviors in your marriage. How you raise your children will be, in large part, born of the decisions you make in this stage. How you treat each other during good times and bad will be influenced by these decisions. The degree to which you stand together in the future is set in motion by how well you are able to stand together at the very beginning.

"You're Letting Me Down"

Another big challenge in the Young Married Couple stage has to do with the couple's conflicting expectations of each other. Many men, even though they insist this isn't true, begin, very soon after marrying, to expect their wife to take care of them in many of the ways their mother did. Be it doing their dirty laundry, filling their empty stomachs, putting away their messy belongings, or soothing their wounded egos, they act as if it's their wife's duty to take care of them. The problem isn't necessarily that she won't do these things (some women enjoy this role), it's that most couples don't talk about their expectations ahead of time or as they arise. Instead, they just expect that what they want to happen will happen and get upset when it doesn't.

Interestingly, men who operate independently do the reverse and expect very little from their spouse. This behavior may be an asset or a detriment, depending upon their wife's expectations of her role: some women find this independence liberating, while others feel isolated. Keep in mind that each of you is likely to have quite specific day-to-day expectations of the other—and sensitive feelings attached to them. Talking about these expectations without anger, resentment, or disdain will help you to avoid many of the skirmishes that can occur in this stage of marriage.

"You're Not Who I Thought You'd Be"

In this phase, most people confront the fact that, no matter how wonderful their spouse is, he or she can't fulfill all their needs. Many women are socialized to believe that their husband will be some sort of a knight in shining armor who will shelter them from harm. But the reality is that neither their husband (nor anyone else, for that matter) can save them from all the bad things in life. They can expect him to be supportive and to do whatever he can to protect them—a good husband will march with his wife through hell—but a woman's true shelter is not her man; it's her marriage. By becoming a strong person who uses her own strength and skill to handle things well, she becomes a confident, high-functioning part of a two-person team where both members commit to operating at their best for a common goal. That's an extremely secure place to be. Equally, many men quickly learn that their wife cannot (and usually will not) treat them the way their mother did. Early on in a marriage, men have to deal with the fact that their wives are not going to care for their every need, overlook their rude or insensitive habits, and view them through the same rose-colored glasses their mother uses. The sooner men realize this and grow up accordingly, the better things go for everyone involved. Those who resist find themselves mired in recurring conflicts.

SUCCESS STORIES: HOW YOU KNOW WHEN IT'S WORKING

I once counseled a twenty-something guy named Rob who was struggling to feel comfortable with many of the aspects of being a Young Married husband. He and his wife had been arguing about many of the issues I've discussed in this chapter. Then, one day, he came in and told me the following story. It exemplified the type of thinking that is required in this stage. It went like this:

"Last week I went to another of the many family functions I was telling you about that I always have to attend, even when I don't want to go. But this time I did something I'd never done before. I was going to my wife's nephew's bar mitzvah. [Rob's wife is Jewish, and Rob isn't, which requires him to attend many religious services that differ from his views.] When I got to the temple, I saw the pile of yarmulkes sitting there at the door and everyone putting them on their heads. Well, as you know, I have long felt that, since I am not Jewish, I was not going to wear a yarmulke—and until that day I never had. I always maintained that my presence at the event was enough, and that I wasn't going to wear something that made me appear Jewish.

"But last week I had a totally different thought. It occurred to me that just because I was wearing a yarmulke, it didn't make me Jewish. And it didn't mean I was selling out my own religion. But it did show respect to the Jewish people in their house of worship (and to my wife's family). I'd never thought of that before. I was always so caught up in how I felt that I never considered that I was there to honor the people to whom that day and that ceremony were special. This event was about them, not me. It wasn't my job to make a statement; it was my job to give the gift of honor and respect to my wife and her family. Now it seems silly that I made such a big deal about it. Why was I only able to see how it affected *me*?"

A Brief Note Regarding Marriages Without Children

Because most marriages eventually include children, Stages Three through Five will focus primarily on the impact children have on a marriage. However, it is important to note that the material included there is still pertinent to couples without children. Childless couples are no different from any other couple in that all couples have to grow and change throughout their marriage. Couples without children still go through each of the stages I've described in this book, with slight modifications during the Then Comes Baby and the Family Ties stages, during which they gain the knowledge and growth of this stage through different experiences than through child rearing.

Couples do not need to have a child in order to find things to bond over, share, or create. Life is filled with opportunities to experience the shared responsibility of caring for someone or something and for nurturing the resulting unity through the years. Couples without children fill their lives with hobbies, volunteer work, friends, careers, adventures, and a variety of other shared experiences, all of which bring meaning and intimacy to their relationship.

Many childless couples do this very well. It may be a passion for travel—one couple I know remember vividly how they sat for several hours gazing at a lake in Maine at sunset, memorizing together all the colors they could see in the water, trees, sky, and land. It may be a shared sport. It may be a love for entertaining, reading, museums, or a collection they nurture and expand. They may be devoted to a pet. Or to a cause. The point is, childless couples, just like those with children, have focal points of common interests that make them laugh, wonder, ponder, work with passion, play with vigor, and marvel.

STAGE 3:

Then Comes Baby

Having children is wonderful and all, but in terms of your marriage and your life, it's like riding along on your bike and having someone throw a stick in your spokes—everything goes head over heels.

—KIM, AGE THIRTY-EIGHT

Many years ago, as a psychology graduate student, I learned that, even though it may appear otherwise, people don't just suddenly snap and "go crazy." They gradually fall into unhealthy or illogical thinking patterns and eventually lose touch with reality. In other words, people dance on the edge of sanity before eventually plunging over the cliff.

After raising two colicky babies, however, I'm certain that whoever came up with that theory never had children. In the middle of the night, a screaming, writhing, inconsolable baby can throw an otherwise sane person over the cliff in a matter of minutes. Sometimes, he can even erode the sanity of two people simultaneously.

One night, several months after our second son was born, after a brutal two hours (2:00 a.m. to 4:00 a.m.) of trying to console my crying, sleepless son, I simply couldn't take it anymore. Head pounding and hands shaking, I gently placed my still-screaming son in his crib and staggered down the hallway toward my bedroom to bury my head deeply under a mound of pillows.

That was wishful thinking. Before reaching the bedroom, I was accosted by my bleary-eyed wife, who, upon realizing that I was coming back to bed, decided right then and there to leap out of bed and have some sort of an emotional breakdown at my expense.

She stood before me in the hallway, hair all messed up and huge circles under her eyes, and began screaming at me feverishly and endlessly about some minor thing I'd done the previous day that I didn't even recall doing.

Not only was I not interested in hearing about this (or anything else) at 4:00 a.m., but with two hours of wailing still ringing in my ears, I *certainly* wasn't interested in hearing how I wasn't helping out enough around the house. But the only thing my beleaguered brain could think of to do to end the madness was to either reach out and put my hand over her mouth (which even in my weakened state I understood to be an extremely dangerous and unwise proposition) or to run screaming from the house and never return.

Since neither option was acceptable, as she stood there waving her arms and shouting about something that was apparently very important to her, I proceeded to have an odd out-of-body experience in which I was unable to hear her words but could only see her mouth moving in a weird slow motion.

Looking back, I'm not sure which one of us was crazier at that moment: the screaming woman with the bloodshot eyes or the strangely detached man with the vacant expression. Either way, it was clear neither of us was functioning very well. We were both overwhelmed people who desperately needed emotional support, but since we both were such a mess, neither of us was in any shape to take care of the other. That left us feeling something we never imagined we'd feel once we had children: alone. It was sad but true: the more people we added to the family, the more alone and disconnected we felt.

Fortunately, we eventually resolved it all, but only after we figured a few things out. The problem was that this was a dilemma neither of us had anticipated. We knew having children would be a lot of work, but we didn't realize how much it would force each of us to change and how, in turn, that would require our relationship to change. Even though we loved each other and had logged years of relationship experience together, over the course of just a few months, many of the building blocks of our relationship had begun to crumble. We weren't communicating very well, and we had stopped listening to each other effectively. We had also stopped explaining our needs well to each other, and neither of us had a clear idea of what the other wanted on any given day. To top it all off, we weren't sleeping or eating very well, and we certainly weren't making enough time for each other.

It took us a while to realize that the babies weren't the problem and we weren't, either. The problem was that our lives were changing very quickly, the things we needed from each other were changing even faster, and we weren't keeping up. Having children required us to change more than just our sleeping schedule, our financial plans, and our social scene; it also required us to make major changes to our relationship.

AN ENTIRELY NEW RELATIONSHIP

The birth of a child typically produces powerful feelings of intimacy that unite a couple in ways they never imagined. However, at times, raising that child produces exactly the opposite feelings—and many couples aren't prepared for the one-two punch. They often feel wonderfully connected at one moment and angry and hopelessly disconnected the next. During this time, many couples find that their lives change so much, so fast, that they temporarily lose control of their relationship—in fact, most report that their marital satisfaction falls to its all-time low. Many spend days either not talking to each other at all or only talking about logistics in ominous tones ("Did you put the diapers where they belong, or did you just throw them in a pile?" "Are you going to pick up the dry cleaning, or should I just do it?" "Are you ever going to get some groceries?").

Paradoxically, many people also find these to be the best years of their lives. Babies have that effect on people. They bring so much joy and so much angst, all at once. Nonetheless, although many people attribute their marital problems in this phase of life to the arrival of children, it's not the children that cause the problems; it's the couple. Babies are usually cute and cuddly enough to make up for the inconvenience they cause. Typically, the issue is that most couples are psychologically and emotionally unprepared to handle *each other* during this period.

Don't worry too much if you find yourself in this position. All of this anguish comes with the territory, and even the best marriages can suffer during these years. Couples *can* find ways to get through this stage and grow and change in positive ways.

THE GOAL OF THIS STAGE

By far the most difficult and emotionally trying period in most marriages is the baby years. Having children requires most people to go through an incredibly challenging transformation, individually and as a couple, in an extremely short time, with virtually no prior experience or training. In most cases, both must become very different people who now have different goals, different communication styles, different interests, different skills, and even different perceptions of attractiveness. It's a tall order, and most of us find out relatively quickly how unprepared we are for this adventure.

Solving this dilemma is of the utmost importance. If the growth issues of these years aren't addressed, things can quickly go awry. Sadly, sometimes the pressures become so great that they destroy a marriage.

The major goal of this stage of marriage is to survive its inherent turmoil without letting it take too big a toll on your relationship. To do this, three seemingly opposing stances must be adopted:

1. Realize that, in many ways, you will be on your own during this time to meet many of your emotional and personal needs.
2. Understand that just because your spouse isn't completely there for you doesn't mean that your spouse has abandoned you.
3. Remember that taking care of your spouse's needs is just as important as taking care of the needs of your children.

One reason it's so important to marry someone who is mature, reasonable, and emotionally self-sufficient is because there are numerous times in every marriage when our partner is unable to support us effectively. For men, one such time is when their wives are pregnant. Sometimes I tell men that they have to think of it as if their wife has the flu for nine months: "Sure, she's up walking (or waddling) about, but she's usually just running on fumes. So, just like when she has the flu, she's not really able to take care of you—and, more importantly, she needs you to take care of her much more than you might typically do."

Equally, there are many times when men are dealing with stressors that make them incapable of being there for their wives. And sometimes, whether because of work, family, friends, chores, or any number of other possibilities, it's impossible for either spouse to be available for his or her partner. It's a reality of relationships that people have to deal with—*as long as it's a temporary and situational experience, not a way of life.*

So, during the low periods, we have to be able to resolve things by ourselves. Remembering this is especially important during the baby years when our partner may be just as overwhelmed and emotionally drained as we are.

Problems arise in this stage when one spouse is too dependent on the other and can't solve problems on his or her own or take care of himself or herself emotionally. Some spouses become needy, depressed, angry, or nonfunctional when their partner is unable to make things better for them. When that happens, the children suffer, the relationship suffers, and the marriage quickly unravels.

That's why couples who do well in this stage accept that, in many ways, they're on their own. This doesn't mean they should expect that their spouse will never be there for them, and it certainly doesn't excuse the spouse who doesn't even try. It just means that you have to cut the well-meaning and honestly trying spouse some slack if he or she lets you down, and that sometimes it is simply your job to take care of yourself.

Children have a way of consuming so much time and energy that spouses often have nothing left for each other. When that happens, spouses grow increasingly more disconnected and, at times, even agitated. So even though we should show some leniency with each other, we should also continue to try extremely hard to take care of each other's needs during this stage. The best spouses make it a point to do this on a regular basis (examples of good ways to do this are outlined later in this chapter).

Here's another way to look at it: if you're playing baseball or football, you don't go up to bat or into the scrimmage assuming you'll hit a home run or make a touchdown on every play. But you always *want* to hit that home run or make that touchdown, and you never quit trying. Your teammates expect that of you, and you expect it of yourself. As long as you both know you're doing your best, everyone learns to accept that we don't always get the outcome we hope for.

The same applies to teamwork in the baby years. However, when one or both members of a couple feel that the teamwork is breaking down, they quickly shift to opposing sides in . . .

The Blame Game

By the time Mitchell and Janice came to see me, their marriage was a shambles. They had two small children ages two and a half years and six months and were barely speaking to each other. Although they felt their marriage had been pretty good before they had children, both agreed it had gone downhill almost immediately after the kids came along. "I knew that having kids was going to be a lot of work," remarked Janice, "but I never thought my marriage would be even *more* work. We loved each other and didn't argue or bicker that much—unlike many of our friends. Sure, we had our issues, but I never thought we'd become one of *those* couples. After we had kids, though, it's like everything fell apart."

Janice was angry at Mitchell for almost everything—and had been for nearly two years. According to her, Mitchell was "basically useless." He would only help out when asked—and then did a horrible job. "I really think he doesn't get it," she said. "We're both gone all day, but when he comes home, he acts like the king of the house. He expects me to take care of him, to make dinner, and to cater to his every need, while he sits there watching television!"

Mitchell countered this by saying that whatever he did to help out was never good enough. "If I watch the kids, she says I'm not watching them correctly. When I play with them, she gets mad because I'm not doing laundry or dishes. And when I play with them *and* do the household chores at the same time, she says that's not good parenting! She's probably right that I could help out more, but why bother, since according to her, I do everything wrong? I've had it. Why should I put up with being screamed at all the time in my own home? I work hard all day to make a living for us. The least she could do is be happy that I'm home."

Mitchell genuinely believed that having kids had somehow made Janice go a little insane: "Janice used to be easygoing and relaxed, but now she's a control freak about everything. I think something hormonal got screwed up in her—I've heard that can happen to women. She cries for no reason, has no interest in sex, and basically treats me like crap. I've started to dread coming home, because I can feel her ready to explode at any minute. I just want my old wife back."

Ending the Blame Game

Both Mitchell and Janice felt the problem with their marriage was that the other person had somehow morphed into someone who wasn't respectful, helpful, or even polite. In short, they both felt abandoned.

But it wasn't a matter of anyone morphing into an alien being who was evil or crazy, anymore than my wife and I were evil or crazy when we had our little emotional breakdown in our dark hallway. The issue was that both Mitchell and Janice were having major identity crises. Both needed to adjust to parenthood, and neither was doing it very well.

Although Mitchell described himself as a dad, he really wasn't doing many things differently in his life now that he had become one. His sales job often required him to travel several days a week, and he still played golf every weekend and poker once a week with the guys. This schedule made him mostly unavailable to Janice during the week and only intermittently available on weekends. Mitchell also still chose to drink heavily during his golf outings and poker games. So when he finally got home, he was (to use Janice's term) useless. When he was home, he frequently had the television tuned to a sporting event, even while watching the kids.

Mitchell insisted he wasn't going to cut back on his activities: "Golf is something you knew I loved to do and poker is mostly during times when the kids are asleep anyway. And so what if I watch sports on TV? I'm not going to give up everything just because I have kids."

Having children doesn't mean, of course, that one can't follow sports—or play them. But Mitchell had made a pact with himself that having kids wasn't going to change *his* life the way he'd seen it change so many other people's lives, so he went out of his way to make sure that didn't happen. He even had a personal motto he was rather proud of: "Hold out, don't give in, be yourself, don't let 'em win." He believed that giving up his identity as an independent, highly active man would diminish his self-esteem. What he failed to see was that not giving it up was killing his marriage.

Mitchell felt he wasn't the problem; Janice was. After all, he hadn't changed, *she* had. "Besides," he said, "how could changing my activities possibly help? I've seen so many guys become miserable, beaten-down slaves who no longer own their own lives when they have children. I can't see how us becoming like that could possibly help our relationship." He felt that if Janice would just return to being the woman she'd been before they'd had kids, she'd be able to handle the children and her own problems better.

In one way, Janice was right: Mitchell clearly didn't get it. But it wasn't that he didn't know how to be a parent; it was that, in this stage of marriage, he didn't know how to be a good husband. Each of his rationalizations served *his* needs, not the family's, and certainly not Janice's.

As a working mother with two young children and a household to run, Janice needed a husband who was committed to being a father—and that meant being a guy who was willing to help out in whatever way he could. She stopped wanting to have sex with Mitchell not because she was crazy, but because the things she now desired most—companionship, appreciation, patience, assistance, understanding, and compassion—were nowhere to be found in Mitchell, and that was an intimacy killer. Worse yet, he was saying their problems were all *her* fault. What's sexy about that?

Although Mitchell wasn't making the right moves to mend things, neither was Janice. Mitchell's perception of her, while certainly extreme, contained some truth. Janice had become a very different woman than the one he had married. She was harried, angry, frantic, and openly critical much of the time. But she wasn't crazy. Like Mitchell, she was having an identity crisis: she was learning how to be a mom and was in a major tailspin as a result.

Before having children, everything in life had come easy to Janice. Now she was exhausted and winging it every day while living in constant fear that she was screwing things up. In her mind, she was on her own with all this. Her mother had been an absent parent (no good advice or help there); Mitchell wasn't coming through (he was being "useless"); all her friends had their own problems (can't burden them); and the parenting books she'd read just didn't seem to help or they contradicted one another (Pick up the baby when he cries. Don't pick him up because that will spoil him. Leave the room and let him cry in the other room for hours to teach him how to cry himself to sleep? Yeah, right!).

All of this left her feeling isolated and overwhelmed. She tried to make use of all the words of wisdom about parenting she'd received through the years, but none of them worked. All that ever soothed her six-month-old son was to hold him. Anytime he wasn't being held, he was screaming. This made her feel like a terrible mom. "What am I doing so wrong," she thought, "that my little one is so miserable?" With the added pressure of having a toddler who also desperately needed time and attention, Janice was at her wits' end.

Janice's solution was to try to control absolutely everything. She figured that if she cranked up her organization and decision-making skills and could get everything organized and done the correct way, life would finally run smoothly as it had before she and Mitchell had kids. As a result, she had become extremely compulsive and had developed unattainable expectations for herself, the household, her husband, and her kids. She had rules for how to do almost everything and felt great distress when Mitchell, or anyone else, didn't follow the plan. Whenever situations didn't go the way she envisioned, she would, in her husband's words, "freak out" and would intervene with a critical hand. It was true that she walked around the house like a drill sergeant, keeping an eagle eye out for infractions: "I realize I do that, but I can't help it. I spend all day trying to get things organized and done right, and then Mitchell comes home and messes everything up in about ten minutes! I can't take it. He only makes things worse."

Janice, like Mitchell, was unwilling to change her style and her method of dealing with problems. In the old days, she'd been able to handle everything smoothly by being highly organized and supercompetent. She'd been easygoing and relaxed because whenever a problem came along, she'd take care of it quickly and decisively and move on.

This strategy wasn't working now, for three reasons. First, there were too many things on her to-do list to ever get everything done. Second, Mitchell didn't operate with her superefficiency—and was never going to—and trying to force him to do things her way only succeeded in shutting him out, leaving them both feeling isolated and misunderstood. Third, kids don't operate that way, either; they're even more unpredictable than adults. That meant, in order to keep things under control, she had to keep an unrealistically tight rein on them on a constant basis.

People who try to control the uncontrollable usually just end up spiraling out of control themselves, and Janice was on her way down. It was clear that she needed to change her expectations and her coping skills. But like Mitchell, Janice was extremely invested in the identity she'd held before she had kids and her expectations of how her world should operate. Since she was unable, or unwilling, to change her outlook, things were only getting worse.

DEVELOPING A NEW IDENTITY

Mitchell and Janice eventually worked things out and their relationship improved significantly. A major first step was for them to realize that they each were contributing to the problem by not keeping up with the changing needs of the other spouse and their life together. Once each decided to change himself or herself and begin doing things differently, their life together improved almost instantly.

Mitchell gave up his motto. He decided that he needed to put his responsibilities as a father and a husband above his own needs.

Janice decided that she needed to relax a bit and that getting less than perfect help from Mitchell was far better than fighting constantly and getting no help at all. She decided to pick her battles and let the other stuff go—with a smile.

They worked out a schedule for taking care of the children that both of them found acceptable. It required Mitchell to spend much more time at home and to be much more productive while there. It also required Janice to let Mitchell parent the children in keeping with his personality and his style.

Mitchell continued to play golf, but he stopped considering it an entitlement and started seeing it as an occasional break from his responsibilities. He played less frequently and he didn't linger or go out for drinks afterward, making sure he returned home refreshed and ready to help out.

Something also dawned on him that he'd never considered before: his golf and poker buddies might be going home to their wives and behaving very differently than he was. They went home and took care of business, whereas Mitchell went home and crashed.

Once Mitchell decided to become a proactive, on-the-ball parent who took care of his responsibilities and anticipated what the kids and Janice needed, his life with Janice improved dramatically. He also found that his poker nights became less of an issue in his marriage. It seems the problem wasn't that he played poker but his insistence about it—and that it was one more thing that pulled him away from taking care of the family. Once he eagerly and effectively took care of so many other things in their life, Janice was happy for him to spend some well-deserved time off with his friends.

Mitchell found that, contrary to his expectations, once he fully committed to this lifestyle, it wasn't all that bad. The trade-offs were worth it because he was so much happier at home—and he was still able to spend quality time with his buddies.

Janice found the same to be true. When she stopped expecting everything to go smoothly and Mitchell to do everything her way, their life didn't fall apart. In fact, she started to enjoy their time together better and appreciated him more. She even discovered that, once she stopped micromanaging, Mitchell had a lot more good family-man traits than she'd given him credit for. She found him to be a loving, motivated father who just did things differently than she did. He had much more patience with the children than she, made everybody in the family laugh (which was good for the children), and actually had many useful ideas for how to handle situations that arose with the house and the kids.

In time, Janice realized that she was feeling much more relaxed and more fun to be with as a spouse and a mother. Sure, the house often looked like a tornado had just blown through, but she found she could live with that—besides, no one but she seemed to notice or care. Most importantly, everyone was happier: she found that her entire family was much healthier living in a happy-but-messy home than they'd ever been in a neat-but-conflict-filled one. Having grown up in an unhappy home, Janice wanted more than anything to provide happiness and stability for her children.

WHY THIS STAGE CAN BE CHALLENGING

Most women are culturally conditioned to sacrifice themselves for others and to be considerate and nurturing whenever possible. As a result, many women develop into selfless caretakers who go out of their way for others. It's an admirable trait that creates a world full of kind, magnanimous women. However, in the world of the new mom, everyone needs her, and they need her right now! On any given day, the mother of a young baby (when she's done with her outside-the-home job) needs to do about fifteen different things all at once to take care of her child, despite the fact that she rarely sleeps through the night and rarely gets a moment to herself. Meanwhile, the laundry pile is always growing, the refrigerator is always empty, the other children are always hungry, the house is always messy, the dishes are always dirty, and the list of things to do is always getting longer.

To someone conditioned to take care of everything, it's a prescription for disaster. Many mothers feel lost in a black hole of caretaking that saps their energy and sometimes even their self-esteem. Imagine how overwhelming it feels when, in a situation that calls for nurturing skills more than at any other time in their lives, women with this conditioning believe they are failing miserably.

Men, too, often feel overwhelmed in this stage, but for different reasons. Men, who in general pride themselves on being powerful and competent, feel constantly confronted by situations they've never before encountered and feel powerless to fix. All first-time fathers, at some point during the first few months of parenthood, are hit with the realization of how desperately in over their heads they are. One day they find themselves with a naked, screaming baby in one hand, a poopy diaper in the other, and a crying wife in the next room. While they realize that something has to be done—and that it needs to be done immediately—they have no idea what to do. Most men have no training in changing diapers or comforting babies, and few are much good at dealing with a tearful, postpartum wife, either. Nonetheless, all that and much more is thrown at them in a matter of weeks, and they feel great pressure to fix all these "problems."

The upshot of it all is that very soon after they have their first child, men begin to feel overwhelmed, incompetent, and powerless. For men, these are especially ugly feelings. It seems particularly unfair that they spend their lives trying to avoid these feelings at all costs, only to have them all thrust upon them mercilessly immediately after reaching the pinnacle of manhood: fatherhood.

THE IDEAL MATE IN THIS STAGE

I always remind the new parents I work with that total competence and control are, in many ways, illusions. The reality is that sometimes, despite everything we do to comfort him, our baby cries and cries. That's normal—and it's not a sign of bad parenting. The same goes for most other parental dilemmas as well. No matter how careful we are, sometimes our children get hurt, and sometimes parents get frustrated and yell or scream when we shouldn't. It's also true that, a lot of times, we don't look our best, our family's clothes could be cleaner, our house could be neater, and we could have fixed a better meal. All of these things are common, and they happen in every household.

No parent ever feels supremely competent or universally effective, and no children consistently behave as one expects, or even instructs. Simply put, children bring chaos, and chaos can only be managed, not controlled. Those who try become swamped. These are all realities of life as new parents, and the best we can all hope for is just to get by.

I realize that this is much easier said than done, and that letting all these things slide can turn even the strongest of people into emotional jelly ("What kind of mother lets her child cry/get hurt/doesn't keep the family pulled together/fixes a bad meal?" "What kind of a father am I when I can't do anything right?"). To help you build realistic expectations, I've put together a description of the ideal spouses in this stage of marriage.

Husband #3: The Ally

Most men realize that, once they become fathers, they'll have to make significant changes in their lives. But few realize that becoming a dad also requires them to become a very different *husband* than they've ever been before. In this stage of marriage, a woman no longer needs a life-of-the-party guy, an absent workaholic, or a cool, aloof loner. She needs a husband who realizes that he is a co-conspirator in creating the chaos they're currently living in and who works willingly to reduce it. That means he helps out in every way he can. He changes diapers without being asked, gets up in the middle of the night when babies cry, and takes the kids for long periods of time on weekends even though he's exhausted—because so is she.

It also means that, like Mitchell, he gives up doing many (not all) of the things that he used to do that kept him away from the house. He understands that many of the attributes that made him special in the past are no longer needed, possibly no longer even desirable. He works with his wife to reduce the madness of everyday life without making things worse and without making everything about him and his needs. He also accepts, without getting angry or resentful, that, as unfortunate as it is, his needs will often drop to the bottom of the list and stay there for a while.

One of the most important things this guy understands is that taking care of his children is as much his duty as it is his wife's. The fact that his father never helped out when he was a kid has no bearing in today's world. Most women have outside jobs in addition to their roles as mothers. So when he comes home from work, she is likely doing the same. Her need for a break is just as pressing as his. Even if his wife works part-time or not at all, this guy recognizes that her household demands are really 24/7: when she's at home, she's not relaxing or doing something that qualifies as time away from work. Therefore, instead of raging or withdrawing when things don't go smoothly, he helps her out just as much as he would if she had a full-time job outside the home. He occasionally volunteers to take the kids for an entire day and encourages her to take that time for herself. And when he is at home with the kids, he's productive. Greeting her at the door with a stinky baby, a hungry toddler, a ransacked house, and a million other undone chores isn't really taking care of her needs.

Wife #3: The Chaos Control Manager

The ideal wife at this stage figures out how to handle the constant emotional and physical demands of motherhood without losing herself in the process. She keeps the big picture in mind and realizes that a functional home with a positive atmosphere is far more important than any other factor in fostering children's long-term happiness and success. She learns to focus on being a good enough mom, not a perfect one.

Many new mothers become harried and have difficulty distinguishing the not ideal from the catastrophic, viewing far too many situations as critical. I recently counseled a woman whose marriage was falling apart because she was a completely stressed-out parent. She reacted to almost everything her husband and children did as if that one small event would ruin the child for life. She and her husband once had a lengthy argument after their three-year-old son wanted to sleep on the floor of his room in a tent he had created out of blankets and pillows. She insisted that it would be bad for the boy's back and was furious at her husband for approving this venture and subjecting their son to "back problems for the rest of his life!" She insisted that their children never be allowed to watch cartoons, stay up past ten o'clock, or eat a meal that didn't include a full complement of vegetables. So she got very angry at her husband when he let the children stay up after ten one night ("They need their sleep in order to be healthy!"), even madder when he let their older son eat pizza at a friend's birthday party without also making him eat something healthy ("He needs his vegetables or he'll grow up being fat!"), and outraged when he let this same son watch *SpongeBob SquarePants* on television one afternoon ("It'll turn his brain to mush!).

By turning small issues into catastrophes and expecting far too much of herself, her sons, and her husband, she was creating much bigger problems for everyone. By the time she contacted me, her husband had asked for a divorce and her children were acting out in a variety of ways.

The vast majority of children in the world turn out just fine even when they occasionally watch mind-numbing cartoons, skip their vegetables, stay up late, sleep on the floor, or wear their favorite shirt four days in a row. Still, it's very easy for new mothers to lose perspective on what is most important.

The ideal wife/mother at this stage is a concerned, competent mother who, like Janice, recognizes how easy it is to get caught in the perfect parent trap. She focuses on keeping the family running as smoothly as possible without becoming controlling, falling apart when things don't go well, or expecting her spouse to take care of her in unreasonable or unattainable ways. On days when she's at home, she doesn't meet him at the door with a crying baby and the words, "It's your turn. I've been in charge all day," and she doesn't get riled when he says that he needs a little time to unwind. She realizes that it is not his job to save her. It is *their* job to figure out to spell each other and take care of each other.

Mothers who recognize that the goal of this stage is to manage chaos, not vanquish it, become excellent chaos control managers and learn to concentrate only on what is most important. In doing so, they find effective ways to take care of themselves, their children, and their husband.

Sometimes You're the Pigeon . . . and Sometimes You're the Statue

A good tip for incorporating give and take into your relationship once you become parents is to remember that, in successful relationships, sometimes you're the pigeon . . . and sometimes you're the statue. What this means, of course, is that at certain times you are simply on the wrong end of things. In all relationships sometimes your needs get met while at other times they don't. It's a fact of life all healthy people learn to accept, and as long as the ratio is close to fifty-fifty, they're probably doing pretty well. Spouses who recognize this and embrace it do far better than those who fight it. These folks don't consider their "statue" moments as a chore; they view them as a gift they give to their partner.

When faced with spending an entire Saturday with screaming children, a house full of laundry, multiplying dishes, and perpetually hungry mouths to feed, mature, responsible spouses jump into this quagmire headfirst and eagerly accomplish as much as they can. They do this happily because they consider it their job to unburden their spouse completely for a while. They understand that these "statue" days are an expected and unavoidable part of parenthood and that, if they do their job well, they will likely be a pigeon soon. Spouses who do this poorly rarely get to be pigeons.

Making It Happen: Mastering the Then Comes Baby Stage

The best way to survive the Then Comes Baby stage is to meet change with change. Once children enter the picture, there's really no way your life will ever be the way it was. Therefore, it's time we discussed specifically how couples in this stage can make the changes they need to embrace.

THE BIG EIGHT: SUPER-COMMUNICATION SKILLS FOR THE THEN COMES BABY STAGE

In working with couples going through this stage, I've found there are eight communication tools that are vital to the success of the new family. In general, they involve becoming highly specific and speedy, which is why I call them "super-communication" tools.

Tool 1: Use clear, direct, detailed statements

Successful couples in this stage communicate highly specific and meaningful information with quick, direct statements that are thorough and unmistakable. Since unattended children can topple a hot pot on the stove or pull down an entire rack at the department store in a matter of seconds, it's important that couples at this stage (1) no longer assume anything, and (2) explain everything that's on their minds with remarkable efficiency. In their prechildren days, an afternoon of shopping used to include statements like "I'll be back in a minute," followed by a fifteen- to thirty-minute disappearance. Now they include detailed exchanges that include information about even the simplest tasks. It's sort of amusing how spouses who used to hem and haw for hours about what they wanted to do for dinner now convey multiple, detailed messages in the blink of an eye. Let's look at some examples:

Example 1:
Parenting in the Department Store without Good Communication

Step One	*Wife* "Where did you go? I was looking at a pair of pants and suddenly out of the corner of my eye I saw Jake at the other end of the store climbing up a shoe rack! I thought you were watching him."

Step Two	*Husband* "Me? I was in the changing room. I know you saw me go in there."
Step Three	*Wife* "But that was fifteen minutes ago! What were you doing in there, trying on the entire store? I figured you had to be out by then."
Step Four	*Husband* "I stopped to look at the sweaters by the door."
Step Five	*Wife* (exasperated) "Why didn't you tell me? Jake could have been seriously hurt."
Step Six	*Husband* (incredulous) "Why didn't *you* tell me you were leaving or that I was in charge? How was I supposed to know you left?"
Step Seven	*Wife* (agitated) "Why would you think you weren't in charge? Do you just assume I'm going to handle everything? I have enough to worry about without having to always remind you that you have children!"
Step Eight	*Husband* (angry) "Why do I get blamed for everything? I just go try on some clothes and suddenly I'm a horrible father and a terrible husband!"

Example 1:
Parenting in the Department Store with Good Communication

Step One	*Husband* "Honey, I'm going over here to talk to this salesperson for two minutes. You've got both of the children. Keep an eye on Jake; he's been eyeing the shoe rack."
Step Two	*Wife* "Got it. Let me know when you're back and I'll take Meghan with me over to the sweaters. That way you and Jake can run around for a minute."

Step Three	*Husband* (upon returning quickly) "OK, I'm back. I've got Jake; do you have Meghan yet?"
Step Four	*Wife* "No, I still need a minute. I'm going over to that table to look at a shirt for Mom; why don't you take both of them over to the shoe area and I'll meet you there in five minutes."
Step Five	*Husband* "OK, I'll be over there with them. Let me know when you're back."

Even though it seems like overkill, this sort of constant checking in is required to make sure no one is making any assumptions about what the other is doing. The two key parts of the process are the giving of details and the completion of the communication loop. It is extremely important that the spouse who is receiving information vocalize that he or she got the information. Many times information is given but not received, even when it seems obvious it was received. Believe it or not, including all these extra words actually shortens conversations instead of lengthening them because it eliminates all the fighting on the back end.

The need for this type of communication happens at home as well. Before children, many couples say things like "I'm going out for a while," and that is perfectly fine, even when it leads to hours of noncommunication and each partner having no idea where the other is. Once kids enter the picture, though, a couple's communication must get significantly more detailed.

Example 2:
Parenting at Home without Good Communication

Step One	*Wife* (upon returning home from the store) "Why's Meghan crying?"
Step Two	*Husband* "I don't know. I was in the garage; you tell me."
Step Three	*Wife* "Me? I was at the store!"
Step Four	*Husband* "When did you go to the store? I thought you were putting Jake down for a nap."
Step Five	*Wife* "I did that half an hour ago and I left you a note to switch the laundry load! Then I went to the store. Don't tell me you never checked on the children the entire time I was gone?"
Step Six	*Husband* "I didn't know you were gone!"
Step Seven	*Wife* "Are you telling me you were *in the garage* and you didn't notice one of the cars was missing?"
Step Eight	*Husband* "Well, yeah, I guess I was kind of aware of that but didn't realize that that meant you wanted me to come in and do things."

Example 2:
Parenting at Home with Good Communication

Step One	*Wife* "Jake is down for a nap. I'm going to run to Target for some diapers. Would you switch the laundry load while I'm gone and empty the dishwasher? Then, when I get back I can fold the laundry and finish the dishes. Meghan is in the living room watching TV; make sure you check on her also. I'll be back in twenty minutes tops."
Step Two	*Husband* "Got it, laundry, dishes, daughter. Take your time. I'll take care of it."
Step Three	*Wife* "Thanks, honey."

Once again, the good communication seems like overkill but it actually is much more efficient than the alternative. This detailed and direct communication doesn't occur by accident. It streamlines over time as couples repeatedly find themselves in arguments over who was supposed to be in charge at a given moment.

There are those who fight learning this streamlined communication method, despite its obvious benefits. I counseled a couple who refused to do it because they thought they would sound like helicopter parents who constantly hovered and fretted over the kids. Their goal was that they weren't going to let their children change them and turn them into nervous, insecure people who got stressed out about every situation.

Well, things didn't work out very well. Trying not to fret about the children turned into screaming fights about each other's ignorance, rudeness, or poor parenting. They also lost track of their children for brief but scary moments and often had no idea who was in charge, what they expected of each other, and what parenting intervention was required at any given moment. When they finally adopted super-communication, their marital life immediately improved.

Spouses can also use super-communication to communicate their feelings and needs to each other clearly: "I'm exhausted. Would you please make me something to eat while I take a quick nap on the couch?" Or "I'm feeling overwhelmed today—could you take the kids for a while so I can get a break?"

While it sounds easy enough, it's remarkable how seldom couples interact in this way—and then how often they are upset that the other person doesn't telepathically know how they feel or what they want.

Tool 2: Evolve your communication to fit the situation

When my wife and I first married, we argued occasionally about how I was supposed to respond when she said, "I love you." She always expected me to say it in return, so as not to leave her hanging, whereas that felt artificial to me. I wanted to say it whenever I felt like it.

As you might expect, I lost this argument, and eventually we settled into a nice back-and-forth repartee that satisfied her needs. But when we transitioned into the child-rearing years, it all went awry. One day I came home to find her looking extremely harried and distraught, with a wailing baby in one arm and a laundry basket in the other. Using my previously learned "I love you" skills, I sidled up to her, looked her in the eyes, and warmly announced how much I loved her. "Get out of my face; you're crowding me," she shot back, followed by, "If you really loved me you'd go do some dishes instead of standing there jabbering on!" Clearly, we had entered new territory.

Good communication isn't only about saying kind things or stating how you feel. It's about meeting another person where he or she is at. It evolves to fit the situation. In this stage of marriage, many couples find that while "I love you" was great before, now

"I love you and you're doing a great job" is even better. Or better yet: "I love you; you're doing a great job. Let me just take ten minutes to relax, and then I'll do the dishes."

Tool 3: Discuss new expectations

Couples should discuss how, now that they have children, their expectations of each other will change and what things will have to give. They should decide:

- What sacrifices will have to be made
- How they will communicate their new expectations
- Why their changed expectations should be acceptable
- How they want to handle life given their new expectations
- How they want to bring up changing them even more if necessary

What follows is a list of questions couples might want to consider together to help facilitate these conversations.

Questions to Consider in This Stage

1. How do you feel your day-to-day life will change now that you have children?

2. How do you feel your extracurricular life will change now that you have children?

3. How do you feel your work life will change now that you have children?

4. How do you feel your social life will change now that you have children?

5. What sacrifices will this require you to make in each circumstance? How do you feel about making those sacrifices?

6. How do you plan on communicating these changes to your spouse and how will those changes impact your expectations of each other?

7. How do the two of you plan on discussing the effect of your changes and what do you expect from your spouse when you make (or fail to make) these changes?

8. How will you handle the emotional impact making these changes will have on you as an individual and as a couple? Will you be positive or negative, resentful or appreciative, blaming or embracing, etc.?

9. How do you want your spouse to communicate his or her feedback regarding your changes?

10. What process will you use to evaluate the success of your changes and how will you develop a new plan if one is needed?

Tool 4: Talk about how you feel about your new roles

No one makes sweeping changes in his or her life without some growing pains. That's why couples should make a point to compliment and affirm each other's new role. Discussing how it feels to be a parent (the good and the bad) helps discharge tension and bring you together. Talk about your mixed feelings about your new identity and encourage each other to grow and blossom in your roles. Remember, just because your spouse feels occasionally overwhelmed or tied down by his or her new role doesn't mean he or she isn't glad to have made this choice. These are normal feelings; they come with the territory.

Tool 5: Time is at a premium, so speak your mind quickly and clearly about your feelings and needs

Discussions about feelings and needs needn't be exhaustive in order to be productive. Couples who communicate well in this stage get to the point in a kind but assertive way. Beating around the bush ("I dunno, I've felt better, but it's not like I feel terrible or anything"), avoiding trouble that is clearly in the air ("Never mind—*sigh*—nothing's wrong. I'm just tired"), or making your partner chase you to discuss your real feelings ("C'mon, honey, what's wrong?") only wastes time and aggravates your spouse.

Tool 6: Make a list of all the jobs that need to be done and prioritize and divide them between you

The couples who perform best at this stage adopt a healthy divide-and-conquer strategy. They make a list of everything that needs to be done (including taking care of each other), prioritize each item, make a schedule, and get busy. They agree on how to complete each task and then put those expectations through their new lower-standards process to make sure this job really has to be done and that they're not overburdening themselves. I always remind couples that they should feel free to reevaluate the plan if things aren't working out as expected, or as their needs change.

Tool 7: Discuss your needs for rest and relaxation

Getting time off for oneself is essential at this stage. Discuss what each of you needs to relax and recharge. It's best to make a schedule for these activities and list what each of you will do to help the other get this time off. Ideas include:

- Brief periods when one spouse is off duty even if he or she is at home
- Full days or weekends off
- Regularly scheduled events like time allotted to watch weekly television shows or nights out with the girls/guys
- Occasional free passes for one spouse to do whatever he or she wants (within reason)

Make sure to divide these times up evenly. Both of you will need them. Even if one of you feels you don't need that much time, take it anyway. It's best to rest and refuel before you're running on empty.

Tool 8: Define trade-offs

Children are adorable, but they're still frustrating and a ton of work. That often leaves whoever is home dealing with them feeling burdened while the other is out playing, working, or even doing the grocery shopping. Many people go into the baby years insisting they won't keep score and that "we're in this together." To that I say, good luck. You'd be better off if you realized that bartering will occur and you *will* keep score. But don't see that as a bad thing or as a sign of selfishness. People keep score; it's simply human nature. It only becomes a problem when people don't talk about their feelings when they feel the situation is unfair, or when the scorecard is skewed too far in one person's favor. I want you to have the best parenting experience you can, and in order to do that, you can't live with blinders on. Scorekeeping and bartering are part of life and relationships. Just do it in a mature and healthy manner.

To an overwhelmed parent, just being in the store with no kids tugging at you can feel like a break. Many husbands don't realize that while going to the store for your wife is helpful, it often doesn't score as many points as staying home with the kids and letting her go to the grocery store. Then again, sometimes your wife will want you to do the shopping.

While one spouse is absent, the on-duty spouse usually looks forward to his or her break time and expects to cash in that chip relatively soon. I call these trade-offs. Couples need to discuss exactly what their expectations are regarding break times and what's considered a break and what isn't (remember the grocery store example—sometimes it's a break; other times it's a chore).

Understanding this is very important. I know many couples where the wife considers her husband's work hours to be break time, whereas he considers them to be on-duty hours. Equally, I know many husbands who consider their wife's caretaking hours as break time, which conveniently allows them to assert that they need some break time, too—like a weekend in Vegas with the guys. So make sure you define trade-offs and discuss your expectations. Those who do this honestly and openly fare far better than those who secretly keep score and deny they're doing it.

TOOLS FOR BUILDING INTIMACY IN THE THEN COMES BABY STAGE

Super-communication will help you navigate the day-to-day aspects of this stage and will go far toward keeping tensions from building between you. But you also need to find new ways to build intimacy at a time when it seems you barely have a moment to think.

During the first two stages of marriage, couples have the luxury of time and many opportunities to build and maintain intimacy: frequent sexual encounters, long conversations, numerous shared experiences and hobbies, lengthy walks in the park, travel, and so on. These experiences continually allow couples to connect and reconnect. When one or more infants begin showing up in their lives (and bed), the opportunities for intimate bonding become, in a word, rare. Time together often turns into tactical planning exercises: working out logistics for who's doing what, who needs to be where, what needs to be done. Tasks can consume so much time and effort that the couple lack the energy to bond in any of their standard ways.

I can remember countless times when my wife and I were so exhausted after a day with the children that we didn't have the energy to talk about ourselves, our days, our feelings, or even complete a short conversation. All we felt like doing was collapsing in bed and, we hoped, getting a good night's sleep. I can't tell you how often my wife fell asleep midsentence while lying next to me in bed, relaxing on the couch, or sitting at the kitchen table. So, despite their best efforts, many couples find themselves slowly drifting apart. Here are a few tips for maintaining intimacy during these years.

Have Empathy Discussions

In some cases, I specifically advise couples to make an empathy checklist and to devote time each week to discussing how it must feel to be in each other's shoes. The idea here is not to fix or critique these feelings, just to create a forum for discussion. This can be an extremely powerful exercise if done well. Most people don't realize how often their spouse is having thoughts and feelings similar to theirs. See the following for a sample empathy checklist you might use.

A Sample Empathy Exercise

When I stay home with the children all day, I feel . . .

- ☐ Overwhelmed, frantic, and hopeless
- ☐ Incompetent, ineffective, and stupid
- ☐ Excited, energized
- ☐ Underappreciated, unattractive, and boring
- ☐ Tired, old, and slow
- ☐ Happy, fulfilled
- ☐ Taken advantage of, manipulated, and cheated
- ☐ Useful, loved, important, needed
- ☐ Other: ________________________________

When I'm at work and the kids are left in day care, I feel . . .

- ☐ Like a terrible mom/dad
- ☐ Like I'm hurting my baby
- ☐ Like I am being judged by others as uncaring
- ☐ Relieved
- ☐ Angry
- ☐ Sad
- ☐ Happy
- ☐ Lonely
- ☐ Guilty
- ☐ Distracted
- ☐ Like I can't wait for the day to end so I can go home and be with my child
- ☐ Other: ______________________________

____

____

Be Present

In previous stages of marriage, being on the computer or hanging out in different rooms of the same house was okay. Now you need to be active in each other's lives. When you're home, be home. When you're tired, it's tempting to zone out on the computer or in front of the TV. Sure, you're there, but that's not the same as *being there*. Go out of your way to connect.

Many men and women bring work home. I realize that work today no longer ends at 5:00 p.m. But there's still a time and a place for it. If you have work to do, designate time for work and time for hanging out, and make sure you do each of them well. Mixing the two usually doesn't work. Some couples make 8:00 p.m. to 9:00 p.m. work time and 9:00 p.m. to 10:00 p.m. hanging-out time.

And while friends, social commitments, or personal projects are important, they aren't more important than your relationship. Don't spend time when you're supposed to be with your spouse chatting on the phone with friends, reading e-mails, working in the garage, or doing other chores. Quality time spent with your spouse is your job. Treat it that way. Note that quality time doesn't necessarily mean heavy conversation or even heavy petting. Many people just need to unwind. It's great to do this cuddled up together in front of a TV show or a movie. That counts.

Make Specific Plans to Take Care of Your Spouse

In this stage, it's a luxury to have time set aside for taking care of oneself. Giving your spouse time to take care of himself or herself is a huge gift. If scorecards are being kept (and trust me, they are), you will receive major points.

Men: This means that you announce (announcing your intentions is very important) that you're going to devote X period of time (hours, not minutes) to taking care of everything in the house (kids, laundry, dishes, and so on) so your wife can get a break. Or tell her that you're going to handle all of the housework and the kids for X number of evenings, and after that you will either give her a little TLC, a night to herself, or time to do whatever she wants. (Note: do not use this as a ploy to get sex. First of all, this is not about you, it is about her. Second, she isn't stupid; she'll sniff out your true motives, and she probably won't be happy about it.

Third, don't be so singularly focused on immediate gratification. A few nights that are all about her often lead to many nights that are all about you.)

Women: Provide him with an occasional guilt-free break. Tell him that you *want* him to go spend time with his buddies or to do whatever he's interested in doing and that you're eager to set some time aside for him to do this. This gift usually goes a long way toward making a husband feel appreciative of his wife.

Avoid Compromises

This may sound like a provocative statement, but it really isn't. The problem with compromises is that neither person typically feels as if he or she wins in those situations. That makes each spouse eager to win the next time—especially during the very hectic baby years when people rarely feel their needs are being met.

The pigeon and the statue philosophy from earlier in this chapter applies here. A great gift of intimacy one spouse can give the other is to fully commit to being a fabulous statue when it's your turn to do so (except in situations where it involves abusive or unhealthy actions). An example: Many men, upon hearing that they have to spend an afternoon at their wife's sorority sister's wedding shower (or some other event they feel completely unexcited about), grudgingly agree to attend—but only if they're able to apply a strict structure to the event: "All right, I'll go, but you know how much I hate those things. Just make sure we're out of there at two o'clock like you said we would be." Then, on the day of the event, they drag their feet on the way to the gathering, disappear into the den (i.e., they find the television) immediately upon arriving, and only poke their heads out to point to their watches at ten minutes to two and give the "let's go" signal. It's a compromise in which nobody wins. He feels he suffered through "her" event and deserves some time of his own now. She feels he was never really present, or even particularly polite, and ends the day feeling her needs weren't met. When the next weekend rolls around, you can be sure each will be looking to finally secure a win.

A better way to handle this particular example would be for the guy to embrace the pigeon/statue concept. Instead of dragging his feet on the way to the event, he could help prepare, be ready to leave on time, and understand that these things occasionally go longer than planned. At the event, he could oversee the kids' lunches, engage in conversation with the host, and spend some quality time in the kitchen talking it up with her friends. If, while all the other guys were in the den watching the local team score, he was in the other room being charming, interested in conversing with the group, and genuinely eager to help out, he'd be scoring far more points for his personal home team.

This doesn't mean he has to miss the entire game or never set foot in the den. It just means that he has to give his wife what she's really looking for: a considerate husband who tunes in to her friends and her family and takes care of her needs before his. That's being a good statue, and it makes a spouse feel appreciated and respected. At the end of that day, most wives of guys who operate this way are grateful and appreciative (especially when every other husband was moody or absent). These wives are usually much more eager to reciprocate and, more importantly, feel far closer and intimate with their husband. This is the sort of guy they want to be with at this stage of life.

Women can do the same thing when it comes to his time with his friends. Instead of attempting to control when, where, and how long he goes out, she could freely embrace his need to be with his friends. That doesn't mean that he gets these free passes every week or that he should be allowed to stay out all night; it just means that when he does get some time to himself, she should, if at all possible, not attempt to squeeze it into a compromise.

Special Circumstances in the Then Comes Baby Stage

Blended Families

One of the fastest-growing types of families in the world today is the blended family. These families contain any of a number of different configurations of family members. Sometimes they consist of stepchildren who suddenly have to share a home with one another; sometimes they involve stepchildren as well as younger children born of their parents' current marriage; sometimes they include other extended family members in the home, such as grandparents, cousins, or foster or adopted children.

Most traditional couples have several years to work through the challenges in the various stages of marriage. Before they have children, they spend years getting to know each other, establishing trust, learning to work as a team, building good communication tools, and developing methods for deepening intimacy.

Blended families don't have that luxury. Imagine having to trust someone to smoothly address the complex interpersonal conflicts common to a blended family when you've had few opportunities to work together solving even minor problems.

The Key to Success

Relationship building progresses along predictable pathways, even when life doesn't. All couples, regardless of their ages or circumstances, still have to start their relationship growth curve at stage one and work their way through all six stages. There's simply no other way. People in blended families have to navigate these stages at warp speed. Many blended families experience significant growing pains as a result of the high-speed transitions they're required to make from stage to stage.

This means they need to familiarize themselves thoroughly with the goals of each stage and what each partner is required to accomplish. Furthermore, they also have to gain some very clear insight into how they participated in the dissolution of their previous marriage (divorced families are the most common type of blended family). I am not saying that people should blame themselves for the failings of their previous marriage; I am saying that they need to identify why their marriage went off track. In doing so, they often find that, despite their previous spouse's unique set of issues, they also likely failed to deal well with some of the challenges of marriage early on. This insight can help them formulate new patterns they'll want to make in their new marriage.

Whatever their particular situation is, it is extremely important to engage in this introspection. As it's often been said, those who don't understand the past are doomed to repeat it, and spouses who fail to recognize and understand their errors do this frequently. If you want your new marriage to succeed, then you must understand the missteps you've made in the past and how not to make them again.

I suggest that couples in this situation sit down and have very serious and specific conversations with each other regarding

1. How well they see themselves functioning as a couple
2. What areas they feel they need help with
3. Personal areas where they each need growth

Having these conversations can be a vulnerable and humbling experience, but it is vital to the success of their marriage. Since children are involved and everyone's well-being depends on getting the marriage and the family quickly onto solid ground, the sooner blended-family couples make these transitions, the better. Those who avoid dealing with the difficulties of this process or who fail to make the appropriate changes can end up in a tumultuous situation.

As challenging as blending families can be, it also has the potential to be a remarkably enriching experience. Those who make this transition well find themselves in a deep and rich marital relationship.

SUCCESS STORIES: HOW YOU KNOW WHEN IT'S WORKING

For most couples, the Then Comes Baby stage is simultaneously the hardest and the most fulfilling period of their marriage. The work required to physically and psychologically adapt and change during these times is tremendous, and even when you think you're doing it as well as you can, you may feel you're just hanging on for dear life. That's why the little moments of joy that get sprinkled in from time to time are so memorable and so powerful. Here's one of my favorites.

When my two boys were very little—ages three and one—my wife and I still hadn't accepted the reality that we couldn't take the kids with us out to dinner at the same upscale restaurants we used to enjoy when we were single. (You tell yourself it will all work out fine, but it rarely does, and you eventually learn to prefer the informality and the promise of fewer embarrassing moments of the diner to the ambiance of the nice restaurant.) We wanted to believe that things really weren't that different now that we had kids, and we told ourselves that all we needed to do was just control them well (hah!) and everything would be okay.

So one Friday evening, we decided to take the family out to one of our favorite places. This restaurant happened to also have a very popular bar attached to it, and the hostess seated us right next to it.

To put it mildly, dinner didn't go as planned. It was one of those meals where the entire table felt like it was constantly exploding. Both of the children seemed to be spilling something, crying about something, or needing something every fifteen seconds. I must have been up and down from my chair about seventy-five times in ten minutes, frantically attending to one disaster after another. During one of those moments, I noticed two young men at the bar watching me with disdain and laughing to themselves as they observed my predicament. I overheard part of what they were saying, but I didn't need to hear it all to know the gist of it. After all, I had been one those guys at one time in my life. I knew they were gleefully making a pact with each other: "Please do me a favor and shoot me if I ever become that guy."

I must admit that it was a humiliating moment to realize that I had become "that guy," but I didn't have much time to think about it, because right at that instant my oldest son announced emphatically, "I need to poop!"

Anyone who knows anything about toilet training understands that that exclamation comes with an extremely small window of opportunity. I dropped everything, rushed over to him, scooped him out of his high chair, and scampered to the men's room with him held high in my arms out in front of me, all the while imploring innocent bar patrons to please let me through immediately.

I'm glad to say that we made it to the bathroom in time. But the story doesn't end there. At that time in his young life, my son only felt comfortable using the toilet if he was completely naked. So as we entered the extremely unclean restroom, he began shedding clothing as fast as he could. As I was chasing him in, I was catching his clothes and draping them over my shoulders and on top of my head as fast as I could. Once he had fully removed every bit of clothing (including socks and shoes), he selected the nearest stall and dashed in. All I needed was one quick glance at the toilet in that stall to realize that there was no way I was going to let his pristine little bottom touch any part of that germ factory.

So, with the window of opportunity closing by the nanosecond, I decided to suspend him in my arms several inches above the toilet to let him do his business. This required me to crouch down in front of the toilet, rest my elbows on my thighs, sweat profusely, and pray for expediency.

Since there was too little room for me to close the door of the stall, the vision of me crouching in front of a toilet holding my naked son six inches above a gross toilet seat with Barney underwear draped over my head was visible to all others frequenting the bathroom at that moment. That's when my son started to cheerfully and loudly sing, "Baa, baa, black sheep, have you any wool? Yes sir, yes sir, three bags full! . . . Baa, baa, black sheep . . ."

I knew this was quite a spectacle, but I had become accustomed to these sorts of predicaments and just figured I'd weather the storm as I had many others. However, just about then, the same two guys from the bar entered the restroom, stopped short, and stood there staring at me with complete disbelief and mockery in their eyes. Clearly, I had reached an all-time low. As my son finished and I got him dressed, I decided right then and there that this was the last time we were ever coming back to this place.

But we weren't finished yet. On the way back from the bathroom, we stopped at one of my son's favorite places: the window near the kitchen where you could watch the pastry man make pizza crust, flipping the dough into the air. As we stood there watching the man spin the disk of dough on one finger, my son reached his arms around my neck and gave me a huge, spine-crushing hug, and said, "Daddy, I love this place. Can I come back here with you tomorrow?"

And that made it all worthwhile. It didn't matter how feeble I appeared to those twenty-something guys at the bar or how little of my meal I actually got to eat. All that mattered was that my son wanted to be with me and he was having a great time. That's why I was doing all this. That's what parenthood was all about. It was a great night.

So was the next night—when we went back again.

STAGE 4:

Family Ties

To live is to change, and to be perfect
is to have changed often.
—JOHN HENRY NEWMAN

If you sat in a therapist's seat day after day, as I do, you'd often find yourself face to face with a fascinating yet troubling phenomenon: in any group of people, be it a family, a couple, or a work group, the person in the group with the weakest coping skills always controls the group (note: I didn't say *leads;* I said *controls*). As emotionally sensitive human beings, most of us go to great lengths to avoid confrontation and conflict, so we acquiesce to the needs of the most volatile or most troubled person in our presence, while telling ourselves that we are just being polite and respectful. The problem is that, when this happens, the entire group becomes dysfunctional.

In my family, there's a person who is chronically late to almost every scheduled event. But the rest of the group, instead of beginning to eat, open presents, or engage in whatever activity we've all gathered for, sit around waiting for this person to arrive because we fear hurting her feelings (and her feelings do get severely hurt on the rare occasions when we start without her). So at every family function we arrive on time and then sit there, putting the meal or the good times on hold or the event behind schedule, inconveniencing everyone in the group, just so as to not offend a person who is unable to respect the time constraints of everyone else and who can't emotionally handle people moving on with their lives without her.

Here's a short list of some of the dysfunctional behaviors people commonly engage in and which others too often put up with. Do any of them seem to fit your family, friends, or relationship?

- Overwhelming anxiety (everyone avoids the anxiety-causing situation)
- Excessive drinking (everyone avoids drinking)
- Picky eating habits (the group only eats what that person can handle)
- Uncontrollable anger (everyone avoids touchy subjects)
- Impatience (people rush to keep things going smoothly)
- Insistence upon cleanliness (others frantically clean up)
- Chronic lateness (everyone becomes late)
- Inability to handle others' emotions (people speak very carefully around them)

We all have certain flaws and vulnerabilities. The problems arise when our issues negatively affect our own life or the lives of others. You can imagine how wearing it is on a marriage when there's constant vigilance to avoid certain situations, discussions, and emotions. Particularly in the Family Ties stage of marriage, any unresolved issues we have become the central theme and the defining problem.

THE GOAL OF THIS STAGE

The goal of this stage of marriage, which begins roughly when the youngest child reaches school age and continues all the way until that child leaves the nest, is to solidly and assertively co-lead a well-oiled machine. With so much going on in the lives of spouses at home and on the job, with children at home and at school, and with the extended family, this is the stage of autonomy, efficiency, and competence. Spouses at this stage therefore need to be securely and successfully coming into their own as individuals, parents, partners, and leaders. In order to accomplish that, they need to have dealt with whatever personal issues they have. If this busy marriage also has to contend with the damage created by unresolved issues, it struggles to thrive.

Typically, before they have children, couples tend to metaphorically place unresolved personal issues in the "yours" or "mine" category and move on. It's as if they're acting according to an unwritten rule that states something along the lines of "That's *your* issue, not mine, so you deal with it. I'll put up with it to avoid conflict and to make you happy, but I am not going to let it affect me."

This "solution" is really only temporary: it works until it starts to unduly affect others—especially children. Once one parent begins to see the impact of his or her spouse's dysfunction on their beloved children, tempers begin to flare and battle lines get drawn. At that point, it's no longer a "yours" issue; it's an "ours" issue, and it needs to get resolved *now*! That's why, during the Family Ties stage, issues that seemed like not that big a deal suddenly become gigantic.

In the Then Comes Baby stage, spouses need to start growing up and putting the needs of others first, even when they are overwhelmed themselves. In the Family Ties stage, that is still the case, but what makes this stage different than the previous one is that one's own emotional issues have to be resolved by this time or the relationship quickly falls apart.

In my practice, I see a great number of children, and invariably their troubles reflect those of their parents. For example, children with separation anxiety invariably have anxious parents who have trouble dealing with their own fears. These parents unwittingly pass these fears on to their children through "the person with the weakest coping skills controls the group" model I just described. The same is true for children with anger issues, boundary issues, and nearly every other type of dysfunction. Almost without fail, whatever problem a child is dealing with can be directly or indirectly connected to a parent who has the same problem.

So don't kid yourself into believing that your children won't be affected by whatever issues you have. Children pick up on their parents' stresses and problems and learn to believe either that they, too, will not be able to handle the problem or that it is okay to handle it in the same dysfunctional manner that their parent does.

Let me say here that "family" in this stage is defined as whomever you and your partner view as your inner circle, as "us." Obviously "us" often includes children. It can also include elderly parents or others for whom you are responsible. Even marriages without children still require, at this stage, two highly efficient and dedicated spouses who are at the top of their game and can pass the baton smoothly back and forth as they navigate the relay race of life in their prime.

Below are three brief examples of couples suffering from some of the most common dilemmas that arise in this stage.

The Woman Who Couldn't Cope

Although Patty is thirty-nine years old and a working mother of three children (aged ten, eight, and six), in some ways she needs more attention and caretaking than all of them. She is often insecure and anxious and, as a result, has great difficulty making decisions because she fears either embarrassing herself in front of others or making a mistake. Since she also has difficulty saying no when people ask her to do things, both her work and home lives are often overloaded with events and activities that she shouldn't be doing and doesn't really want to do. She ends up spending most of her days frantically running from one place to another.

Patty fears that her children won't like her or that others will perceive her as a mean parent if she sets limits with her kids, so she coddles them, waits on them, and allows them to get away with far too much. All of this causes her to be an ineffective and overwhelmed mother.

But this is not why Patty and her husband Bill came to me for marital counseling. They came because Patty was extremely angry with Bill for a variety of actions that she deemed unacceptable. Patty had always leaned on Bill for emotional support. It had long been their pattern that if Patty was feeling overwhelmed or highly emotional, she would become tearful and withdrawn. Seeing her distress, Bill would drop everything to nurture her. As their lives had become more and more demanding, this pattern had extended to Bill's comforting Patty on a daily basis and, when she was especially distraught, consoling her into the wee hours of the morning.

Patty now felt very anxious when she couldn't get hold of Bill or when he branched out to meet new friends. She was increasingly suspicious of his interactions with other women and insisted that he not talk to them unless she was present. In order to keep his wife happy, Bill had to limit his social activities and carefully nurture her whenever they did accept social invitations.

Patty was upset because over the past few years, Bill had become progressively less responsive to her distress, which left her feeling angry and even more needy, leading to accusations of lack of interest ("You don't love me anymore"), dishonesty ("You're just not the husband I thought you were"), maliciousness ("You don't care if I suffer"), and even infidelity ("If you're not taking care of me, you must be taking care of someone else"). Finally, she insisted on therapy to get to the root of the matter.

I'll bet you aren't as surprised as Patty was to hear that these weren't the real problems in her marriage. What Patty didn't understand was that, in this stage of her life and her marriage, *her* issues were dragging down her family and her relationship.

Before they married, and when the children were very young, Bill felt good about taking such diligent care of Patty because he liked to feel needed. But as Bill's career revved up, the family grew up, and the children began to need a more emotionally self-sufficient mother and an efficiently running household, things began to unravel—and Bill, empathetic though he was, began to resent the situation. "I just want things to be handled smoothly," he said. "There's so much going on in the family, between our jobs, all the kids' sporting events, music recitals, homework, friends, birthday parties, sleepovers, doctors' appointments, and whatever, I can barely keep up. We're all so busy that I hardly get to see the kids anymore. I can't spend time that should be devoted to my children scraping my wife off the floor for the hundredth time. I won't blow off my kids to help her deal with issues she should be able to handle herself. I'm tired and I'm frustrated. And the kids are affected by it. I see them limiting themselves and the things they do so as to not make their mother anxious. That's what bugs me the most."

Bill and Patty had run into a roadblock that strikes many couples in this stage: the character traits that at one time had brought them together were now pushing them apart.

To Patty's credit, after some time and discussion, she began recognizing how her insecurities and her unreasonable expectations of Bill were negatively affecting their relationship. Together, they decided to change how they dealt with Patty's anxiety. Patty took it upon herself to get some counseling and began learning ways to handle her anxiety on her own. She decided that, as a thirty-nine-year-old woman, it was time she learned how to solve her own problems—and that it wasn't Bill's job to do it for her.

Once Patty began working on dealing with things herself, Bill had to learn to let her. Even though this freedom was something he wanted, letting go wasn't so easy for him. He realized that he prided himself on being able to take care of Patty. Without this role, he struggled to feel needed. As they searched for their new roles, they felt even more disconnected for a while, but things eventually worked out well for them and they conquered this stage of marriage successfully.

The Woman Who Married Peter Pan

Gabe is a fun-loving guy. He's gregarious, entertaining, and makes most people laugh with ease. He's the type of guy who stays up too late, enjoys life a little too much, and always has a funny story to tell or an exciting event to attend. All of which means he's an awful lot of fun to be around—unless, of course, you're his wife or one of his four children. Often they find his actions irritating and irresponsible. Of course they have their good moments with Gabe, but these days, they want more. They want a husband and a dad who's more than just the life of the party; they also want a responsible, grown-up role model.

His wife, Carolyn, describes Gabe this way: "I feel like he's my fifth child. He's completely irresponsible and undependable. I can't leave him at home at night with the kids because he's likely to just fall asleep on the couch instead of helping the kids with their homework. He has no idea what the kids are doing on any given day, so nothing important gets done unless I handle it. I have to initiate all their activities, organize their entire day, and remind him repeatedly where he's supposed to be and when. We have a wall calendar in the kitchen with every activity written on it, but does he ever check it? Of course not! I don't think he even remembers it's there. And he never spends any quality time with the kids. He's always dumping them off on friends or sending them off to entertain themselves so he can hang out with his buddies. I'm beginning to wonder what we actually need him for."

Gabe's career was sputtering as well. Although he continued to hold a good job, he was repeatedly passed over for promotions. Although this upset Gabe, he viewed his bosses' feedback that he needed to improve his performance and take his career more seriously as attempts to "turn him into a boring, paper-pushing stiff" like his father was.

When Gabe and Carolyn were dating, she found Gabe's adventurous ways energizing, exciting, and entertaining. At that time, Carolyn, like many people, found Gabe to be one of the most enjoyable men she had ever met. They got married, lived a great life as a young married couple for several years, and eventually had kids. During the early baby years, Gabe's irresponsibility caused some problems, but Carolyn managed to handle the extra load and their relationship weathered that storm. But once the kids got older and started needing a more mature and responsible role model, things fell apart.

Gabe was unable, or unwilling, to change his fun-loving and live-for-today nature, and it wasn't long before Carolyn went from loving and admiring her free-spirited husband to seeing him as a liability. What Gabe didn't recognize was that, in many ways, having a spouse who was fun and free-spirited was no longer his wife's top priority. To put it bluntly, he had outlived his usefulness in the marriage. With two preteen children and two younger ones, Carolyn needed a husband who acted his age, who set a positive example for the kids, and who stood united with her as a parent and partner.

Gabe didn't see what the big deal was. According to him, "The kids are healthy and happy, the bills are paid, and there's food on the table. Life can't be about deadlines and schedules. If the kids don't do their homework, they'll get the natural consequences from their teachers, and that's how they'll learn. If they miss a soccer game, we'll make the next one. I'm not going to be a policeman running around here yelling at everyone the way you do, and I'm not going to work myself to the bone in a dead-end job for a boss I don't like."

Gabe's marriage was in big trouble, but he either didn't seem to notice or didn't seem to care. His wife was no longer attracted to an "I-gotta-be-me" guy, and her marriage and family were no longer capable of dragging that guy along with them.

In therapy, they worked on these issues, but sadly, Gabe was unwilling to change and stopped attending therapy. Carolyn eventually decided that she was not going to change him but that she was not going to divorce him, either. That left her with only one option: swallowing all her feelings and doing all the work to keep the family functioning effectively.

Carolyn paid a price for that decision that left her never quite happy with her life or her relationship. Through the years, she became that all-too-familiar woman who complains to anyone who will listen about how miserable her life is and how awful her husband is. I'm not suggesting that she should have divorced him; I think her desire to stay for the kids was noble, selfless, and mature. I am saying, however, that people in her circumstance must realize the difficult path they are taking. In most cases, down that road are some major problems that only get worse as the years pass and you move into the next stages of marriage. Typically, couples who are unable to resolve issues in one stage of marriage do not thrive in the next, either.

The Case of the Invisible Husband

When Don and Joelle came to see me, Joelle had served Don with divorce papers after almost twenty years of marriage but had, as a last-ditch effort, agreed to try marriage counseling. The problem was that, through the years, Don had become an invisible man in his family. He worked all the time, and when he wasn't working, he was on the phone dealing with work-related problems. But even when he wasn't on the phone, he was barely present. Don's moods alternated between extreme depression and extreme stress, and he was essentially caught up in his own world. His preoccupation resulted in him frequently putting his own needs ahead of his children's. He turned down their requests to go on camping trips because he didn't like all the work involved and because he needed a good night's sleep to be at his best at the office. He told his daughter that he didn't have time to help her practice for her driving test and that he was too nervous to take her out to practice on the road.

Since he constantly felt overwhelmed, Don's way of handling conflict at home was to ignore it and hope it would go away—until he couldn't take it anymore. Then he'd explode, yelling at Joelle or reprimanding the children.

Before Don and Joelle married, Don's issues with stress and anger had been present, but they'd only caused minor inconveniences in their relationship. Joelle was a very competent woman and had been able to overlook or at least compensate for Don's inadequacies. However, despite her strength, Don's issues began to take a toll on her, as she attempted to juggle her own career and shoulder all of the family demands. As time passed, she began to wonder whether she could tolerate his behavior.

What she hadn't calculated was the impact all this would have on their children. It devastated her to see her children make attempt after attempt to bond with their father, only to be rejected. She saw her children becoming progressively less connected to Don and how much this hurt them. She sat Don down repeatedly to discuss these issues, but despite saying how much he loved the children and wanted to do right by his family, Don was unable to change. Because Don was failing to grow and develop as his relationship moved into a new stage, his marriage and his family were suffering.

Joelle and Don ended up divorcing, but that's not as bad as it sounds. In the long run, this was a good decision for them and, believe it or not, for their children. Don wasn't emotionally equipped to be a highly functional, full-time dad. Once he was only required to perform his fatherly duties sporadically, he became a much better father, and his relationship with his children improved a great deal. In time, he and Joelle found other partners and, last I knew, were both enjoying much healthier and happier lives, as were the children.

Summing It All Up

In each of these cases, you can see how the spouse with the fewest coping skills placed a great deal of pressure on the other spouse and on the children to modify their lives in order to accommodate their lack of maturity. That is never good for a marriage, and it's devastating for a family. That's why it's so important that spouses at this stage of marriage embrace change. They need to develop a new identity, one that is consistent with the changing needs of their relationship.

DEVELOPING A NEW IDENTITY

In my early twenties, before I became a psychologist, I worked as an account executive for a large advertising agency in downtown Chicago. What I remember most about those years was how disappointed I was in one of my clients. This particular guy was an incredibly smart and personable man in his early forties who lived in the distant suburbs with his wife and two young children. Of all my clients, I liked this guy the best. He was the one who clearly got it, and he was the only one who I thought could really go places in that profession, unlike many others I knew who were more hot air than substance but who somehow managed to get themselves promoted. But, to my dismay, this guy was also the only one who didn't pursue a bigger job or a more prestigious position in the field. In fact, he worked as the marketing director for a small company on the outskirts of town and never got too involved with the highly sophisticated and exciting world of advertising that was right at his fingertips.

While all my friends and I, along with our like-minded clients, would work all weekend on creating the greatest advertising campaigns in history, this guy would leave at five, take the weekends off, and usually stayed at home with his family doing "nothing." It bugged me for many years that he would just allow himself to lose out to the blowhards I had to deal with every day who held the high-powered, high-profile jobs.

Many years later, when I had children of my own, I finally understood that he wasn't losing at all; he was winning. I just didn't understand that he was running in a different race than I was.

During those years, I was in a different stage of life than my client, and his stage had significantly different goals, measuring sticks, and rewards. He was in the Family Ties stage and was fully invested in his identity as a husband and a father. He went home to his wife and kids each evening, coached their baseball games, played with them in the yard, and helped them with their homework. He was an integral part of their lives and, as a result, his kids were happy and his marriage was healthy. I had been right about one thing, though: he really was the one who got it.

The Family Ties stage can be one of the most rewarding periods in a marriage, if couples fully embrace the new identity that comes with it. Couples with children must realize that their children are watching them very closely. Everything they do, everything they say, and even everything they overlook is minutely observed and processed very personally by the little sponge brains who are wandering around their home every day. That's why it is vitally important that, at this stage of marriage, both parents be strong, mature, and responsible role models. They must embrace their identity as competent, authoritative (not authoritarian), flexible leaders, realizing that when they get bogged down in unnecessary quarrels, immature issues, or pointless dramas, the family suffers. Happy, mature children come from happy, mature homes, and it is the parents' job to make the home environment reflect this mood.

Whereas the previous stage of marriage was fraught with newness and insecurity, this one should contain boatloads of confidence and security. In these years, couples should function as fully competent adults who rise to the occasion to bounce career and life decisions off each other, run interference for each other, run errands, play good cop/bad cop with the world at large, mend a scraped knee, rescue a late Sunday night science project disaster, and comfort a broken-hearted teenager.

Here's another reason why self-confidence is essential during these years: children test boundaries by nature, and even the best of parents are cast aside from time to time by their teenagers. Parents who can't accept periodic rejection as part of the healthy life cycle can get sucked into the dramas of their children. That is never a good place to be. Good leaders take periodic push-back and displays of attitude in stride and know when it is and isn't to be tolerated.

THE IDEAL MATE IN THIS STAGE

Husband #4: The Family Man

A few chapters back I portrayed marriage as a decathlon rather than a marathon. My point was that marriage, instead of being one long, steady race, should be viewed as a series of smaller, diverse events, each with different goals and requiring different skills for success. The advantage of viewing marriage through this lens can be clearly seen during the Family Ties stage.

The ideal husband at this stage, just like during the Then Comes Baby stage, has evolved from someone who was all about himself into a guy who is all about the family. But there is one important difference. During the previous stage of marriage, this husband, much like a rocket trying to blast out of Earth's atmosphere, consumed a great deal of energy at a rapid pace. He was sleep deprived and worn out most of the time, but he still managed to power his family through to the next stage. These days, while he's still all about the family, he has to operate in a different way. He is less focused on the quick burn and more focused on long-term stability. Now he's concentrating on keeping the family moving steadily in a smooth and functional orbit instead of rapidly ascending. In other words, he's working smart rather than working hard.

This guy realizes that his wife and family need him to be a steady, well-balanced person and a good father more than anything else. His family still needs his energy, but they also need his brains, resourcefulness, and wisdom. With that in mind, he finds a way to be a nurturing, connected, and kind parent to his children, a motivated and enterprising worker, a staunch team player with his wife, and a tolerant member of his family and hers, even when he feels stressed or mistreated.

When his children are very young, he has boundless patience with them, even when getting hit over the head repeatedly with a toy hammer. When they are a few years older, he finds a way to be enthusiastic about school art projects, alert and focused during long pointless stories about dinosaurs, and interested and excited about whatever they are interested in, even if he can't quite follow why they find that particular item so thrilling. When the children are teenagers, this husband wisely looks past their irrational and selfish behaviors and finds ways to make them feel supported and respected even when their decisions are immature, lazy, or self-centered—while holding fast against their tirades and calling them on their more egregious transgressions. In short, he treats his offspring as if they are his most prized treasures and devotes his energy to raising happy, well-adjusted children.

He also treats his wife and his life differently than he did in previous stages. He eagerly and forcefully supports his co-leader when she needs it and steps aside when she's running the show. He still keeps an active life outside of his family, but he always considers ways to put his family first when events or circumstances cause his individual needs to conflict with those of his family, because he recognizes the important role his emotional and physical presence plays in the lives of his children and his spouse. He understands that his children need a positive relationship with him and that, more than any other factor, their feeling of being connected to and loved by him determines how well they will do in life.

Wife #4: The Chief Operations Officer

In this stage of life, most husbands need a wife who organizes, manages, and executes like a pro. This woman no longer bounces ideas off her husband for approval or acceptance—now she just gets things done. These days, she knows the plan (she probably came up with it) and knows how to pull it off. During these years, life is *busy.* While millions of fathers participate in child rearing more fully than ever before, many women will tell you that the lion's share of the responsibility—and the worry—still falls mainly to them. On any given day, life consists of several kids running around who all need to get out of bed, eat, shower, and dress, make it to various educational, social, and athletic activities, get homework done, feed and walk the dog, and snuggle with their mother. This, of course, all needs to be organized and completed on time, even when she is also packing their school lunches and backpacks, talking to their teachers, arranging their schedules, signing off on their homework, transporting them around, and catering to all their unpredictable daily physical and emotional needs.

These mothers must also carry an immediately accessible mental library of information on each and every child: what each one eats, when they eat it, when they're going to buy lunch, when they're going to pack lunch, who is dating whom (this week!), who broke up with whom (and why), who has to go to the doctor, friends, stores, activities, and anything else that comes up.

A woman who gets all this done is awe-inspiring. And men find these skills to be irresistible, even if they rarely say so. A woman who handles the many difficulties of juggling a busy family is far more interesting and desirable to a mature husband in this stage of life than a young, immature woman with few of these abilities. Even though this woman may not look as young and fit as she did fifteen years ago, what she has to offer these days is maturity, competence, and confidence. In the hectic life of a family, a woman who knows what she's doing—and who can fake it like nobody's business when she doesn't—is far more valuable than a fun but high-maintenance woman.

This woman has developed a strong sense of self. Despite everything that's going on, she doesn't lose herself in these responsibilities. She recognizes that she has to be strong and capable and that it is her job to take care of herself and to build a life of her own as well.

This woman also handles her extended family much better than she did during previous stages. She is growing into her role as the matriarch of the family and has become much more confident knowing exactly what she wants, when she wants it, and how she wants it done. That confidence enables her to communicate her wishes kindly but assertively, and she deftly handles many of the intrafamily politics.

Making It Happen: Mastering the Family Ties Stage

COMMUNICATION SKILLS FOR THE FAMILY TIES STAGE

In line with the need for competence and autonomy that dominates this stage, successful couples learn during these years that there is no room for the immature conversational games that sometimes plague earlier years in a marriage. Here are a few of those games and tips for how to avoid them:

Game 1. "Guess What I'm Thinking"

Many people (often women) develop a passive communication style derived from their fear of simply speaking their mind. Instead of getting directly to the point, they drop hints, hoping the listener will figure out what they need, so they don't have to assert themselves. This communication style often sounds like this: Mary, on the phone with her husband, says, "When are you leaving the office? The children have a lot of homework tonight and I need to go grocery shopping later." While this statement sounds clear enough, it really isn't, because what Mary is trying to communicate is that she wants her husband to get home on time that night and help her out. She is hoping he'll say something like, "I can stop at the grocery on the way home. I'll head out soon. What do we need?" Since all he hears is a laundry list of things that *she* is doing, he's likely to miss that message and say something like, "OK, I'll probably see you around eight after I work out." This response makes her angry, and she might say something like, "All you ever care about is the gym and working out." Now, thoroughly confused, he returns her volley with either anger or a demeaning shut-down: "Whatever."

In the Family Ties stage, spouses typically have no emotional tolerance for these antics. It is not appropriate for a competent, high-functioning adult to beat around the bush and revert to sulking when things don't go his or her way. As you learned in earlier stages, the process of communication is always changing, which means that *how* one communicates has to change through the years just as much as *what* one communicates. This stage of marriage calls for leadership, and leaders speak their mind. In the example above, Mary just needs to say, "Will you come home early tonight so I can get a few things done?" or "I need to get the kids started on their homework. Can you get home early and stop for groceries on the way?" It sounds simple enough, but you'd be amazed at how often couples waste time chasing each other around these immature interactions.

Game 2. "My Feelings Get Hurt When You Don't Listen to Me"

Before we each had children, my brother and I used to have long, detailed phone discussions about each other's lives. Then, once we both had young children running around, our phone conversations changed significantly. At that time, it was not uncommon for either one of us to quickly interrupt the other with, "Oh, gotta go," and then abruptly hang up. And that was perfectly fine. We both knew that times had changed and that our abruptness was nothing personal. Neither of us was offended by it because we were both in the same situation and, more importantly, we knew we weren't responsible for taking care of the other's emotions.

Unfortunately, this degree of understanding is not always in evidence in relationships. Often, early in the marriage, couples fall into communication patterns that require each spouse to listen at great length to the everyday dramas of the other. While this kind of confiding is important and necessary in general, not a lot of time is available for it to happen with any regularity during the Family Ties stage. I can't tell you how many times during this stage I came home from work and began telling my wife a story about something that happened to me during the day, only to find that I had to restart the story numerous times due to constant interruptions by children, phone calls, or a variety of other things. All these years later, there are still many stories hanging out in Untold Story Limbo simply because we never got around to finishing them. When we were newly married, I would feel hurt by these cutoffs (so would she when the tables were turned). But once we reached the Family Ties years, we put all that behind us. We knew that our intentions were always good but that circumstances weren't always in our favor.

Couples who don't evolve this sort of acceptance can become mired in hurt feelings on a regular basis. Similar to what we saw with Patty, many partners expect their spouse to be at their disposal for any number of their emotional and physical needs. I am not saying that couples shouldn't take care of each other or talk deeply and intimately with each other—of course they must and they should—but there's a limit to what another person can do and what a partner should expect, especially during these years. Spouses like Patty who expect that their spouse will be their emotional be-all and end-all, providing undivided attention on demand, are not being reasonable.

Game 3. "Just Do It the Way I Say"

Some relationships are more dictatorships than democracies: one spouse or the other has no patience for things being done differently than how he or she wants them done. For such people, a supportive spouse doesn't argue, he or she just does. It's a style that develops between two insecure spouses. The controlling one insists that things go as he says because he feels uncomfortable when things don't go his way (remember: the person with the fewest coping skills controls the relationship), and the passive one feels that she will be unloved if she argues. Together, they create a communication style fraught with power plays and insecurity.

While this style may work before the couple has children or when the children are young, it never works once children become old enough to speak their mind and develop their own opinions, particularly during the preteen and teenage years. At that point, rebellion is part of the daily fare, and "my way or the highway" parenting usually leads to constant battles, deceptive behaviors, and possibly extreme acts of defiance.

Couples with this communication style must evolve if they hope to survive those years with any degree of sanity and marital satisfaction. To these couples I suggest that they quickly examine and reevaluate their definition of respect and support. These concepts can be defined many different ways, and those who want to receive appreciation must learn how to give it as well. Imbalanced power relationships like this commonly lead to children who embody the same insecurities.

Game 4. "If You Loved Me, You'd Chase Me"

This technique, although similar to "Guess What I'm Thinking," is slightly different in that it involves a spouse who measures how much her partner loves her by how many hoops that person is willing to jump through in order to communicate effectively with her. It often looks like this:

Denise, when asked by her spouse how her day was, says with a big sigh, "Fine." When pressed by her spouse as to what that means, she often says, "Well, it's really nothing." This goes on for several exchanges until she eventually pours out how she's really feeling.

Young couples engage in this style of interaction frequently, and before their lives and careers get hectic and complicated, they have the time and the energy for it. Once they hit the fast lane, particularly when children are involved, those days should be put behind them; otherwise they'll find themselves angry, disconnected, and frustrated with each other in the Family Ties stage.

To these couples, I often point out that they are actually mistreating their spouse by asking him or her to continually prove his or her love through this game. No one wants to spend his entire life proving himself. Those who choose to behave this way usually get exactly what they fear the most: a spouse who eventually abandons them.

Game 5. "Feed My Ego"

Many people rely heavily on their spouse to complete them. Most of their interactions are thinly disguised attempts to get their spouse to boost their self-esteem. It often looks like this:

Suzy, after a long day of work, describes to her spouse in great detail all of the things she had to do that day just to survive. He hears all this and begins offering suggestions (remember he's a man, so he's a fixer) as to how she could do things differently. But she doesn't want advice. She is very proud of herself and wants him to acknowledge what a good job she did and stroke her ego. When he fails to do this, she gets angry and feels he doesn't understand her. Later that night, she acts cold and withdrawn toward him because she expects her spouse to affirm her good traits and feels lost and alone without that. The problem is that he never knew what he was supposed to be giving her. In most cases, if he knew that was what she was looking for, he easily could have met that need.

It happens also when dad takes the kids for the afternoon. Many dads return from these escapades desperate for some atta-boys from their wives for how well they did, but if dealing with the kids is something she does every day, no rewards are likely to be forthcoming. Many dads feel hurt by this, but in this stage of marriage, spouses need to be assertive enough to state what they're looking for and secure enough not to sulk or fall apart when they don't get what they want.

To these couples I often point out how they are failing to achieve the primary goal of this stage of life, co-leadership, and that if they don't find a way to become competent, autonomous, and functional of their own accord, their relationship—and their children—will suffer.

TOOLS FOR BUILDING INTIMACY IN THE FAMILY TIES STAGE

As you probably remember from the Young Married Couple stage, one of the problems newly married couples face is that they have limited shared experiences through which to achieve intimacy and need to seek out opportunities to create intimate moments. In the

Family Ties years, a couple's lives have become so interwoven that they can find many different avenues for building intimacy, provided they take the time to do so.

Building Intimacy Through Shared Life Experiences

When a couple become parents, they are immediately intimately bonded simply through the process of having children together. But as the children grow, they develop lives, personalities, and interests of their own, and that creates an entirely new set of bonding opportunities. As certain activities become extremely important to them—from snuggling on the couch every Friday night with a movie or spending an entire weekend carving a pinewood derby car—spouses begin to witness how well each partner interacts with the children and how well the children bond and grow in each spouse's presence. When this happens, a deeply felt intimacy occurs. There are few things more wonderful than seeing your children grow through the process of being loved by your spouse. It's those connections that build a deep and lasting bond in this stage of marriage. In our hearts, our children mean everything to us, and when we trust that our co-parent will love and cherish our children with the same boundless love that we feel, it creates a deep bond. Parents also need the energy and unity this bond provides in order to keep going during the teen years, when these moments of closeness tend to become far less frequent.

This point also illustrates why change is so important in a marriage: those who fail to reach an appropriate level of competence in co-parenting will not experience this unique and powerful bonding.

Building Intimacy Through Shared Emotional Experiences

As couples in this stage begin to achieve deeper levels of communication, they can deepen intimacy through their ability to share common feelings. The following pages explain the different levels of communication couples can reach as their intimacy grows.

Level One Communication—Surface Interactions

At this level, people exchange pleasantries and discuss mildly personal subjects. This is the level at which most strangers interact. It is polite and informative, but it lacks detail and deep emotion. Some examples are:

Spouse 1: "How was your day today?"
Spouse 2: "Fine; how was yours?"
Spouse 1: "Good. What's for dinner?"
Spouse 2: "Spaghetti."
Spouse 1: "Sounds good. I'll be on the Internet; let me know when it's ready."
Spouse 2: "OK."

or

Spouse 1: "Did you see the new James Bond movie is coming out this week?"
Spouse 2: "No, I didn't."
Spouse 1: "Yeah, it's coming out Friday."
Spouse 2: "We're busy Friday—the Wilsons are coming over for dinner."
Spouse 1: "Oh, yeah. We'll go next week then . . . I think it's going to rain all weekend . . ."

This level of interaction is necessary for communicating basic information, but if couples communicate mainly on this level, their relationship stagnates quickly. Successful couples in the Family Ties years interact at this level only as necessary and then move on to deeper conversations.

Level Two Communication—Facts without Feelings

Level two is a slightly deeper level of communication that contains many of the details of a person's daily life, from the contents of the workday to the contents of the refrigerator. Married couples can fill hours of time talking at this level, but the subject matter usually lacks an emotional connection of the kind that builds intimacy. In a stereotypical example, a spouse, returning home at the end of a long day, will talk at length about all of the details of the workday, including who said what, what product was purchased by whom and for what price, which meetings lasted too long, which boss is behaving poorly, which client is being irrational, and on and on. While this monologue certainly contains many details of the spouse's life, it contains none of his or her feelings. It's the absence of those feelings that causes the other spouse's eyes to glaze over halfway through the story because there's little to relate to of any lasting importance.

Similarly, long stories about how many diapers were changed, how many errands were run that day, and detailed explanations about overflowing laundry baskets, sinks, and closets all contain no emotional component and usually cause the other spouse's eyes to wander back toward the television set.

If a couple spends too much time in level two, the lack of shared emotional connection will cause one or both spouses to withdraw and return to level one communication, and they eventually lose each other. That's what brings us to level three.

Level Three Communication—Facts with Feelings

Level three contains much of the good stuff. At this level, couples share the events of their day but stop short of exhaustive detail. Instead, they insert into the discussion how they felt in a given situation. So, in the workday example mentioned above, the spouse talks about feeling frustrated with unappreciative clients, feeling ignored by the boss, and the feelings of futility attached to failing to get anything productive done during the day as a result of countless interruptions.

In the stay-at-home-parent example, instead of spouting off an endless litany of boring chores, now that spouse shares his or her feelings of frustration with unappreciative children, feelings of being ignored by those same children, and the repeated feelings of futility at failing to get anything done because of countless interruptions.

As you can see, when couples interact in this way, they soon realize that they often share similar or identical feelings throughout the day. That gives them something to identify with and bond over.

Level Four Communication—Identification and Intimacy

At this level, couples begin to have a deep intimacy that can only be found when each spouse feels that his or her partner truly understands and connects with him or her. Level four communication comes as a result of the strong bond that couples build in successful level three interactions. Couples who successfully master the Family Ties stage find themselves frequently interacting at this level and experiencing this level of intimacy. Insecure, domineering, or selfish spouses have difficulty allowing themselves to acknowledge the vulnerability that this level requires. In these interactions, couples move beyond describing the details of their days and even the emotions attached to those events and begin talking about how good it makes them feel when their partner understands and really connects with them. They are able to talk about how important this makes them feel to their partner and how special it makes their relationship.

Couples who interact well in level four talk about how much they appreciate their spouse's empathy, awareness, and interest in getting to know them. They also talk about how loved, respected, and understood they feel. Interactions like these are the ones that build lifelong relationships. By the time they reach the Family Ties years, couples need to communicate at this level in order to achieve intimacy.

DEVELOPING NEW ACTIVITIES

As a young single adult in my late teens and throughout most of my twenties, weekends (and occasional weekdays) were exclusively reserved for activities like parties, spontaneous out-of-town trips, nights at loud singles bars, and hours of recreation. During those years I couldn't imagine anything more boring than spending an entire weekend sitting around with the family and couldn't possibly fathom how anyone could enjoy that. I even made a promise to myself that when I had kids I wouldn't become one of those people.

Then, of course, when I reached the Family Ties stage, things changed completely. During those years, I found it hard even to remember why I enjoyed some of the things I did when I was younger (what did I possibly enjoy about standing around sweating in a loud, crowded bar, screaming at people just to have a conversation?), and I couldn't possibly remember why going out all the time to talk to strangers was so fulfilling.

I guess what happened is that I grew up. When my children were babies, I had no time for all those extracurricular activities, and when they got a little older all I wanted to do was to spend time with them. When given the choice, I took spending time with my family over most anything else. I began looking forward to weekend-long Monopoly games and G-rated movie marathons with the entire family curled up on the couch eating popcorn and fighting over the blanket. I found that Wiffle-ball games in the backyard and messy cake-making adventures became the things that kept me going day to day, not late-night dance marathons or even romantic dinners at expensive restaurants. The memories of those days with the family are some of the best memories I have of my kids, and I wouldn't trade them for anything.

All of this serves to make the point that, as we grow and change through the years, the activities we need to engage in with our spouses change as well. We all grow up—or most of us do—and the things that give us energy and excitement change with us.

Spouses need to recognize this and adapt their interests in order to keep pace with their marriage.

Not all activities at this stage have to do with children or with family time. Couples both with and without children often find other activities to occupy their time and emotional interests.

As healthy and enjoyable as this process should be, I find that adopting healthy new activities in this stage is one of the biggest hurdles couples face. Even though the world is filled with interesting adventures to explore, hobbies to pursue, and challenges to meet, many couples simply fail to engage in new activities at this time in life. It's amazing the number of previously active people who, upon having children, find themselves only interested in watching television, working, or surfing the Internet. I've outlined below four important factors for couples to think about when taking on new activities in this stage. I suggest that couples entering this stage of marriage review this list and decide how best to adopt this new thinking into their lives.

1. Spend Time Together as a Family

At this point in my life, I've sat through more Little League baseball games than I thought humanly possible. And even though it often consists of just sitting around watching the budding superstars walk twenty-five batters in a row, being there still serves a wonderful purpose for my children and my spouse. Some people make the mistake of believing that we attend these events for our kids, but it's not only my kids who appreciate my being there; my wife does as well. As we huddle side by side on unforgiving metal bleachers, we share the experience together. That time together keeps us far more connected and happy than earning a few more dollars or going out for nice dinners ever does.

In this stage, it's often easy to identify the couples with the good relationships. They're the ones who attend every activity they can, and they sit together, enjoy their time, and rarely talk on their cell phones. These people realize that family time is family time and that these are moments to be cherished.

2. Spend Time Together

It's vital that you make it a nonnegotiable priority to carve out alone time with each other on a regular basis. While this may seem a slight contradiction of my last point, it isn't. Even though family time is important, couples still need specific alone time to spend with each other. Some couples make it a priority to go out to dinner or a movie or some sort of event each week, just the two of them. This plan sounds easy enough, but as life gets hectic, it's often the first activity to get tossed from the schedule. That's typically a mistake. I find as a couples therapist that most of the couples who are in trouble have, somewhere along the way, cut this particular priority out of their lives. Even just one night a week can go a long way toward keeping couples connected. This date night idea can work for couples without children, too: I know one couple who eat dinner together every night at home but make it a point to dress up a bit and go out to dinner each Saturday night. The change of scene and ambiance spurs them to talk about dreams, plans, aspirations, and worries that have been on their minds—level three and level four topics they might never discuss over leftovers at home.

Another good way to meet this goal is to consciously insert bonding moments into each day. What I mean here is that couples carve out specific time during each day (say 9:00 p.m. to 9:30 p.m.) exclusively dedicated for them to communicate with each other without other interruptions—no cell phones, Internet, children, television, or anything else but each other. During that time, the couple has to sit down, talk about whatever is important to them, and simply spend time together. Believe it or not, very simple actions like this initiate progress because they force the couple to work on their relationship on a daily basis.

3. Set Aside Time to Talk About Your Relationship

Intimate connection need not take a long time, especially if it's frequent. Now that you know how to engage in level three and level four communication, use these techniques to move quickly to an exchange about something you appreciate about each other, or something you recently noticed your spouse say or do that impressed you or that you wondered about, or a memory of a wonderful time when you felt beautifully connected, or a request for something that would help you keep your connection strong. Make these conversations calm and affirming, even when you're talking about something that needs improving in your relationship. This is not a time for logistical discussions of who will do what in the household. It's also not a time for complaint, whining, or airing a list of grievances. If you're really doing this every day, you won't have a list to air.

4. Support Each Other in Individual Endeavors

Everyone needs time alone and the space to have a life outside the one he or she shares with his or her spouse. It's important to have activities that are uniquely yours that you engage in without your spouse or your family, and each spouse should agree to pull extra time with family duties to support the other's "me time." Without this, spouses have nothing new to bring to the relationship to keep it energized. I like to think of two people in a relationship as two oars on a rowboat. They have to work together, but they also each have their own water to churn, their own goals to meet, and their own unique responsibilities. Without them each fulfilling their own separate duties—yet still working together—the boat would be dead in the water (or go in circles). That's why marriages that contain two people who are emotionally strong enough to be their own people fare far better than marriages in which a couple becomes hopelessly enmeshed, doing everything together yet bringing nothing new to the table.

Make it a point to embrace and encourage each other to take on hobbies, activities, interests, jobs, or even friendships that are uniquely your own. I recommend that couples sit down and discuss what each would like to do and what each can do to support the other (within reason) as he or she embarks on these activities. Spouses whose emotional needs are so great that they restrict their partner from growing beyond the relationship limit the relationship from growing as well. Couples who encourage outside growth in each other experience far more satisfying marriages and have a much easier time transitioning into the later stages of marriage, which require an infusion of new energy and new attitudes.

TROUBLESHOOTING IN THE FAMILY TIES STAGE

As we've seen so far, each stage has its own set of challenges. Following are several common scenarios that arise in the Family Ties stage, due to the unique circumstances and dynamics that people encounter at this time in their lives.

"I Don't Want Dad Coming to My Game"

There's a troubling presence at almost every one of my children's sporting events: the overbearing, highly critical father. This is the guy who screams at his children and berates the umpires, ruining the game not only for his children, but also for everyone else. Many men have a love of sports and a highly competitive spirit. Mature men don't lose that fire; they just realize that it has a time and a place—and that place is certainly not in the bleachers at their fourth grader's baseball game. Guys who act this way certainly don't personify the mature, role-model responsible leadership of the Family Ties stage, and their behavior usually negatively impacts more than just their children and the eardrums of innocent bystanders. Just like Patty, who unloaded all her emotional baggage on her family, these dads unload all of their insecurity on their kids, and it becomes a tremendous intimacy killer in their relationship. Most wives want to feel proud of their spouse, not have to apologize for him or worry whether he'll embarrass them in public. When they experience him acting this way they feel angry and disconnected from him. Most of the men who behave this way defend their actions as "just being competitive" or "just trying to teach their children discipline" or "just showing a winning attitude," but they're none of these. They're the tantrums of an immature man who hasn't learned that he's not a loser if he (or his kid) loses—and who hasn't figured out that how he behaves is a reflection of his spouse as well.

"Help! I've Become a Nobody"

Many people (usually women) who give up highly successful careers to become stay-at-home parents eventually begin to feel like they no longer have anything important to say, any important place to go, or any impressive accomplishments to discuss other than "Well, I got Justin and Emma to every one of their events on time this week!" The problem is that seemingly mundane tasks like successfully cleaning all the Cheerios from between the cushions in the backseat of the minivan or perfectly synchronizing the completion of laundry loads with naptime feel insignificant in the grand scheme of things. Considering this, it's understandable why many stay-at-home parents end up feeling as if they no longer contribute to the world in any meaningful way.

To combat this tendency, couples must remember the importance of setting goals and continually working toward them. Those who get bogged down in feeling useless and unattractive should recognize that finding activities that satisfy their own interests is just as important as finding activities for their children. Children get bored without activities, and so do stay-at-home parents. If you're bored, do what you'd tell your kids to do if they were bored: "Go find something to do!"

"Poor Me"

Many people (usually women) suffering in bad marriages come to therapy at this stage of their life looking for a therapist to sympathize with their plight. Usually the problem is that their husband is mean, irresponsible, incompetent, unfaithful, or all of the above. Now don't get me wrong; I am very sympathetic about these situations and spend a great deal of time helping people work through the many difficult feelings that dysfunctional relationships create. But more needs to be done than just hand holding or teaching spouses how to keep the peace in their marriage (many therapists do exactly that by teaching victimized spouses to just accept things and find positives in other areas of their lives). Typically, both spouses contribute to bad marriages. Sure, the mean or inappropriate spouse is the obvious violator, but the victim spouse is dropping the ball also. As you know by now, the goal of this stage of marriage is to be a fully autonomous adult. That means that you handle problems that need to be handled and make tough decisions when tough decisions need to be made. Spouses who are only willing to adopt passive stances are failing to take charge of their lives. I always say, "You only live once. If things aren't going well, fix them. If they can't be fixed, try a little harder." In the end, though, if it becomes clear after your best effort that things aren't going to change, it is your responsibility as an adult either to get divorced or find some other assertive solution. Floating along through the rest of your life depressed and resentful in a miserable marriage is not a solution. Remember, you spend a great deal of your parenting hours imploring your children to step up to the task at hand and be responsible, even if it's unpleasant. If you have problems you don't deal with, your children will likely do the same. I know it's tough, but you can't point the finger at your immature spouse if you aren't willing to grow up a bit yourself.

"I Get No Respect Around Here"

Teenagers are notorious conflict starters, and parents are almost always pitifully willing to take the bait. Parents often come to see me specifically because their unruly teenager is destroying their marriage. Most of the time, these parents have wildly conflicting opinions of how to deal with the volatile child and end up fighting constantly about how to handle him or her. I find that most of the time they should do nothing and that they should concentrate more on healing their marriage than trying to straighten out someone who doesn't want to be straightened out.

I'm not saying that serious problems like drug abuse, violence, or failing out of school should be ignored; I'm talking about all the other, smaller things, like sloppy dress, messy room, poor grammar, surly attitude, chronic lateness, and the like. The simple fact is that, with adolescents, many of these traits come with the territory. Many parents find themselves at odds because they take all of these behaviors personally and consequently feel disrespected, mistreated, or ignored most of the time.

The solution here is not to accuse your spouse of creating the problem or to attempt to control the uncontrollable child. The best solution is to develop thick skin and a short memory. Parents of these types of kids usually have difficulty in both of these areas, but trying to control things only makes the child more rebellious and the marriage more contentious.

Special Circumstances in the Family Ties Stage

Marriages That Occur Later in Life

While most people marry in their twenties or thirties, many people get married much later in life. Nevertheless, they still have to go through the same adjustments all married couples do.

The good news is that some people who marry later in life have already worked out a number of the personal development issues that can affect a marriage. Often, these folks already understand the importance of being independent, autonomous, and of having their own separate interests to bring energy and intrigue to a relationship. These people tend to settle quickly into a marital style that is appropriate for their phase of life and begin building a deeper relationship through various experiences and challenges.

The greatest hurdle couples who meet and marry later in life typically have is that both are usually very set in their ways. What appears as an appealing maturity during dating can become a hazardous rigidity in a committed relationship. When spouses marry at a younger age, they may be less skilled in relationship strategies, but they are, in a sense, more malleable and able to accommodate the growing pains of togetherness. A great deal of learning about each other goes on in the early years as younger spouses grow and change together. Even though the process can cause a certain amount of conflict, it also affords excellent bonding opportunities. Couples who marry later in life don't have these common experiences and occasionally find themselves feeling remarkably disconnected from each other as a result of not having experienced a particular growing moment together. When not handled well, these situations can lead to insecurity, hurt feelings, and a rift in the marriage.

The Key to Success

Couples who marry later in life don't have the luxury of many years of trial and error learning. They have to transition through the early stages of marriage very quickly. Therefore, it's important that couples who marry later in life discuss key issues such as negotiating the conflicting rules of families and friends and learn how to speak very precisely and clearly to each other about what they want and how they feel during moments of stress. These tools often come in handy during stressful or crisis moments in later years, such as when dealing with aging parents, career upheavals, or personal health issues. Couples who marry later in life may have long-established communication patterns that they've never questioned but that now don't serve them as well as they used to. Reprogramming one's thinking can be challenging, but it can be done, and here again, it should be done *before* the problem or crisis hits, since learning new skills in the heat of the moment adds stress that no one needs.

Families Taking Care of Elderly Parents

Many families have elderly parents who need caretaking. Families in these circumstances are challenged not only by the difficulty of their situation, but also by the chronic nature of it. They feel like they never get a break—and unless they take active steps to avoid that outcome, they're basically right. The physical and emotional drain is enormous and can be unrelenting. Spouses not only have to adapt to the caretaking role itself but also need to find a way to cope with the chronic nature of it.

The Key to Success

Couples in these situations need to become specialized versions of the ideal spouses in each stage. Caring for elderly parents, depending upon the nature of the caretaking, is in some ways similar to dealing with small children. It often requires constant, highly efficient communication between spouses, as this additional responsibility is absorbed into what is likely already an extremely busy life. And it only adds to the need for the couple to arrange for time off—both alone and together as a couple. All people need a break now and then, and healthy couples make it a point to provide each spouse with time away from his or her daily responsibilities. For couples with chronic family issues like caring for an elderly relative, these breaks are even more important because of how easy it is for the pull of chronic responsibilities to consume our lives.

Couples who are dealing with parents with chronic needs fight this battle for many years (as opposed to just during the infant years). That makes it extremely important for them to embrace and continue implementing the strategies that work during the baby years throughout the course of their marriage. Doing so ensures that the couple will not lose themselves in their roles and will continue to work on growing as interesting and complex individuals. It also provides renewed energy to the relationship and encourages the spouses to continue to grow together as a couple, separate from their many duties and united in their identity as a force together.

SUCCESS STORIES: HOW YOU KNOW WHEN IT'S WORKING

Several years ago I gave a speech about relationships to a group of parents. While the speech I gave seems like a story about parenthood, it's really a story about achieving unity in a marriage through mastering the goals of this stage. It's about how an aligned marriage built by competent, mature spouses allows good parents to love their children and make them a priority above all else. As such, I think it embodies the main task—and rewards—of this stage well.

The Day I Grew Up

If you knew me today, you would find it hard to believe that as a child I was incredibly shy. As an adult, I speak comfortably and engagingly in front of large audiences and wish I could do more of it. I love people. I love attention. And I love the limelight.

As a young boy, though, I was small, scared, and passive. I took very few risks and, consequently, had very few opportunities. At school, I was often overshadowed by my brothers and my peers. I always felt that I had nothing to say and that no one would listen anyway. I was afraid.

But one day, something happened that forever changed who I am and how I look at the world. It changed my life in a way I never expected. This is the story of that day.

We all grow up and we all have life-changing experiences—things that forever shape who we are and who we become. For some of us, such an experience may come in the form of a book, a song, a poem, or an event. For others, it is a person, a place, or a spot on an X-ray. For me, it was a fish.

When I was eight years old, I spent a week at a YMCA camp with my two brothers and my parents. One day my mother took my brothers and me horseback riding for the afternoon while my dad stayed back at the cabin to fish off of the dock. After about three hours, we returned to find my father sitting quietly on the dock by himself with his fishing rod. These days, viewing the scene through the eyes of a parent, I recognize the incredible relaxation my father must have felt from three hours of summer sunshine on a dock with no screaming children at his feet. As children, of course, my brothers and I were unaware of these benefits and found it hilarious that Dad had spent all that time sitting there with his line in the water without catching a single fish. We mocked him mercilessly and demanded to begin fishing ourselves. My dad agreed to this idea, and amid the chaos of getting everyone's line in the water, he handed me his rod as he prepared one for me.

Well, within seconds of his handing his rod to me, the bobber disappeared, the line ripped out, and we all started screaming. Several minutes later the largest fish any of us had ever seen was flopping around on the deck, and *I had caught it!* High fives were passed around, pictures were taken, and I was the envy of my father and brothers. We told the story to everyone we saw, and I was repeatedly asked to reenact the event in all its details and glory.

But it didn't end there. To this day, using that little internal movie projector of memories we all seem to have, I can still see my father pulling the director of the camp aside and whispering something to him in the dining hall. I can see the look of pure pride on my father's face when I looked down at him as I stood on my chair telling the story to the entire cafeteria, as the camp director had asked me to do. And I can hear the roar of the crowd as they stood up and cheered for me after hearing that I had caught the largest fish ever to be taken from that lake.

Things changed after that. Everyone at camp knew me. Everyone wanted to see the pictures and everyone wanted me to tell the story. I made a bunch of friends that week even though I had never made a single friend in all my previous trips to camp. I went back to camp every year after that with my new friends and kept many of them as friends for years.

My life at home changed also. I started that school year as

a new person and never looked back. I made friends, I became popular, and I started opening up to the world. In the years to come, I grew into a confident, outgoing kid. I starred in school plays and musicals, played on a variety of sports teams, got good grades, made good friends, and enjoyed life. I was (and am) outgoing, friendly, and not afraid to take risks. Today, people remark that I don't seem to have a shy bone in my body.

Now, I don't want to give you the impression that growing up was all that easy for me or that I somehow arrived at adulthood without significant emotional baggage. Even though my father is a good man, I never was very close to him. He's a quiet man who's not all that affectionate, and he keeps his emotions well hidden. When I was a kid, he didn't spend a lot of time filling me up with long conversations about how much he loved me. But that's okay; I turned out all right, and I learned not to expect those things from him.

However, as I continued to grow up and grew more and more social, I found that we had less and less in common. In fact, for most of my adolescent years and into my early adulthood, I felt that we had nothing much to say to each other at all. I felt that he really didn't know me and certainly never understood me. I was sure that I didn't really know or understand him. We lived side by side in the same house for years and rarely ever talked about anything other than sports and the weather. I eventually concluded that he really didn't love me all that much.

Then one day all that changed.

When I was twenty-eight years old, I dropped in on my parents one day while they were visiting with some old friends. As the conversation turned to old times and old stories, we revisited the fish story for the hundredth time. As we were reminiscing about it, one of my parents' lifelong friends got very confused about the story. The way she understood it, she said, was that *my father* had caught the fish when he first started fishing three hours earlier, and that he had then rehooked it and waited for me to show up. She remembered that he had purposely given the rod to me and not my brothers because he wanted *me* to catch the fish.

The room was silent. My father was embarrassed and fumbled about as he tried to cover it up and change the subject. I was floored. Here I had learned that my father, the most avid fisherman I have ever known, had given up the catch of a lifetime because he realized that it was a bigger fish for his son than it would ever be for him. This, from the man who I thought didn't love me.

At that moment I realized that I didn't understand parental love at all. I see now that when two spouses are able to put their personal issues aside, it opens the door for unconditional love to flow between them and their children. When wholeness and personal integrity prevail in a marriage, parents are able to rise to a higher level of sacrifice and awareness, to a level that I had no idea existed. Mature, responsible parents, secure in themselves and their marriage, are able to joyfully put the welfare of their children ahead of their own needs. These well-balanced individuals are capable of seeing the bigger picture at all times. This allows them to recognize that some things, while important to them, are often much more important to their children. They know this by already having applied this rule to their marriage.

When the truth of this story dawned on me, I realized that throughout my life, I had only looked for love to come to me in the ways I wanted to see it. I had yet to understand the kind of love that is built in a healthy marriage and how that love carries over into parenthood. I was unable to see that love comes in all different ways and in all different forms, and just because I wasn't tuned in to my father's particular channel didn't mean the love wasn't there.

I realized then how selfish I was and how much I had misunderstood about the man and the husband my father was. I also realized how little I knew about my relationship with him. That was the first time I realized that he did want me to shine—he *really* did—and he really wanted to be a part of it. But he wanted to be the man behind the scenes who built the set, made sure the lights worked, constructed the stage, and then sat back and watched me perform. He hated the limelight, but he was thrilled to see me bask in it. I believe that he worked so hard to make sure he wasn't seen because he wanted *me* to be seen. It occurred to me that, throughout my life, he really had always been there for me—it was just that he'd been in the background, when I was looking for him in the foreground.

I realize now that I couldn't have done all the things I've done in my life without my father providing me with that foundation. For the first time ever, it occurred to me that although he certainly grew up in a very different world than I did, I had never bothered to try to understand him or that world. He came from a generation of men who were told never to show their emotions and grew up in a family that punished him when he did. Despite this, he was able to put these issues behind him and find another way to express his love for me—one that wouldn't violate the rules he had been taught but would still allow him to put my happiness above his. Although he didn't give me love the way I was used to getting it—through public attention, praise, and social approval—he gave it to me in a much more meaningful way because it was truly selfless. He gave it in a way that had ten times more impact than all the praise I'd gotten in my entire life. He worked hard to become a complete and competent person, and that process allowed him to joyfully give up important things in his life so that my life could be fruitful and happy. It had always been that way. The responsibilities of parenthood and the give and take of marriage had taught my dad to be selfless. I was just never able to see it until that day.

And that is the day I grew up.

STAGE 5:

Empty Nesting

There is nothing noble in being superior to some other man. The true nobility is in being superior to your previous self.
—HINDUSTANI PROVERB

My wife and I got married on a Saturday. On the Sunday morning following our nuptials, I awoke to find my wife in tears. "What's the matter?" I asked. "It's nothing," she said. "I'm just sad because I realized that now the only thing I have in life to look forward to is waking up next to you each morning."

Shocked, I stammered, "Did you really just say you were crying because now the only thing you have to look forward to is waking up next to me?"

"Yes," she said, still not entirely grasping how her words sounded. "I've dreamed about getting married my whole life, and now that dream is over. I'm married. Now all I have to look forward to is you."

I told her that if she thought she had it bad, imagine how I felt: "All I have to look forward to is waking up each morning to you crying about how bad it feels to wake up next to me!"

Eventually we laughed about the whole thing (and she hasn't cried about that since—that I'm aware of!), but the scenario stuck with me, not because I was hurt or worried that she secretly was unhappy, but because of how interesting it was to me that she was moved in that way. Since then, I've often imagined what it would be like if it were true. What would life be like if the only thing someone had to look forward to was waking up, once again, next to the same tired old person with the same stinky breath, the same messed-up hair, and the same frumpy pajamas? And what if that person said the same stupid things every morning, took too long in the shower every day, and stared at me in the same annoying way time and again? How would I stay in love with that person if that were the case? How do people who've lived together for many years manage to still want to be with each other when this is what they get day after day?

Welcome to the Empty Nesting years. These are the years when my wife's statement looms large and many people wake up and say to themselves, "I've lived all these years, and now all I've got to look forward to is him/her? Now what am I going to do?"

THE GOAL OF THIS STAGE

In some ways, this stage is similar to the Young Married Couple stage. The goal then was for couples to make their relationship a priority over everything else, building a strong, well-functioning team able to deal effectively and efficiently with life's inevitable ups and downs (babies, jobs, in-laws, financial challenges, and so on). Couples who've executed that stage well realize that it was the strength of their relationship that got them through, not just their love or their individual skills.

The same goes for the Empty Nesting years. The goal in this stage is to reconnect with your spouse and rebuild a powerful two-person team that can weather any storm. During these years, couples need to refocus their attention on their relationship, ensuring that they are on solid footing when they enter the next stage of their lives, the Golden Years, a time when companionship, mutual respect, and shared intimacy are the hallmarks of success.

Of course, the day-to-day challenges of this stage are different than the team-building years of the Young Married Couple stage. Nowadays, issues like adjusting to the kids being gone, approaching retirement, and dealing with aging and possibly health issues are paramount. But the need for couples to reconnect—and go forward with hearts and minds as one—is just the same. In these years, it's time, once again, to flex the muscles of a tightly bonded team.

DEVELOPING NEW IDENTITIES

People need a purpose. Without one, they feel adrift and struggle to find things to look forward to on a daily basis. During the first four stages of marriage, it was relatively easy for couples to find a shared purpose. When newly married and then as a young couple, they focused on nurturing their budding relationship and smoothly blending their separate lives into one. During the baby years and family years, they focused on forging their careers and meeting the needs of their children and each other. But when children grow up and move away and old age starts looming in the not-too-distant future, people begin to experience a sudden loss of purpose. This creates a powerful existential anxiety, and it compels them to search for meaning. The first place most people look is to their relationship. They examine the strength of their bond and evaluate what the rest of their life with their spouse will be like. If their assessment of their future offers few opportunities for them to share and enjoy life together as a couple, they become agitated and distraught.

The Couple Who Had It All

Jeff and Suzanne had been married for twenty-five years when the youngest of their three children left for college. Until that point, their marriage had been "above average" according to Suzanne; overall, things had gone relatively smoothly and they were happy. Jeff was a very involved father and had coached both of his sons' baseball teams for many years. He'd also been a major supporter of his daughter's acting interests, volunteering to help out in whatever way he could with set construction, lighting work, or any odd jobs when she landed roles in a variety of local theater productions.

Suzanne, too, had been very involved in the lives of their children. She'd been the manager for the boys' travel baseball teams and was well known for the terrific costume work she did for her daughter's shows. She'd also been a very active participant in the kids' school functions and served on the board of the PTA for a number of years.

Jeff and Suzanne were lucky enough to have kids who didn't mind hanging out with their parents, so they went out to dinner together often as a family and spent many nights home together playing games, exercising, or hanging out. Jeff and Suzanne were also fun-loving, gracious hosts and, as active, tuned-in parents, usually had a house full of kids. On weekends they would split their time—one going to one child's event and the other attending a different one—and then would invite all the kids and their friends over in the evening. Their house was "the neighborhood house," so much so that often other children would come by just to hang out, even when Jeff and Suzanne's kids weren't around.

"It was a great run," Jeff said when he sat in my office describing those years. "There was always so much going on and the house was always full of noise and excitement." Suzanne echoed the same sentiment: "I loved having the kids around. Those years were the best years of our life."

The Day the Music Died

Despite their long history together and all those wonderful memories, once all the excitement that was generated by a houseful of kids died down, Jeff and Suzanne's marriage had steadily drifted apart. By the time they came to see me, they were living active but separate lives and rarely did anything together. Suzanne had many friends and, when not working, pursued a variety of interests and hobbies. In the past few years Jeff had picked up an additional job in the evenings umpiring baseball games in the summer and basketball games in the winter. This kept him busy most evenings and often throughout the weekends. When he wasn't doing that, he had an old car in the garage that he was refurbishing.

The distance that had grown between them was unacceptable to Suzanne, and she found herself feeling lonely and isolated most of the time. She also was becoming increasingly angry with Jeff: "I'm basically invisible to him. He never kisses me hello or goodbye, never checks in with me, and we rarely have sex. We don't go anywhere or do anything together, we seem to never have anything to talk about, and he's always busy doing other things. Sometimes I think he just doesn't love me anymore. I want a marriage where my husband loves me, spends time with me, and cares about me."

Jeff scoffed at these ideas. "Of course I love her, and of course I want to spend time with her. We're just not interested in the same things. She alternates her evenings between knitting, shopping, and reading. I'm just not into those things. I'd love to spend time with her, but come on—it's not like I'm going to go to her knitting class or develop a sudden interest in shopping!"

Jeff didn't see what the big deal was. "We've always had busy lives with lots of things going on. We still do. Isn't that good for a marriage? Nothing has changed except that the kids are gone. Every marriage goes through some difficult times when the kids leave. It'll work itself out; it always does. We've gotten through rough patches before. I think the real problem is that Suzanne just misses the kids. She's the type of person who needs something to fret over, and the kids were it for her. I think she should volunteer at the school in her free time or find a child to take care of on the weekends. Then she wouldn't feel so lonely."

Although Jeff was right when he said that being active was good for a marriage, he was missing an important point. Being active is a good thing, but it's not the only thing. At this stage, rebuilding a connection with your spouse is much more important than just being active. That's why I call this stage Empty *Nesting* as opposed to Empty *Nest*. It's a dynamic time rather than a static continuation of the things you've been doing.

Finding Common Ground

Suzanne and Jeff still loved each other, but at that point they were anything but a tightly bonded team. They had devoted so much time to their children and to their individual pursuits over the years that they had lost touch with each other. Repairing their marriage involved a two-step process.

First, they had to recognize that rebuilding their team was essential to the success of their marriage, which meant they had to change their focus and attitude and no longer concentrate so single-mindedly on separate goals and interests.

Second, they had to rediscover their trust and respect for each other. It turns out that one of the reasons they'd gotten into this predicament in the first place was that many years ago, in the Young Married Couple stage, they'd had many conflicts over their different interests and perspectives on life. In the early days of their marriage, Jeff had been a highly competitive and driven young man convinced that "second place was for losers." He pushed himself, his friends, and his wife very hard to excel and was prone to angry outbursts when he, his wife, or his friends performed below his expectations. Needless to say, this attitude and behavior created many conflicts in their marriage.

Suzanne, as it happened, was almost at the other end of the

spectrum: she hated competition. She enjoyed activities that allowed people to share their creativity and time together. To her, life was too short to get agitated about a game, a job, or a hobby, and she could never understand why winning really mattered.

Jeff found Suzanne's attitude passive and thought it meant that she was unmotivated and destined for a life of mediocrity. He often voiced his disdain for her perspective, which hurt her and caused her to withdraw from him. Eventually, they stopped discussing any subject that involved a competitive activity, since it always ended in an argument. Each felt the other just didn't get it. Instead of working through their differences and finding common ground, they chose to agree to disagree and spent the next twenty or so years of their marriage pursuing separate interests, other than the children. They were still working under the same assumptions of twenty-plus years ago. But if they wanted a successful, loving relationship, the old model was just not going to work.

Since they took their differences as givens, when we revisited these issues together, it came as quite a shock to them to learn that each had softened his or her opinions.

Jeff reported that raising children had made him realize that he was wrong all those years ago. "I learned that win-at-all-costs crap from my dad when I was growing up, and I never really questioned it until I had kids of my own, especially after I started coaching their baseball teams. That's when I realized that they can't win all the time and that they're still successful even when they don't come in first."

Suzanne had a different opinion as well. "I realize that I was a bit naïve back then. Life isn't just about good intentions. My kids got so much self-esteem from setting goals and reaching them—that's winning, too."

Realizing that each had changed over the years opened the door for Jeff and Suzanne to rejuvenate their marriage. Once they knew that sharing a passion would not place them in the same awful conflict it had twenty years before, they were much more willing to find interests and activities to share. Their relationship took a turn for the better as they slowly began the process of building a life together. Eventually, they found several activities to share and their marriage blossomed.

Suzanne was the one who came up with the best idea for them. She had always been interested in dancing, and Jeff, while not an avid dancer, was athletic and good on his feet. Suzanne had a friend who was attending dancing classes, and she suggested they go together to learn ballroom dancing. That progressed into learning several different kinds of dancing and even participating in a few competitions over the years. Eventually, they purchased some equity in their local dance studio and ran that business on the side.

They also began to take a greater interest in each other's hobbies. Suzanne attended some of the games Jeff refereed on weekends, and they would go out to eat after each one and he would talk about the game. When Suzanne opened her mind to how difficult Jeff's job as referee was, she learned to appreciate what he was doing. Jeff started to invest some energy in learning about Suzanne's knitting. He even helped her find a place where she could donate some of her knitting projects to underprivileged individuals in need of extra clothing. Suzanne also started knitting various items they could sell at their dance studio. All of their efforts rebuilt their foundation as a couple, and their relationship was revitalized.

DEVELOPING A NEW IDENTITY

Most people, when they reach this stage of life and confront the hurdles that accompany it, do one of three things. The psychologically unhealthy shut down, give up, and become depressed, lonely, and bitter. These folks view their better days as behind them and they spend the majority of their time looking back on all that they have accomplished, failing to develop any meaningful new interests in the meantime. Partners (and parents) who operate from this perspective can be extremely boring, and relationships with them tend to be strained and unfulfilling.

Others, like Suzanne and Jeff, build new lives, but they do so in a way that is separate from that of their spouse. These people end up with more meaning in their lives individually but find themselves disconnected in their marriage. The third group work hard at building a shared life together, no matter how difficult that process may be. It starts by recognizing, once again, that each partner must construct a new identity.

Many spouses struggle in this stage to find an identity. They aren't old, yet they certainly aren't young anymore. For many years, they have defined themselves as a young married couple, as career builders, as parents, or as a family. Now, with those stages behind them, they find themselves with no clear idea as to who they are. They've probably achieved mastery in their careers and are either interested in new horizons or thinking about how they'd like their later years to look and feel. Their parental responsibilities have significantly declined. They're still a family, but their role in that system has changed as well. The long and short of it is that they have to find a meaningful identity that gets them excited and engaged.

Couples who view these years as an opportunity to do something different fare far better than those who view it as a loss and sit around mourning their old identity.

With that in mind, here's a good way to think about the challenges of this stage.

Expanding vs. Condensing

When spouses first get together as a young couple, their combined world is a small circle of two. As their lives continue to evolve, and especially if children are added to the mix, that circle, like a balloon continuing to inflate, expands to include all of the new family members as well as all their interests, activities, and friends. The couple's circle also includes neighbors, work colleagues, bosses, members of clubs and associations, and members of religious groups.

During these early expansion years, successful couples find a way to operate productively within this large circle without their own issues weighing them or their family down. Many couples are excellent "expanders," and it brings joy and energy to their lives. They find a way to include everyone in their circle with enthusiasm and ease. But marriages require people to play many roles throughout the years, and those who are good expanders often are poor "condensers." When the primary focus of the couple's attention goes away, the couple experiences a major void in their lives and they feel lost.

But there is no reason to think that one's life has to condense. Life is as big and interesting as we want to make it, but doing so in this stage requires a conscious effort on the part of each partner. Voids don't have to remain as empty spaces in our lives. Find things to fill them and life will remain as rich as ever. The key is recognizing that you will have to seek out activities and interests; they won't come to you. Keep your mind open and you'll be amazed at what you can find.

THE IDEAL MATE IN THIS STAGE

Husband #5: The Revitalizer

The ideal husband at this stage is full of ideas. He appreciates how good he and his wife were at leading the family team and navigating their large circle of people, activities, and responsibilities, and he strives to find new teams and new adventures for the two of them to engage in as a couple. He regularly goes out of his way to discover new activities, interests, or events for the two of them to share and is ready, if necessary, to give up some of his old ways and embrace life in a variety of new and different ones. He seeks the positive in life and welcomes almost every idea his wife brings to the table (that doesn't mean he agrees with everything, but he listens and looks for ways to build on her thoughts). He also finds ways to enjoy her interests and to share them with her as much as possible.

All this can be done far more easily than one might think. For example, Jeff didn't have to take up knitting in order to bond with Suzanne over her hobby. Just listening to her ideas, affirming her work, and learning a little of what knitting is all about and why it's meaningful to her was enough. Most spouses, if they're being fair, recognize when their spouse is meeting them halfway on an issue, and they deeply appreciate it. The ideal husband in this stage realizes this and understands that there are many ways to connect with his spouse's interests beyond literally sharing the same experience. Instead of viewing these years as an opportunity to "finally do everything *I* have always wanted to do," he views them as a time to "finally do everything *we* always wanted to do."

If they have children, this husband is keenly aware of the emotional loss both he and his wife are feeling as a result of their children leaving the nest. Instead of dismissing her tears or the loneliness she may feel, he listens to her, comforts her, and shares his similar feelings. He also encourages her to try new things, to discover new interests, and to embrace new ideas.

Most of all, this man is a companion. He understands that happy relationships are fed by people who are enthusiastic about building and sharing things together. He understands that the success of his partnership, now and in the years to come, is based upon how willing and able he is to create an even tighter bond than the one they shared as a young married couple.

Wife #5: The Renewer

The ideal wife in this stage of marriage, like her spouse, realizes that the success of her marriage in this phase of life depends upon how well she reconnects with her spouse and renovates their relationship. She understands that the key to success in all stages—but especially this one—is to be both interesting and interested. As an interesting spouse, she recognizes that it's her job to continually re-create herself as an individual, and she makes it a point to find pursuits and activities that push her to embrace new responsibilities beyond her role as a mother and a career woman.

As an interested spouse, she seeks and finds ways to share enthusiastically in her husband's interests. Every hobby, no matter how dull or unappealing it seems on the surface, has aspects that can be appreciated by the nonfan. For example, in my marriage, I've witnessed my wife, through a process of focusing on the human-interest aspects of sports rather than on statistics or game strategy, evolve from being completely uninterested in sports into an eager follower of several teams. While she rarely knows or cares who's winning, she does seem to know an awful lot about the players and has favorites she roots for on a regular basis.

Another couple I know began long-distance biking together in their fifties. When they had kids, the wife rarely, if ever, got on a bike, whereas the husband rode frequently. At the onset of the Empty Nesting years, the wife decided to join him in this activity. Even though the enjoyment she took from riding was certainly different from his (she liked the scenery and the fresh air, while he liked the vigorous workout), that didn't matter. What mattered was that she found a way to enjoy an activity with him that was important to him. This type of proactive, mature commitment to one's spouse goes a long way in this stage of a marriage.

This woman also understands that her husband, like her, may be dealing with some of the emotions that come up as people in midlife contemplate the passage of time, especially if either spouse has noticed a decline in physical or mental capacities. She recognizes that these changes can be rough for both sexes in our competence-focused and looks-obsessed society. She encourages any reasonable attempts on his part to strengthen or maintain his vigor through exercise, work projects, hobbies, or exciting adventures. Note that I said *reasonable*. This does not mean that she embraces his desire to quit his job, buy a motorcycle, and travel the world. Although that sounds interesting, it's often a singular fantasy that rarely supports the building and joining of the couple.

Making It Happen: Mastering the Empty Nesting Stage

COMMUNICATION SKILLS FOR THE EMPTY NESTING STAGE

I am always fascinated to listen to couples who've successfully reached this stage of marriage: they can communicate vast amounts of information through the simplest comments or through subtle words or gestures. It's ironic that spouses who, during their early years of marriage, had difficulty clearly communicating to each other about dinner (including who was going to shop for it, who was going to cook it, and who was going to clean it up) can now communicate multiple, detailed messages with the smallest of glances. You'll notice the contrast between the couples in previous stages and couples in the Empty Nesting stage in the following example of an exchange between a couple in the car on the way home from a social function. The couple from the earlier stage fails to recognize many subtle cues occurring between them, which results in an argument, whereas the couple in the Empty Nesting stage is recognizing and reacting to a variety of cues. First, the Young Married Couple:

Spouse 1: "I can't believe how rude you were in there, yakking away, when you could see that I was ready to go an hour ago."

Spouse 2: "Are you crazy? My back is killing me, I was ready to go a long time before that, but you were chatting it up with that blonde you work with."

Spouse 1: "I can't stand her. I was only talking to her because you were having such a good time talking to that pretentious guy about his sailing adventure."

Spouse 2: "Why didn't you say something? You looked like you were having a good time."

Spouse 1: "I did! I kept looking at you, remember?"

Spouse 2: "How was I supposed to know that meant you were ready to leave?"

Here's how the postparty discussion goes when couples get the Empty Nesting years right:

Spouse 1: "Boy, I could tell when I looked at you that you were done. You looked totally bored talking to that pretentious guy—just ready to go home. By the way, how's your back doing? It looks like it's killing you."

Spouse 2: "My back is really sore, and talking to that windbag didn't help. You didn't look too happy, either, trapped in the corner with that woman from work. You always get that crazy look in your eyes when you're trying desperately to be polite to someone who's really bugging you."

Spouse 1: "Yeah, she drives me nuts. And I saw you doing that affirmative head nod thing you do when you're completely uninterested in what someone is saying. I wish I could perfect that. You're very good at seeming like you care, but I know you were secretly planning your day tomorrow while he was droning on. It'll feel great to get home and just relax."

Spouse 2: "Yeah."

This sort of high-powered communication doesn't occur by accident. It happens over time as couples come to know each other very well. Despite its advantages, however, this level of familiarity can sometimes cause problems.

Familiarity Can Become Boring

As much as we all dislike conflict, it does engender emotion, and emotions bring spark to our lives. By the time a couple know (or thinks they know) exactly what the other is thinking and feeling, their relationship can feel mundane.

I suggest to couples that they periodically change things up a bit and force themselves to have conversations they may not normally have. One suggestion is to put time aside specifically to talk about their future instead of their past. Ask each other thought-provoking questions that generate intimate discussions, such as:

- What goals would you like to accomplish during the rest of your life, and what do we need to do to make that happen?
- What new challenges would you like to take on, and why are you not taking them on now?
- What are some things you've always wanted to do, say, or accomplish? What's keeping you from doing them now?
- What places have you not visited that you'd like to see?
- What are your fears about the future?

When couples get to the Golden Years stage, life is full of both hopes and fears. Sometimes these can be difficult conversations to have, and it's best to begin having them during the Empty Nesting stage, rather than waiting until it's too late to fulfill the hopes and avert the fears. Mulling over life's big questions with someone who knows you well and who is going through the same process can be fascinating and comforting.

Familiarity Can Be Used to Manipulate or Hurt Each Other

When you know someone very well, you also know how to hurt him or her. Couples who reach this stage with unresolved issues or anger can use their sophisticated communication skills and intimate knowledge of their partner's hot buttons to wreak havoc on their spouse's psyche. Spouses in this stage can hurl incredibly hurtful nonverbal insults across a room at each other without anyone else being aware of it. They can also resort to verbal barbs in front of others with the specific intent of causing emotional distress in their spouse.

Spouses who engage in this behavior are typically people who avoid engaging in mature, appropriate conversations because they fear vulnerability, change, or taking responsibility for their own actions. The best remedy is to let the behavior have no impact on you at the time it's occurring (remember my earlier warning that the person with the fewest coping skills in a group gets the most attention) and then call it out privately when you get the chance. In the end, you must not let this passive-aggressive behavior control how you behave. If you and your spouse need to talk about something, then do so directly and maturely. Make it clear that these games will not be tolerated. Spouses who stand firm on this may not succeed in changing their spouse's behavior, but by refusing to accept it, the toxic impact of the message is greatly diminished.

Familiarity Can Create Patterns That Inhibit Growth

Through the years, as couples come to know each other well, they also learn how to avoid conflict with each other. And most people avoid conflict whenever possible. It's amazing how skilled some couples can be at avoiding even the most glaring of issues simply by following their habitual communication patterns. One of the most common examples is a couple's failure to openly discuss their sex life with each other. For most people, what they find enjoyable in their intimate life changes subtly through the years. Still, a remarkable number of people feel uncomfortable discussing this very intimate topic with their spouse and end up spending years unsatisfied in the bedroom. Instead of simply talking about these things, many spouses rely on hints, innuendos, or sarcastic barbs to get their message across. Surprisingly, couples do learn to read these coded messages, but the tendency is to react nonverbally instead of maturely talking about an important subject. In this way, familiarity inhibits the couple from engaging in more productive conversations. In many cases, this same communication style plays out when discussing household issues, finances, future plans, and interactions with relatives.

Familiarity Can Produce an Environment That Inhibits Change

Often, people change their minds about things after many years of believing and acting in one specific way. Look at what happened with Jeff and Suzanne. When people believe they "know" what their spouse is feeling and thinking, they fail to account for the possibility that their spouse's opinion may have changed. As we've learned, change is very good for a relationship. It introduces energy and excitement. When a couple's accepted communication pattern inhibits or overlooks change, many opportunities for growth are lost. I counseled a couple who spent many years watching television together in the evenings after the children went to sleep. During those years, the husband found the television to be a pleasurable distraction and a way to wind down from his day. However, once the children all moved away, he started to despise the time he and his wife spent watching television. At that phase of his life, with much more time on his hands, he felt that watching television was just wasting time. His wife felt the same way—but neither had mentioned it to the other. They continued doing what they'd always done because they assumed they knew how the other felt. This went on for years until they finally realized how the other really felt.

TOOLS FOR BUILDING INTIMACY IN THE EMPTY NESTING STAGE

It's not uncommon for couples to suffer from a sudden lack of intimacy when they enter this stage. Many of the situations that produced profound feelings of intimacy and connection during the Family Ties stage may no longer have the same impact. When spouses confront the idea that living with their spouse for another thirty years may be all they have left to look forward to, they begin needing some very different messages from that spouse to help them absorb this reality in a positive way.

That's why a wife who never cared before if her husband kissed her hello or good-bye becomes angry and distraught when he now fails to do so. It's also why a sex life that used to be adequate becomes completely unsatisfactory. Most of all, it's why couples who have small rifts in their relationship become highly conflictual. When confronted with the possibility that they will have to put up with this bad attitude, poor sex life, lack of social graces, or whatever other problem is at hand for the rest of their life, they start needing things to change . . . *now.*

To help you quickly move out of the starting gate with these changes, I've compiled a list of tips and tactics below. Ideally each of these changes will have been happening naturally in one way or another as you and your spouse approach this stage. However, once your youngest child has left the home, it is definitely time to sit down and begin making these changes. I usually suggest that couples take a weekend away (or set aside some other time) to mark the start of this new stage. And, at that time, they should begin using these tools.

1. **Explore your new feelings.** Figure out what you need in order to feel intimately connected in this stage and find a way to explain those needs carefully to your spouse. Remember, your spouse likely has no idea that you have

changed or that you now want things to be different. In fact, he or she probably still believes that what worked in the past will continue to work today. Therefore, it is your job to kindly yet clearly report that things have changed. Note that you must also listen with an open mind to what your spouse wants to change as well.

2. **Make it a point to put romance back in your life.** Kiss each other hello and good-bye whenever you can. Call to check in during the day. Embrace each other "just because." Make it a point to sit next to each other on the couch instead of in two separate chairs. Organize date nights and make sure they involve new and interesting restaurants, activities, and adventures. The last thing you want to do in this stage of life is demonstrate that things are going to be exactly as they've always been. That doesn't mean they need to change drastically. It just means that adding some spark and variety will go a long way.

3. **Ask not what your spouse can do for you; ask what you can do for your spouse.** In these years it is always advisable to approach your spouse and engage in a conversation about change that commits you personally to change. Ask what you can do to help bring the two of you closer. Just letting your spouse know that this is on your mind does wonders and opens up conversations for new things to explore as a couple.

4. **Rekindle your sex life.** This is easier than you'd think. Typically it just involves initiating more conversations, engaging in new behaviors, making specific romantic gestures, and reassuring each other that you still find each other desirable. Much of being desirable has to do with *feeling* desirable—and if you don't, you probably already know what you need to do to change that, too, so make

a start and keep at it. You deserve it. And remember, not all changes need to be big. Getting rid of those tired old pajamas, losing a little weight, or just becoming more active can make a big difference.

5. **Create new adventures.** The same old stories and the same old nights out can become boring. Those who successfully generate new sparks in this stage always seem to have a new adventure on the horizon. It's a good thing to actively think and talk about ideas, dreams, and even pie-in-the-sky adventures. Even if a lot of them never happen, it's still good to discuss them and imagine them together, as you never know where your conversations will lead. Intimacy doesn't only occur between two bodies in the bedroom. Sharing your mind, your life dreams, and your fantasies with someone can be a very intimate experience.

DEVELOPING NEW ACTIVITIES

For many years, most couples have had such an extensive to-do list that they may have forgotten how to make a want-to-do list—and how necessary it is for their continued happiness as individuals and as a couple. Couples who succeed in the Empty Nesting years make it a point to introduce new activities into their relationship. Below is a short list of some activities I find especially useful for spouses in this stage of marriage.

1. **The bucket list.** A lot of people have already heard of this. Each spouse should create a list of things they want to do before they die. Then they compare their lists and pick at least two or three goals on the list to accomplish. Make sure the items are reasonable (no space walking or time travel) and find ways for the two of you to reach these

goals. While engaging in the process, remember that the energy couples gain from shared experiences does not necessarily come from the moment of accomplishment. The majority of the impact comes in the planning and anticipation of these events. That's really what the two of you are achieving through this exercise: you are finding something to devote energy and resources toward as a team.

2. **Start a business together.** Remember that not all businesses have to make it big to be successful, and that satisfaction is as much a part of success as moneymaking. Many businesses are just glorified hobbies. The Internet has made starting and operating these types of businesses relatively easy. Consider starting a business in something you've always been interested in doing. With the relatively small start-up costs most of these ventures have, what have you got to lose?

3. **Initiate "blind" activity nights.** Similar to a blind date, you have no idea what you are in for on blind activity nights. Couples who do this alternate roles of planner on a monthly basis (or whatever timetable fits) to plan a night out where their partner has no idea of the itinerary.

4. **Scan the community newspapers for ideas.** Local artsy community newspapers are good for more than just reading racy personal ads. They're also good for finding obscure movies to see, new restaurants to try, unique art shows to tour, and seasonal street fairs to sample.

5. **Try anything.** Life is an adventure. There are always new card games to learn, books to read, book clubs to join, sporting events to participate in, or art classes to take. I know of one couple who started their own book club—for just the two of them—each reading the same book, with a rule of no talking about it until they'd finished by

an agreed-upon date. Then they'd go out to dinner and discuss it. Another woman I know is thinking about asking her husband to start a tai chi class together. She has no idea what tai chi is and neither does he, but why not? Remember, no one expects you to be an expert. Check your ego at the door and learn new things. For example, I can't draw or paint to save my life, but I think it would be fun to take an art class someday. The same goes for photography. I'm fascinated by how people who know what they're doing can take a picture of exactly the same thing I'm taking a picture of, yet theirs looks interesting and mine looks flat and boring. I have no intention of ever becoming a professional photographer, but I'd like to see what I could learn.

TROUBLESHOOTING IN THE EMPTY NESTING STAGE

1. **Arrested development.** In some families, the children either don't move out for many years or don't move out at all. Couples in these situations need to make a conscious effort to move their relationship into the Empty Nesting years—empty or not—and begin the process of rebuilding their bond. Again, doing so is important because the reconnecting that occurs in this phase sets the stage for a strong relationship in the Golden Years.

2. **The delayed divorce.** Many couples find after only a few years of marriage that they have very little in common and don't even particularly enjoy each other's company, yet they stay together for the kids. While I think their motivation is admirable, staying often only postpones the inevitable, while creating numerous other problems in the

meantime. Many such couples find themselves, once the children have gone, with little to say to each other and little interest in rekindling the spark they originally had. I usually suggest that these couples get some counseling. While many do end up getting divorced, others find that, considering they made it through all these years, their relationship has more going for it than they thought it did. Divorce can be difficult, even for those who've planned on it for many years, because it always involves the tearing apart of two lives. Those who've come this far owe it to themselves and each other to do whatever they can to save their relationship. Many find through counseling that it's just a matter of working through unresolved issues and making a concerted effort to change and grow together.

3. **A failure to launch.** In some relationships, one spouse or another fails to effectively move into the next stage of life, desperately clinging to parenthood. I once counseled a woman who insisted on spending time every day with her daughter even though her daughter had recently moved out and had a job and a life of her own. This woman reported that she did this because her husband was "boring and never did anything anyway." She failed to see that she was not helping her relationship with her husband (or her daughter) by clinging to the past. Successful Empty Nesting wives make it a point to invest in new activities, new interests, and new adventures. This woman was heading for a life of loneliness if she didn't start embracing change.

4. **Sudden, unexpected anger management issues.** Many couples find themselves surprisingly angry with their spouse during these years. Often their anger is the result of old hurts that are finally coming to the surface after the many preoccupations of the Family Ties stage have ended. Many spouses feel blindsided by this anger and ac-

cuse their partner of being unable to let go. But it's often not that simple. Many people don't deal with important issues in their marriage simply because they either don't have the time during the Family Ties years or they don't yet have the emotional fortitude to address the problems. When they reach the Empty Nesting years, they finally find themselves able to tackle these problems—and as I've mentioned, there can be a pressing sense of urgency in this stage. In these circumstances, I usually suggest that couples receive marital counseling. The goal of this counseling is not to fix an ailing marriage, but to help create a healthy environment for working through some old issues.

Every few months in my practice I seem to get a couple in precisely this situation. They come in with their marriage intact and their love for each other still going strong—but they need a referee to help them take care of stuff from their past. Couples who engage in counseling at this stage usually learn how to work through these difficulties very quickly. They usually come in for five or six sessions (if that) and move on. It's nice to see them take command of their relationship and take flight again. These couples are making their marriage a priority and recognize that counseling is not just for people who are contemplating divorce.

SUCCESS STORIES: HOW YOU KNOW WHEN IT'S WORKING

Amy and Andy entered the Empty Nesting stage with the specific intent of finding a hobby the two of them could enjoy together. Even though neither had much experience with sailing, both wanted to learn more. So they bought a sailboat, joined a boating club, and decided to see what that adventure would bring.

Through the years, they suffered a number of harrowing encounters at sea, as well as adventures in docking and maintaining a forty-foot boat. Still, they came through it all loving the experience and eventually bought a bigger boat that they could take on longer trips. In time, through many costly errors and heated arguments, they learned how to sail their boat like pros. They also made many new friends at their boat club, started spending long weekends there, and eventually began helping other couples learn how to sail and navigate the seas. Amy even held a position on the board of the club for many years. They are still dreaming of new places to go and new adventures to take together.

In a way, their boat was their second family. To this day, Amy and Andy are one of those couples who seem ten years younger than they really are. When you spend time with them, you feel how much they care for and appreciate each other. It wasn't just the ups and downs of the high seas that fueled their energy and zest for living. It was navigating the ups and downs of their relationship, never abandoning their ship, that has kept them forever engaged, forever interested, and forever interesting. That is Empty Nesting at its best.

STAGE 6:

The Golden Years

An archeologist is the best husband any woman can have: the older she gets the more interested he is in her.
—AGATHA CHRISTIE

Several years ago, I was asked to give a speech to a group of elderly women on marriage and relationships. Given the warm response my "I'm My Wife's Third Husband" speech usually elicits, I gladly accepted and prepared my standard speech about change and the power of change in a relationship. I figured these women had been through a great deal of change over the years and would surely relate to what I had to say.

I finished my points, all of which exhorted spouses to encourage each other to change, wrapped up with my humorous-yet-inspiring finale that never failed to get a laugh followed by enthusiastic applause . . . and was met with total silence.

In all my years of public speaking, I can't remember a speech that bombed quite as badly as that one did. When I pressed the group to comment, I heard statements like "My husband died last year, and the only change I want is to have him back" and "My husband couldn't hear me tell him to change even if I wanted to!" One woman remarked, "I spend most of my days hoping nothing changes! I don't want anything to change."

Woman after woman chimed in with their fears surrounding change. Those whose husbands were alive and functioning well were just glad to have them around, and those who were widowed longed for companionship far more than for any other changes in their life. Over the next hour, as they shared their fears, needs, and dreams, they taught me a profound lesson about life and relationships in this stage of marriage.

I had forgotten that during this period of life, change can bring hardships, causing some to view change as an enemy. Spouses in the Golden Years particularly need dependability, reliability, and constancy. Anything else can cause trepidation and discomfort. If one spouse does seek changes, they must be undertaken with care and clear communication so that the other spouse doesn't feel distressed or abandoned.

While this is a stage when spouses depend on each other more than ever, paradoxically, it's also a more self-focused time than any other stage. Spouses are often consumed by their own issues and yearn to have their own needs addressed or anxieties comforted. It's not that they become selfish or stop caring for others' needs and feelings; it's just that their own concerns about companionship, health, death, and loneliness become very consuming.

THE GOAL OF THIS STAGE

Even the healthiest and strongest people confront a variety of discomforting feelings during the Golden Years. As their bodies and minds continue to show signs of age and they mourn the illness, incapacitation, or death of friends and loved ones, it's all but impossible to avoid struggling with their own fears of these sobering life passages. No one wants to grow old, lose their faculties, or become a burden to others. Perhaps most of all, no one wants to be alone.

That's why the Golden Years can best be described as the age of companionship. When we feel increasingly vulnerable, nothing beats a partner who, despite his or her own fears and vulnerabilities, stands resolutely at our side. The paramount goal for each spouse in this stage is to become a caring, kind, and dependable companion as together they face the greatest life change of all.

Couples who successfully navigate this stage will tell you that what keeps them going is their deeply felt faith that their spouse will love and take care of them no matter what happens. Whatever fears they have of what may lie ahead, they know, in a deep and comforting way, that they are not alone. Their strength comes not from all their years together, but from their realization that they are *still* together, and will continue to be.

DEVELOPING A NEW IDENTITY

In this stage of marriage, just as in every other, spouses develop a new identity. But unlike the others, this identity is not one based on turn-on-a-dime self-change, but rather on standing firm as a solid, unchanging force that can weather any storm. Healthy spouses in the Golden Years see themselves as strong, caring people capable of keeping things going, no matter what.

One of my wife's grandmother's lifelong friends embodied this phenomenon perfectly. When young, she dropped out of high school to work and raise money for her family. Despite her regular statements that she was going to return to school to continue her education, life continued to get in the way, and many years went by. Then, at the age of seventy, she became a widow. Soon after that, she decided it was time to return to school to finish her high school courses. Twenty years later, she had accomplished far more; at age ninety, she received her doctorate. When pressed, she always said that she kept going because she didn't want things to change. She figured that she still had many things to accomplish in life and that sitting around doing needlepoint wasn't one of them. The best way to live her life was to forge on as if she was still as young as ever.

Many people at this age seek this kind of constancy. They decide that you're only as old as you let yourself feel, and they go about making sure they continue to be as active as possible in body, mind, and spirit. As long as they remain that way, they feel as if they are winning the battle against time.

Note that I'm talking about constancy, not predictability. Many people think spouses in this stage yearn for predictability in their partners and in their lives. That couldn't be farther from the truth. Predictability is boring and is an unhealthy change from how things were in previous years. Couples at this age want constancy—the belief that their significant other will be their constant companion and that life will go along as it always has. That's why, in order to keep life rich and varied, more and more seniors are getting part-time jobs while in retirement, picking up new hobbies, volunteering, and taking courses at local universities. All of these activities enable them to continue living rich and varied lives.

WHY THIS STAGE CAN BE CHALLENGING

Many people are shocked to learn that even couples in the Golden Years receive marital therapy. John and Sally are a typical example. Even though they'd been married for forty-seven years, they came to me struggling with a variety of issues. Sally, it seems, had become furious with John over the past few years, and now it seemed that John was very upset with Sally as well.

John had worked long hours up until the day he retired about two years earlier. His concentration on business to the exclusion of nearly everything else meant that he had few hobbies, few nonbusiness interests, and few friends outside those both he and Sally knew. This narrow focus made him overly dependent on Sally for social, physical, and emotional support. In retirement, John suddenly found himself with a lot of time on his hands. Without a strong and independent life outside his wife and his job, he expected Sally to drop everything and spend time with him.

But Sally had other ideas. For the past forty-seven years, even while working a full-time job, she had cultivated an active social life and had many friends and activities. While she loved her husband, she had no interest in sitting around with him all day.

John was hurt by her attitude and felt she was abandoning him to be with her friends. As we talked, it became clear that, to John, Sally's behavior was much more than just an occasional social blow off; it was a mortal wound. Ever since retiring, John had been feeling increasingly old and useless. He feared that he wasn't as attractive to Sally as he used to be—he certainly knew that his "equipment" wasn't working as well as it had in the old days. He also wasn't as mentally sharp as he had been even a few years earlier, and he knew Sally was aware of it. He felt as if he were slipping a little further into oblivion each day, while she was out having lunch with her friends. He felt lost and alone. "How could she just cast me aside like that?" he wanted to know.

Hearing this made Sally even angrier. She also was struggling with fears having to do with old age, but she had chosen not to talk to John about them because of an event that had happened about five years earlier when she had undergone major surgery. During her recovery, she had been confined to a wheelchair for several weeks. According to Sally, John had been very upset with her during that time. He'd been critical of her neediness and openly angry that she was unable to interact with him and take care of him as much as he wanted.

John's response had been devastating to Sally, and it had scared her. She was also getting older and was not nearly as energetic and sharp as she used to be, but she had always believed that John would be there for her no matter what. John's reaction to her surgery shook her to the core. It made her fear that if something ever happened, John wouldn't be there for her. It was at that point that she became highly productive in building a social network and a strong support system. In her mind, she needed to surround herself with people who would be there for her in case the time came when she couldn't do things for herself.

So, over time, Sally had built a life quite separate from John's. She considered her friends to be her main companions and devoted most of her energy to being with them. When John finally began pushing for a closer relationship, Sally had already moved on and viewed his neediness as pulling her away from the people with whom she most wanted to spend time. Ironically, just at the stage when companionship becomes paramount in marriage, John's desire for closeness had become a burden to Sally.

As in the other stages of marriage, when couples have difficulties at this time in their lives, it's typically because they failed to properly resolve relationship issues that may have existed for many years. John and Sally had failed to reconnect well during the Empty Nesting stage; when they should have been solidifying their relationship and reestablishing their bond, they were each concentrating on other priorities.

When Sally was recovering from her surgery, John had failed to recognize that both he and Sally were dealing with the physical and emotional transition to old age and that she needed his support just as much as he needed hers.

Sally had dropped the ball, too. Instead of talking with John about her anger and despair over his failure to take care of her after her surgery and finding a way to work through it, she just moved on and found other companions.

That left them with a strained relationship, even though they weren't aware of it until the Golden Years, when they found themselves angry and resentful of each other—not a good place to be during a time when you need each other more than ever.

THE IDEAL MATE IN THIS STAGE: THE COMPANION

Happy spouses in the Golden Years seem to truly love each other, despite each other's obvious failings and persnickety ways. They also seem relatively energetic and carefree, despite the unmistakable advance of time. How do two people after many, many years together still manage to love and respect each other as much as (or even more than) they did thirty, forty, or even fifty years ago—and celebrate the gift of life, whatever it brings?

Many people think that the secret lies in the strength they derive from sharing many years together, but it can't be only that. Memories, however wonderful, can't erase the fears and struggles of the present. And many people who meet and marry late in life attain the same deep love and companionship as couples who've been together for decades. So it must be something more than shared history.

I believe that "something" is a couple's ability to fulfill the three primary needs of people at this age: loyal companionship, patient caretaking, and a bit of selective amnesia. It's these traits that make the difference during these years, and both spouses must strive to achieve them. That's why the ideal husband and ideal wife in the Golden Years have the same name—the Companion—and identical goals. Let's take a closer look at the three jobs of the ideal spouse in this stage:

1. Companionship

One of our greatest needs in this stage is a best friend with whom to share our life—yes, a warm body, but also someone with whom to enjoy life, have meaningful conversations, and share memories and special occasions. This person listens well, communicates well, and knows his or her spouse extremely well. This person has reached a point where he or she accepts the other spouse's weaknesses and is comfortable with the decline of his or her strengths.

Good companions in this stage develop a mutual acceptance and respect that say, "I know who you are, who you've become, and what you look like—and I'm okay with it. Even though you may not be proud of your body or your mind these days, I love them both, and I always will."

Spouses in this stage also serve as memory keepers for each other—not only enjoying shared memories, but also helping each other remember friends' names, appointments, events, and so on. They're also great comforters, seeming to know, after all these years, just the right thing to say when we are upset, how much to say, and even when not to say anything at all. This is a stage of life when friends and loved ones often become sick and even die. Good companions help each other accept these losses and cope with their fears of the same happening to them.

The best companions at this age, while devoted to each other, remain very independent and encourage each other to be independent as well. They each still need to have their own lives and to give each other space. That helps them feel alive and interesting, both to themselves and to each other.

The ideal husband at this stage appreciates what is meaningful to his wife and goes out of his way to make her happy. He may do simple tasks like running errands or cleaning up a bit around the house or more time-consuming activities like babysitting the grandchildren or going shopping with her. He does what needs to be done because he understands that these are more than just duties and chores; they are ways of demonstrating that she is important to him. He looks forward to spending time with his wife even if it's only reading the newspaper together on a Sunday morning or going to watch their grandchild's orchestra recital.

The ideal wife at this stage is virtually the same. She sees her husband as her best friend and companion and goes out of her way to make him happy. She has learned what things are important to him and takes pleasure in being able to provide them. That means she may make his meals for him even when he is certainly capable of doing it himself or may fold his laundry while he watches television. She may join him on whatever errands he is running just so they can spend time together. This woman realizes that both of them need to feel important and productive. Thus she enthusiastically supports whatever venture he takes on, from tinkering around the house to planning and taking long vacations or other adventures. As long as she's not required to give up her independence and lifestyle for any significant period of time, she is all for it.

2. Caretaking

Couples at this stage of marriage live daily with the fear of infirmity and loss of independence and dignity. Sometimes that fear is very acute—striking hard when someone close to them falls ill or dies—while at other times it is more distant, yet still present. Knowing this is something that is always on their minds, loving spouses serve as selfless caretakers for each other. It is extremely comforting for each spouse to know that the other will be there to take care of him or her whatever fate may bring.

Great spouses at this age have patience with each other's failings because they realize they could be in the same situation at any time, and they have great sympathy and understanding of how it feels to be dependent upon another person. Thus they are happy to help each other put their socks on, drive to doctors' appointments, bathe each other in those hard-to-reach spots, and in general be available for whatever comes along.

In this caretaking role, the ideal husband at this stage helps his wife do whatever it is that she needs done and lets her know that he is willing to do whatever it takes to care for her. They may be simple things like lifting heavy objects, helping her get into and out of the car, assisting her in getting dressed, helping her care for any of her medical conditions, or accompanying her to appointments, or it might be more significant actions like nursing her through a serious health problem, assisting her with her daily hygiene, or visiting her at the hospital or nursing home. He understands that it is his job to take care of her, and he lets her know in every way he can that he will fulfill this duty with kindness, patience, and relentless effort to the best of his abilities.

The ideal wife, too, recognizes and embraces her role as caretaker, nurturing her husband with the same tenderness and zest as when she took care of their children. She sees this as a gift she gives to her husband and communicates to him that she loves him and will be there for him no matter how ill or incapacitated he may become.

3. Selective Amnesia

Even though we realize that with advanced age comes a decline in our physical health, the reality of a failing body and faltering mind still comes as a shock to most of us. Many people will tell you that, while they knew things would change when they got older, they still never expected their bodies to feel so *old*. It's easy to see why the best spouses at this age look for ways to help their partner see beyond the inevitable consequences of aging. The ability to live life without feeling overshadowed by these reminders of mortality is priceless. That's where selective amnesia comes in.

The best spouses in this stage of life live in a healthy defiance of their age and all that comes with it. During this particular stage of marriage, this type of selective denial is extremely beneficial, and the positive energy and attitude that come with it help offset the fear that can easily overwhelm aging couples.

People in the Golden Years are often so intimately connected that they affect each other in a mysteriously symbiotic way. When one is down, the other may stumble, too. In fact, it's not uncommon for Golden Years spouses to become sick, confused, or even emotionally distraught when their spouse is gone for any length of time. When one spouse becomes consumed with depression or merely stops pursuing joys and activities in life, it can be extremely draining on the other spouse. That's why spouses who approach everything that comes their way with the attitude of a person half their age are so valuable. They're eager to try new things, enjoy life, develop new hobbies, go on trips, spice up their sex life, and experience new adventures. Their refusal to relinquish their youthful spirit is infectious and helps keep their spouse energetic and young at heart.

The ideal husband at this age recognizes that his youthful attitude will rub off on his wife, so he makes a point of taking care of his health and his outlook, keeping both as energetic and positive as possible. He stays in shape as best he can and rarely lets himself be sidelined from an activity simply because he might be considered too old to do it. He finds his wife sexually desirable and gorgeous regardless of her aging appearance and embraces sex in whatever form it may take these days—including trying new things if there's been a decline in his ability to perform. In his mind, you're only as old as you allow yourself to be, and he wants both of them to live as vitally as they can, right to the end.

The ideal wife, like her husband, is highly committed to maintaining an energetic and youthful disposition. Like him, she goes out of her way to accept new challenges and to live her life actively and enthusiastically. She works at keeping both of them as active and alert as possible. At regular intervals, she provides strong reminders that age is just a number. She finds her husband sexy because she still sees in him what she saw in him when they fell in love: a strong, caring man who loves her and is willing to do anything for her.

Making It Happen: Mastering the Golden Years Stage

There is nothing quite as endearing and uplifting as spending time with two elderly people who clearly love each other. The charm of this experience comes from more than just the enjoyment of spending time with people who finish each other's sentences. It comes from the remarkably comforting feeling one gets from being with two people who thoroughly enjoy each other's company and are such beautiful examples of loving companions.

Couples who make it to the Golden Years do so through being more than just familiar with each other. They accomplish it by attaining a new level of communication.

COMMUNICATION SKILLS FOR THE GOLDEN YEARS STAGE

By the time couples have reached this stage, most have worked out the majority of their communication issues and are able to convey a great deal of information to each other simply through a glance or a brief comment.

There are, however, some very important priorities during these years in the content of a couple's communication.

1. **They communicate with complete frankness.** Healthy couples at this stage speak openly with each other about their physical ailments, their worries about the future, and their expectations of each other. It's a time when couples need to be able to bare their souls in a way they may never have done before.

2. **They remind each other of the good times and actively plan future good times.** Earlier I mentioned the need for selective denial at this stage. With that denial comes a great deal of hope and future planning: couples talk about all the things they want to do, focusing their attention on those fun activities and on their continued growth. Together, they plan upcoming events. They continue to establish goals for themselves and encourage each other in reaching them. Couples who remind each other how

fortunate they are to be able to accomplish all the things they're planning to accomplish can feel a great degree of contentment despite infirmity.

3. **They openly comfort each other in tough times.** Healthy couples in this stage do not shy away from giving each other comfort when things get tough in their lives or in the lives of loved ones. This sort of communication can be both verbal and nonverbal. Often the latter is even more powerful than words—think of a time when you've seen an elderly couple quietly holding hands and you'll know what I mean. They also make a point of focusing primarily on the positives instead of the negatives: instead of moping about having to get a hip replacement, for example, they focus on how they'll be able to get around more easily and accomplish so much more afterward.

TOOLS FOR BUILDING INTIMACY IN THE GOLDEN YEARS STAGE

Down the street from me lives a man who turned ninety-three a few months ago. When I talked to him recently about what gets him excited these days, he said something very interesting: "I just want someone to talk to, someone to spend my days with. That's what jazzes me up. I look forward to any time spent with people."

His response exemplifies what brings intimacy in the Golden Years. Whereas things like sex, partnering, crisis management, co-parenting, and reconnecting brought intimacy in previous stages of marriage, just spending quality time talking or doing things together does the trick here. People who aren't yet in this stage have trouble understanding this, but it's precisely why you shouldn't break your scheduled lunch date with your grandmother and why you should call her just to say hello whenever you can. It's also why Grandpa will spend hours fishing with his grandkids or long afternoons discussing with his granddaughter whatever subject a seven-year-old wants to discuss.

I've talked in previous chapters about ways to deepen intimacy, but in some respects, the opportunity is most profound during this time: when spouses know their partner is there for them and will love them no matter what happens, it creates a bond unlike any other bond, one greater than the bond forged even through raising a child or surviving a trauma. Traumas are usually beyond our control, and while having babies is certainly a choice, there are strong social and cultural supports for that decision. But caring for an aging, dependent, self-soiling spouse is purely a choice. It's something a spouse *chooses* to do out of love and respect—and that's what makes it so wonderful. It says, "I've been with you through everything, and I will continue to be with you until the end, even when it gets rough. And if you get to a place where you can't take care of yourself, I will do that for you as well, gladly and proudly. That's how much I love you."

DEVELOPING NEW ACTIVITIES

Given their strong need to remain active and have their life be the same as it has always been, it is very important that spouses in the Golden Years fill their time with a variety of activities. Since I assume that we're all familiar with the common activities couples at this age engage in during their spare time (such as playing cards, walking, Bingo, vacationing, spending time with the grandchildren, and so on), my list contains only the newer or more interesting ideas I've heard in recent years. Talk to the most vital Golden Years folks you know and you'll probably hear more—plus get some good ideas for how you'd like your own Golden Years to unfold.

1. **A ROMEO club (Retired Old Men Eating Out).** This is a weekly meeting of senior men at different restaurants in town. The ROMEOs pick new places each week and then bring a variety of topics for the group to discuss during their time together. Often they rotate leadership, and each week's leader assigns a new topic a week or so in advance, which gives them time to search the Internet or visit the library to read up on the subject.

2. **Senior book clubs or movie clubs.** An organizer picks a book or movie and then provides a variety of questions for the members to discuss ahead of time. Joining a club whose members are a variety of ages can also be worthwhile. People's reactions to books and movies vary significantly depending upon their stage of life and their experiences. These different perspectives can enrich everyone in the group.

3. **A women's coffee klatsch.** This is the female version of the ROMEO club, but with an interesting twist. I've heard of several groups who arrange with a local coffee shop to come in every Saturday afternoon and bring with them a speaker to talk briefly about a subject in which they are well versed. As a psychologist I've spent a few Saturday afternoons with groups like this answering questions and giving a brief overview of what I do and how I do it. A few of the groups I'm familiar with have had speakers on needlepoint, local sports, the stock market, restaurant tips, wine tasting, child rearing, woodworking, and art.

4. **A spiritual eldering group.** In these groups, which are usually led by an experienced facilitator, the members read inspirational books and discuss their lives in terms of the inspirations found in the book. One group I know had

members write down important memories from their lives, one decade at a time, and share them with other members. It's fascinating to hear what others have accomplished, and people usually also derive a great deal of fulfillment in completing this exercise themselves. This is also a great experience to share with children and grandchildren, and those who engage in this exercise can follow it up with a sharing episode with their family as well.

5. **Information desks.** Many hospitals, malls, medical centers, and other institutions need people to help out. These "jobs" provide seniors with a terrific opportunity to meet others, exercise their brains, and feel useful, and they help out the community as well.

6. **Restaurant tours.** Most larger cities now have organizations that provide guided bus tours of local restaurants. Usually they rotate through different themes (Italian, Chinese, wine, desserts, and so on) each week.

7. **Driving.** People always need to get somewhere. Many seniors start casual driving services for people in their neighborhood or surrounding communities. If done well and safely, this can be a very rewarding and involving activity.

8. **Hospital volunteering.** Hospitals are always in need of volunteers to transport and greet patients and otherwise help out. I know one senior who rocked premature babies in her local hospital's neonatal unit. Contact your local hospital to see if there is anything you can do to help out.

TROUBLESHOOTING IN THE GOLDEN YEARS STAGE

"After All I Did for You . . ."

Some couples fail to build a fulfilling life separate from that of their children. My mother told me that when she and my father were newly married, my grandmother expected to come by every day to visit. My grandmother didn't have a very close relationship with her husband and had very few friends of her own, so she turned to her daughter for companionship, caretaking, and entertainment. To her, it was her daughter's (not her husband's) job to take care of her. If my mother had to go somewhere, my grandmother expected to go along, and whenever my mother and my father would go out, she would implore them not to stay out too late, since she wanted to check in with them before bedtime. When my parents had children, she spent even more time in their house and often expected to spend the night to help out with late-night child care. Until the day she died, my grandmother, although loving and caring of her daughter and her grandchildren, was also, in some ways, a burden on the family.

These situations are very difficult for adult children to negotiate. While on the one hand they know that they can't be their parent's full-time companion, they also realize that, without them, their parent has no one. Such situations highlight the need for couples, during both the Empty Nesting and the Golden Years stages, to build and maintain an independent life. Those who fail to do this become overly dependent upon others.

I usually tell adult children with an overly dependent parent that it is imperative that they either get their aging parent to turn to their spouse for companionship (assuming they have one), assist them in developing a life of their own, or instruct that parent as to how they see their role as part of their family. Those who take their parent in must do so without the parent controlling or overpowering the family.

"Give Up Your Life For Mine"

Some couples find that, soon after retirement, they begin to get on each other's nerves. Usually the cause is conflicting expectations of each other during their retirement years. Many spouses expect to spend a great deal of time together, while others find that prospect suffocating. When couples have widely differing expectations of each other, the sparks can really fly. Why? Because they believe these attitudes indicate how much the other is really going to be there for them when the going gets rough. Sometimes, as happened with John and Sally, there are issues from previous stages that need to be resolved before the couple can agree on the kind of time and support each expects of the other.

Many husbands retire and eagerly start planning what they're going to do with all their free time. Although this is great, it can also create problems. I know one couple who, soon after the husband's retirement, took a two-month trip in their motor home. The husband was enjoying himself so much that he persuaded his wife to extend the trip. After almost six months of this, his wife nearly left him. What he didn't realize (and she hadn't felt able to tell him) was that she had a life of her own outside of their marriage, and she needed to participate in that life for her own mental and physical health. On this trip, she was on full-time doting duty, and it was wearing her down.

This sort of tacit arrangement among Golden Years couples is common and often leads to problems like this one. Couples should, before one or both retire, have detailed conversations about exactly what they expect of each other emotionally, physically, and socially. They must be careful not to remove themselves abruptly from the rest of their life—attempting to do so can carry significant, unanticipated consequences.

"Now I'm Really Alone"

Some couples have bad marriages that last for decades. Instead of fixing their problems or getting divorced, they build separate lives within their marriage and keep pushing on. One couple I counseled recently were in their seventies and had been sleeping in different bedrooms for twenty years and taking separate vacations for even longer. They had separate phone lines, different friends, and spent very little time together even though they lived in the same home and remained married. When the Golden Years arrived, their lack of connection caught up with them. As they began to fail physically and mentally, they each realized, with horror, that their partner clearly was not going to take care of them should something catastrophic occur. They ended up divorcing after more than forty years of marriage, which happens more often than one would like to think. This dilemma underscores the extreme importance of couples dealing with their marital problems realistically and completely when they occur. Any issues that are left unresolved only become more consequential in later years.

"It's Not Your Place"

One of the great challenges of the Golden Years is tolerating the behaviors of one's children, in-laws, and grandchildren, and it's often a cause for great disagreement among couples. Figuring out how to put up with your daughter's boorish husband, her offensive in-laws, and her spoiled children without alienating yourself can be very difficult. Many couples at this stage seek counseling specifically for advice on how to talk to their children about what they see as all the mistakes their kids are making with their own marriage and children. The problem, of course, is that it is typically not one's place—even as a grandparent—to provide unsolicited feedback. Often a spouse makes comments in the heat of the moment that cause great distress for all involved, particularly since most Golden Years couples have a strong need for companionship and connection with their children and grandchildren. Couples at this stage should realize that their children's children are not theirs and that, despite their strong emotional attachment, they are not responsible for the upbringing of those children. Their commitment needs to be to each other, not to the generations that follow. They will be far more powerful as role models of a warmly loving, dedicated couple than as critical authority figures.

Nonetheless, in circumstances where serious intervention is needed, Golden Years parents must take it upon themselves to tactfully and respectfully sit their children down and explain their point of view. Then, if their perspective is ignored or dismissed, they must find a way to support their child in whatever way they can. Alienating your children, regardless of the reason, is not a good idea. You will likely need those children at some time in your future, and you want them to feel as though they can come to you no matter what.

SUCCESS STORIES: HOW YOU KNOW WHEN IT'S WORKING

In my wife's family there's a long-standing joke that my father-in-law has no idea where the dishwasher is and no clue how to use it even if he could find it. He also seems to have no idea how to make a bed or turn on an iron. Sometimes I rib him about this and offer to teach him the difficult tasks of turning the dial to On and placing dishes in the rack. My mother-in-law does all of these chores, but their domestic arrangement works well for the two of them and they seem to have a strong marriage.

A few years ago, my mother-in-law fell and broke her ankle. This incident caused them to miss a vacation my father-in-law was dearly looking forward to, and it put my mother-in-law out of commission for three months. Well, I wouldn't have believed it if I hadn't seen it myself, but my father-in-law leapt into action. He took care of his wife with the skill and care of a highly trained nurse. He cooked all their meals, did all the dishes, washed all the clothes, ironed everything that needed ironing, vacuumed the entire house, drove her to all her appointments, and did all the grocery shopping—and he did it all with a smile. Once she got up and began to get around, he drove her to her bridge club, to lunch dates with her girlfriends, and to get her hair and nails done. He also helped her get dressed, propped up her feet when she was reading or watching television, and brought her whatever she needed, whenever she requested it. All of this happened so seamlessly and with such ease that a casual observer would have assumed it had been happening that way for years.

When I asked him about it, he told me that he knows that the time he and his wife spend together is more than just time; it's an investment in each other. "I can't think of anything I would want to do more right now. I'm glad this happened after I retired, because it gave me the opportunity to care for her. This is what relationships are all about. The rest of the stuff we do together are all placeholders that bide time until we can really be there for each other."

Now that she has recovered, once again he seems to have no idea how to do any of the tasks he did routinely while she was laid up. But now we all know better. She cares for him in particular ways and he cares for her in others. It's wonderful to witness.

I suggested to my wife that we ought to try to emulate their day-to-day relationship by dividing the household tasks in a similar fashion, but it didn't fly. Apparently, she feels things are just fine the way they are now.

INEVITABLE BREAKS IN THE BOND:

The Unavoidable Breaches of Trust That Occur in All Relationships, and How to Deal with Them

Many people, after reading the title of this chapter, experience a moment of discomfort or angst. The idea that "breaks in the bond"—threats to your relationship—are not only possible but also inevitable can be very frightening. But let's get something straight, if it hasn't been made clear so far in this book: healthy marriages are always a work in progress, and *no* marriage operates over time without the partners having to deal with a wide range of problems, some of which are mild and some of which can cause serious threats to the relationship. I wish this weren't the case, but it's true. Two people can't possibly spend years intimately intertwined with each other without experiencing any number of hurts between them.

That's the bad news. The good news is that these difficulties are normal and they are manageable, if handled well. Actually, that's the ultimate point here: hurts are unavoidable, but they don't have to destroy everything (no matter how deeply they cut). Many couples overcome even the gravest of emotional wounds. The secret lies in understanding three things: one, that all emotional conflicts, despite what they seem on the surface, are, at their core, betrayals of trust to one degree or another; two, because of this, it's inevitable that both you and your spouse will, from time to time, damage the trust you share; and three, how well you handle these trust issues is what determines the health of your marriage, not whether or not the violations occur in the first place. In other words, if you base the success of your relationship on the hope that you can avoid issues that threaten your sense of trust, you will likely fail. But if you base your relationship on figuring out how to work through the inevitable hurts that will occur through breaches of trust, you'll probably do well.

Despite its ominous title, this chapter is designed to provide you with hope. In this section you will learn two things: one, how to identify the three different types of hurts that occur in most relationships, and two, how to respond in a healthy way when these events occur.

THE THREE BIG HURTS OF MARRIAGE

We all know that the key component in any successful relationship is trust. For any meaningful degree of intimacy to occur, partners must place a large amount of faith in each other to provide unwavering love and protection. This creates an extremely fragile sense of security for couples, yet it is the foundation upon which all relationships are built. Because of this, despite what a particular conflict may appear to be on the surface, when you boil it down to its basic elements, the central issue is invariably that one or both members of the couple feels as though his or her spouse has violated his or her trust in one way or another. When one trusts that his or her partner will always be there to provide emotional support, comfort, and intimate connection whenever it's needed, he or she invariably feels as though his or her most basic level of trust has been violated when a spouse is either emotionally unavailable, harsh and critical, or dishonest in any way.

When someone feels like his or her trust has been violated, not by a stranger, but by his or her own lover, emotions can run high and feelings can get hurt very quickly. These situations can easily spiral out of control and, unfortunately, often result in even greater hurts and violations of trust occurring between the couple. In an effort to help identify these potential land mines and help you avoid them, I've divided them into three categories:

1. Occasional painful periods of emotional distance (sometimes minor, sometimes severe)
2. Occasional feelings of discontent, resentment, regret, anger, and/or hurt (sometimes minor, sometimes severe)
3. Occasional threats of emotional or physical infidelity (sometimes minor, sometimes severe)

1. Occasional Painful Periods of Emotional Distance

All couples experience periods in their relationship when they are less emotionally available to each other than they are at other times. These episodes of emotional distance can be painful and, if handled poorly, extremely damaging to the relationship.

When Dan and Christine came to see me, they were deeply involved in just such a problem. For many years, Dan had been highly connected to Christine and was able to meet her emotional needs on a consistent basis. And she was able to do much the same for Dan. But then, during their fourth year of marriage, when Dan's mother became seriously ill and his career took a turn for the worse, their relationship unraveled rather quickly.

The problems started with Dan, but both of them were ultimately responsible for the issues that occurred between them. In Dan's case, the collective emotional burden of his work and family stressors overwhelmed him and, in response, he became distant, reclusive, and minimally communicative with Christine. Although Christine was aware that Dan was going through some tough times, she still needed and expected him to be a strong emotional support for her. Thus she experienced Dan's withdrawing behavior as abandonment and became desperate and demanding of his time. In turn, Dan, in his already overwhelmed state, experienced this as an additional burden and withdrew even more. By the time they came to my office several months later, both of them felt deeply injured by the other and unable to trust each other. In just a few short months, they had reached a point where they were both questioning the future of their relationship.

The problem, of course, was that they were not prepared for how to handle the periods in their relationship when a partner was unable to provide the emotional support and emotional intimacy he or she needed. Both of them felt as if the other had violated their bond by failing to be there when they needed it most.

In therapy, Dan and Christine learned that, like many couples, they each fully expected their partner to be intimately and inextricably bonded to them at all times. It was as if they believed that the act of getting married produced "emotional super glue" that permanently bonded them tightly together so that the other would always be there whenever they needed him or her. The problem with this belief is that it isn't very realistic. It's impossible for someone, no matter how much he or she loves his or her spouse, to continuously maintain a tight emotional bond with that partner and unfailingly meet all his or her emotional needs.

When Dan and Christine finally understood that, even though being emotionally supportive and reasonably well connected was very important, expecting a spouse to provide a deep and all-encompassing degree of emotional bonding at all times was unrealistic and even dangerous to the overall health of their relationship.

Through a process of developing more realistic expectations of each other and pledging to discuss their feelings more maturely when these types of breaches occur in the future, they eventually worked things out and repaired the damage that had been done to their relationship.

The story of Dan and Christine is a classic example of a situation where either one or both spouses engage in a period of emotional distance that separates the partners from each other. The catalyst for their experience was a combination of work stress and family illness, but there are many other circumstances that result in similar scenarios.

As a spouse, it is imperative that you recognize that both you and your partner will engage in behaviors from time to time that emotionally push the other partner away. Even in healthy marriages, spouses can be distant and emotionally unavailable to their partner at certain times, despite their good intentions. We all experience a wide range of emotions and have to cope with any of a number of different emotionally charged situations in life. Depending upon the intensity of those situations, our own ability to handle emotionally volatile circumstances, and our previous life experiences, we all react to these events differently.

And they won't always be catastrophic events as with Dan and Christine. Sometimes they occur merely as the result of people settling into emotional ruts in their life, or becoming depressed, lonely, or unchallenged. It is your job to recognize that you *will* do this to your spouse and that it's your responsibility to minimize its impact on him or her. It is also incumbent upon you to limit the intensity and frequency of these episodes. In other words, accepting the reality of these incidents is not a license to become a chronic emotional loner or an emotionally abusive person. Healthy relationships experience *occasional* periods of emotional distance and, upon returning to a more connected state, each spouse must take responsibility for his or her actions and make amends.

I know that, despite how much I love my wife, and how close we are, I can also be distant and cool at times. Usually these episodes have nothing to do with her; they're more about what's going on in me emotionally at the time. My wife would also admit that she occasionally does the same to me. We also both acknowledge that whenever these moments occur, the spurned spouse experiences a rush of anxiety that is directly related to the fear that we may be creating a rift that might become too difficult to pull back together.

But we also know that these fears are natural and normal parts of a relationship. Sure they're painful moments, but we also recognize that they are bound to occur from time to time and we make it a point to address things directly and responsibly when they do occur. That allows us to mend the damage as soon as possible. Moreover, we use these events to understand each other more thoroughly and to learn better ways to behave as spouses. It doesn't always go smoothly, but since we expect these periods to occur and address them maturely when they do, we continue to learn from them.

Overall, successful couples recognize and accept that occasional periods of emotional distance occur in relationships and they anticipate that those periods will feel threatening to the emotional bond that exists between them. It's when these moments are seen as catastrophic or handled irresponsibly by either party that problems persist. As a healthy spouse, you must understand and embrace the idea that even lovers with extremely tight emotional bonds have ebbs and flows in their connectedness. The difficulty is that, given our own fragile emotions, when these brief periods of emotional separation happen they feel to us like abandonment, uninterest, or even outright rejection.

To aid you in the process of working through these issues,

below you'll find a summary of the six most common unhealthy tactics people use when dealing with these particular breaches of trust. Following each item are suggestions of healthier ways to approach these situations.

Unhealthy Ways of Reacting to Emotional Distancing

1. **"Let's see how *you* like it."** Many people react to their partner's temporary emotional distance by giving the partner "a taste of their own medicine" and emotionally removing themselves from the relationship as well. This rarely works and, in fact, usually only creates greater problems. If you think about it for a moment you will realize that if your spouse is emotionally distant, it probably means that he or she is dealing with his or her own emotional difficulties. Piling on more emotional baggage is only going to make things worse for him or her. Operating in this way typically results in either creating more distance between the couple, sparking repeated angry conflicts between them, or coercing the initial distancer into acquiescing, but only after he or she chooses to avoid dealing with the problems that started the entire process. This only pushes those problems off till another time, often making the issues worse.

   A healthy alternative: Resist the urge to punish your spouse or teach him or her a lesson. Remember, as I mentioned above: if a husband, for example, is being uncharacteristically distant, it probably means he is grappling with some emotional pain of his own. Empathizing with him, comforting him, or being available to help him in whatever way he needs goes a lot farther in mending the relationship than punishing him or attempting to teach him lessons he either already knows or is unequipped to learn at that time.

2. **"What about me?"** This occurs when one spouse, after sensing his or her partner's distance, becomes emotionally distraught and makes desperate attempts to get his or her own needs met. In these situations, the spurned spouse makes constant, repeated demands for attention out of proportion to the situation at hand. He or she floods the temporary void between them with his or her own neediness, thus forcing his or her emotional needs into the forefront of the relationship. In this way, the more distance that occurs, the more the spurned spouse's emotional demands overpower the relationship. When this tactic is used, marriages become very strained and the ensuing power struggle often results in either the termination of the relationship or the distancer forgoing his or her own needs in order to make peace. While this serves to reduce the immediate conflict, it doesn't bode well for the long-term health of the marriage.

   A healthy alternative: In healthy relationships there is a good balance of neediness between the couple. This means that, at alternate times, one spouse's needs are more pressing than the other's. You have to allow the space in your relationship for your spouse to be the more needy one from time to time. That will sometimes require you to sit with your own difficult feelings. If you find yourself unable to handle these periods, a therapist can be a good resource. That doesn't mean you are crazy or incompetent, it just means that you may need someone to help you deal with your own feelings during the periods in your relationship when your spouse is unable to do so.

3. **"Just deal with it."** In an alarming number of relationships, both spouses have surprisingly little ability to empathize with each other. Many people expect their spouse

to fully empathize with them no matter what the circumstance is—and they get very angry when their spouse fails to do so. Ironically, these are usually the same people who lack patience or sympathy when their spouse experiences the same emotional quandaries. When these situations occur, it usually results in further distancing between the couple. If you think about it, failing to empathize with your partner is bound to put further distance between the two of you. And advising your spouse to leave you alone, solve his or her problems by his- or herself, or get sympathy from someone else can only make things worse.

A healthy alternative: Empathy is a wonderful tool that heals relationships in amazing ways. Do your best to develop some empathy for your spouse, even when you find it difficult. Most people, if they really try, can find meaningful ways to empathize with a loved one's predicament. If often takes patience and imagination, but it's always worth it. If you honestly and openly listen to your spouse's feelings and then communicate your support and understanding, you will find your relationship blossoming even when his or her feelings are difficult to hear or understand.

4. **"This marriage is never going to work!"** A dangerous method for handling stressful marital situations involves all-or-nothing thinking. Those who respond to temporary emotional distancing with catastrophic proclamations only make matters worse. It's important to remember that occasional periods of distance are a normal part of a relationship. During these episodes, emotions are already running high. Adding to this volatile mix the threat of divorce or separation only puts greater pressure on the relationship. It's also an example of failing to see the bigger picture. When you see these situations as the normal unhealthy pe-

riods within a larger, healthy relationship, they don't feel as overwhelming.

A healthy alternative: Keep things in perspective. There will always be ups and downs in your bond. Unhealthy relationships operate in a black-and-white world where everything is either catastrophic or perfect. As long as the rest of your relationship is solid, emotional distance, while difficult, should not be a deal breaker. Remember, it's not breaches of trust that ruin things, it's how they are handled. If their existence throws you into turmoil, then you have to evaluate your own sense of insecurity in the relationship or why your expectations of perfection are so great.

5. **"He hates me."** It is vitally important to your relationship to recognize the times when you should take things personally and when things aren't about you. Unfortunately, people often personalize things even though very few things that others do have anything to do with them. This is often a difficult concept for people to grasp, especially when they feel threatened. It is important to remember that everyone has his or her own personal demons. Even if you are specifically being blamed for someone else's feelings or behavior, you must bear in mind that he or she is actually struggling with his or her own issues or poor coping skills.

   A healthy alternative: Realize that, in the vast majority of situations, when you take things personally you are being both inaccurate and unproductive. Thus, your responses are likely to be inappropriate or even damaging to the relationship. Your spouse, no matter how wonderful he or she is, has his or her own flaws and immature reactions. While many of these feel directly related to you, they likely aren't. Try to accept that most of the time, your spouse's hurtful behavior, no matter how painful it feels, has very little to do with you. When you keep that in mind, and keep your own insecurities out of the process, it's easier to empathize with your partner and deal with the real issues at hand.

6. **"You have to talk about it with me right now."** Many people attempt to assuage the anxiety *they* feel when their partner is temporarily distant by demanding that their partner solve his or her issues immediately. However, since magically resolving most issues right away is not possible, it only adds more pressure on the distancer, thus pushing him or her further away. Often, that fuels the spurned spouse to chase the distancer even harder. It's easy to see how this can easily push tensions to a breaking point.

   A healthy alternative: Negative emotions are almost always difficult to process, and many people feel compelled to rid themselves of these feelings as soon as possible. However, we all have to realize that, no matter how unpleasant it is, sitting with difficult emotions from time to time is part of being in a relationship. That means that not only do we have to learn to sit with our own emotions, but we have to learn to sit with our partner's negative feelings as well. That can provoke a great deal of anxiety, but it's necessary. When we can't handle our partner having overwhelming emotions, we end up throwing our discomfort into the mix and only overwhelm our partner more. Keep in mind that most emotional issues can't be solved easily or quickly. You have to allow your spouse the time and space to work out whatever he or she needs to work out, and you have to avoid putting more pressure on him or her. There are, of course, limitations to these circumstances; a relationship can't live in a perpetually disconnected state. However, keep in mind that each situation is different. Again, if you are struggling with something along these lines, a therapist is a good resource for helping you identify what is reasonable or unreasonable to expect in your relationship.

2. Occasional Feelings of Discontent, Resentment, Regret, Anger, and/or Hurt

Another commonly held belief about intimate relationships is the notion that "if someone loves me, he or she won't hurt me emotionally." It's as if people believe that being in love magically strips their spouse of having any negative, immature, or selfish traits that could result in hurtful behavior. This perspective, like the one I mentioned earlier in this chapter, is based upon an unrealistic view of relationships. Unfortunately, for most people, the person who hurts them the most emotionally is usually the person to whom they are most intimately connected. If you think about it, it really can't be any other way. The more emotionally invested a person is in another person, the more emotionally vulnerable he or she is and, consequently, the easier it is for that person to hurt him or her. Unfortunately, this creates a number of ways in which partners can violate the trust they have in each other.

I wish it weren't the case, but I am just as guilty of this as anyone else. Despite my easygoing and friendly personality, I can also be angry, resentful, selfish, unfair, needy, demanding, and critical. No matter how much I try, I just can't seem to keep from occasionally taking a variety of unpleasant feelings out on my wife. And my wife does the same to me. When we do it, these experiences are both painful and damaging to our relationship. I know that whenever she's the one doing it to me, I find myself equally filled with hurt, anger, resentment, and an unhealthy desire to run from the relationship. Sometimes I translate these emotions into my own inappropriate responses, and sometimes I am able to take a breath and let the situation pass. I'm sure she would tell you that she goes through the same process when I'm angry or hurtful to her. Either way, these situations always hit us at the core trust level of our relationship. Every time these experiences occur, I know my wife, just as I do, feels very violated and questions how much she can truly trust me to be there for her and if she is safe with me.

Unfortunately, this is all normal. In addition to the occasional emotional distancing that occurs in relationships—which I discussed above—occasional hurtful emotion dumps occur between spouses as well. And just like we found with emotional distancing, these too are perceived as breaches of trust when they happen in a marriage. When one spouse, for example a wife, expects that her lover will always be respectful of her feelings and that he will never say or do anything hurtful, she is bound to find herself feeling as if her spouse has violated the basic tenets of their relationship far too often.

In the case of Lisa and Aaron, this was a frequent problem. Aaron grew up in a household in which, good or bad, people expressed all their opinions and feelings. Lisa loved his generous praise and enthusiasm but bristled at his all-too-frequent criticisms. Lisa had come from a family with exactly the opposite culture regarding the expression of emotion. Her family rarely, if ever, raised their voices with one another, and Lisa found Aaron's direct negative statements to be incredibly hurtful and disrespectful. She also believed that they were an indication that he didn't love her. In her mind, there was no way he could love her if he was often critical of her. Aaron, on the other hand, found Lisa's indirectness and tendency to withdraw as equally indicative of her lack of love for him and their relationship. In his mind, anyone who would clam up and give a virtual silent treatment for days was choosing to disengage from the relationship and was, therefore, not being a committed wife. He even went so far as to accuse her of infidelity. He based this upon his belief that if she was so willing and able to disengage from him, she must be able to forget about him in other ways as well.

Clearly, Aaron and Lisa were in trouble when they came to

see me. Their problems, however, were not the result of a lack of love between them; they were a result of their failure to recognize that spouses can *and do* hurt each other emotionally from time to time through their inappropriate ways of handling their own emotions. When the two of them were able to understand that highly charged emotions are a normal part of a relationship and that it was their responsibility to learn how to communicate those emotions maturely and appropriately with each other, their relationship improved dramatically.

The key factor for them was the recognition that there was no possible way to have the intimate relationship they desired without negative emotions cropping up from time to time. They also learned to accept that the existence of those feelings and the inappropriate expression of them was not an indication that either one of them didn't love the other; it was merely an unproductive (and unhealthy) way of expressing themselves that happened on occasion. Once they established that hurts were bound to occur, they were able to develop more appropriate rules for handling those emotions with each other. This changed their relationship dramatically for the better.

Unhealthy Ways of Reacting to Hurtful Emotions

1. **An eye for an eye.** Many people choose to respond to their partner's anger with their own anger. This rarely works and typically only makes matters worse. Adding more anger to the mix—fighting fire with fire—only sets both people ablaze in a number of different ways. That's why, when you're on the receiving end of your partner's anger, it's important to hold your tongue as best you can.

   A healthy alternative: Unpleasant emotions are contagious, and when we have them, it's difficult not to spread them around. However, in healthy relationships, partners are able to resist the urge to treat their spouse with equal disrespect. Thus, it's important to allow your spouse to have his or her anger without giving your anger in return. Sometimes it's helpful to remember that powerful emotions are part of everyone's makeup and we all need to have them and express them, even though they're unpleasant. That said, anger is extremely damaging to those who receive it. Therefore, expressions of anger, while normal, must be curtailed whenever possible. In other words, occasional anger is significantly different from chronic anger. Healthy partners recognize that they are required to tolerate occasional anger, but not chronic anger. Partners who engage in chronic, destructive outbursts of anger usually damage their relationship beyond repair.

When your partner gets angry, encourage him or her to have and express that anger in healthy ways—no threats, intimidation, or violence. Allow him or her to get out whatever anger he or she is feeling and try to get him or her to explore the deeper emotions (hurt, sadness, etc.) that are fueling the anger. This process, while difficult, is still far more productive than hurling anger back and forth between your spouse and yourself.

2. **Withdrawing.** It's difficult not to pull away emotionally from your loved one when it feels as though that person is bombarding you or assaulting you with anger, criticism, or blame. However, pulling away usually only makes matters worse. In some cases, the root cause of your spouse's anger has nothing to do with you. He or she may have had a bad day at work or an argument with a family member or may have simply gotten up on the wrong side of the bed. If you withdraw from your spouse when this is occurring, your spouse may feel even more alone in his or her upset and feel that you're not there for him or her. Then, your spouse may feel hurt or get angry with you for abandoning him or her in his or her misery. In other cases, your spouse

may be directly criticizing you or may be angry with you for some perceived wrongdoing or violation on your part. If you withdraw here, he or she will see it as a defensive maneuver and this will likely exacerbate his or her anger. These examples illustrate why withdrawing, while common, doesn't tend to work as a strategy for dealing with someone else's anger or criticism.

A healthy alternative: When your partner is guilty of occasionally expressing criticism or anger toward you, working to achieve understanding is far more productive than withdrawing. It is helpful to not take what he or she is saying personally or, if it is personally directed at you, to be open to the comments. Most of the time, anger is not a primary feeling. It arises due to an underlying hurt or struggle. When you recognize this, and work with your partner to identify his or her hurt and then empathize with it, you will most likely not only diffuse the anger, but also bring the two of you closer together. Similarly, when your spouse is criticizing you, it is often about something that he or she finds unacceptable in himself or herself. Again, if you are open to hearing what your spouse has to say, he or she is often willing to hear your side of things as well. In most circumstances, your loved one does not really *want* to hurt your feelings but is overwhelmed at the moment by his or her own feelings. Of course, there are times when we each need to withdraw emotionally to a small degree in the aftermath of an argument. But both of us must come back soon and be ready to have an open conversation about what is really troubling each of us. If you stay away too long, there is a good chance your spouse will interpret your distancing behavior as rejection and lash out again.

3. **"Spouse bashing."** Some spouses seek to heal the wounds created in these situations by trashing their spouse to

anyone who will listen. Usually their confidants tend to be close friends and family members. While this enables the spurned spouse to feel better, it only further distances the couple. The last thing your spouse wants is for you to shame him or her publicly every time he or she behaves poorly, especially if your spouse is struggling with difficult emotions or circumstances. While occasionally turning to friends and family for advice is appropriate—as long as it is done respectfully—repeatedly bad-mouthing your spouse to others only puts a greater strain on your relationship.

A healthy alternative: Whenever possible, it's always best to be empathetic with your spouse in these situations. If your spouse is angry, critical, rejecting, or exhibiting any other unpleasant emotion, keep in mind that he or she is likely doing so because he or she is struggling with his or her own issues. It is always best to attempt to get your spouse to talk about his or her underlying feelings. If you feel you must talk to others, be careful whom you choose to speak with and remember to always be respectful. Make sure you tell those in your support system that you want them to help you solve the problem, not just engage in a bash fest. Also make sure you keep the number of people in your inner circle small and that you set limits with them. Remember, you and your spouse may heal the relationship, but the ones you confide in may hold a grudge forever, creating problems for all of you. This does not mean that you can't occasionally discuss your marital issues with your friends and family, but it *has* to be occasional and it *has* to be respectful to your spouse. Remember that you are still part of that relationship and thus have to maintain the integrity of that bond. A good rule of thumb to use is to think about whether or not you would want to be discussed in that manner to others. If you would find it offensive that your spouse talks about you in that manner, chances are your spouse would feel the same way. Remember, even if you feel that your spouse violated your trust by distancing him- or herself from you, you will be breaching his or her trust in a different way by disparaging him or her to others. Two wrongs never make a right, and in relationships they only add fuel to the fire.

4. **Fighting fire with fire.** Many people respond to their partner's outburst of negative emotion by going on the attack. In these situations, the victimized spouse attacks the aggressor in return. Typically this tactic is designed to punish the one who started the fight and, ideally, get him or her to cease the upsetting behavior. This rarely works and, in fact, tends to escalate the conflict to potentially damaging heights.

   A healthy alternative: Healthy relationships require both spouses to behave in an emotionally mature manner. If you can't handle your spouse having occasional periods of emotional distress without feeling the need to punish him or her, it is you who is damaging the relationship, not your spouse. It is imperative that you learn how to control your own emotions and that you treat your spouse with respect. If you find you are unable to do so, seek some professional help. Therapists are great resources for helping people learn how to recognize and balance their own needs in a relationship.

5. **Engaging in unfair fighting.** Many people, in the midst of an argument with their spouse, resort to blaming, name-calling, or "piling on" behaviors. All of these are considered unfair fighting. No good can come out of an argument when one or both partners muck up the process by engaging in any of these behaviors. Typically, it only leads to escalating the argument and compounding the problems.

A healthy alternative: Arguments, while certainly difficult, do not always have to be brutal showdowns. Many people can have healthy, heated disagreements without ever engaging in inappropriate or hurtful behaviors. Even though it can feel awkward, take the time to make rules for yourself and your spouse to use during arguments. Many people agree to write down each person's point and address the items one at a time. Others find it more beneficial to divide the argument into brief segments in which one partner gets to express his or her opinion without interruption followed by the other receiving the same courtesy. Most people, however, find that consistently using good active listening skills (described beginning on page 73) can be one of the most effective tools for ensuring that the couple argues fairly and respectfully. Remember that it is very important, even when you are angry, to fight fairly and respectfully with your spouse. Things said in anger tend to last long after the situation is over, which causes hurt far beyond the original encounter.

6. **Seeking solace elsewhere.** When victimized by their partner's anger, resentment, or criticism, many spouses find it difficult to resist the urge to turn to opposite-sex sympathizers for support. While having a shoulder to cry on or hearing comforting words from a caring friend can certainly ease the pain of these situations, engaging in this behavior is, obviously, a very dangerous path to take. Choosing this direction rarely works out well. The emotional bonds created in shared misery are often unhealthy and do more damage than good. Furthermore, people usually engage in this behavior in lieu of directly dealing with the core issues in their relationship. In this way, well-meaning friends who provide this type of support are not really making things better, even if it feels that way at the time.

A healthy alternative: Your marriage is your marriage and no one else's, which makes you and only you responsible for fixing it, changing it, or even getting out of it, if there are no other options. If you find yourself unable to deal with the difficult feelings you are experiencing in your relationship, it's your job to get help from qualified, unbiased individuals who are trained to help you learn how to deal maturely and directly with whatever problems you face in your relationship. Opposite-sex friends, while certainly comforting, are usually biased and unqualified to offer any meaningful assistance. Try this: ask yourself what you are truly searching for when thinking of securing the sympathy of a friend. If you are only searching for comfort (meaning you aren't really looking for professional or meaningful intervention), then turning to an opposite-sex sympathizer is clearly not a good idea. Likewise, if your answer is that you truly want serious help regarding the best course of action to take, turning to an unqualified and biased friend also won't get you what you need. Instead of embracing this dangerous and unproductive path, make the commitment to work it out with your spouse, for better or for worse, either on your own or with a counselor. While you may have uncomfortable interactions that occur along the way, in the end, you will have dealt with and resolved the problem head-on, no matter what the final outcome.

3. Occasional Threats of Emotional or Physical Infidelity

The subject of infidelity is a difficult issue to discuss with couples because there is no greater fear at the heart of all relationships than the fear that one's spouse will stray. Many couples even refuse to entertain discussions about infidelity because of the intense emotion attached to the subject. This is unfortunate because infidelity happens in many more ways than just physical affairs. While research reports that, in the United States, physical infidelity touches 1 in every 2.7 couples, it's clear that the other forms of infidelity occur even more frequently. Infidelity happens anytime a spouse engages in a secretive behavior or relationship, or when a spouse fails to share important information, experiences, or feelings with his or her partner. Some examples include the following:

- **Emotional affairs**
    - **Minor**—when a spouse has crushes, feelings, or attractions to others that exist in his or her mind but aren't discussed or pursued in any manner.
    - **Major**—when a spouse shares intimate feelings with another person even though he or she refrains from becoming physical.
- **Financial infidelities**
    - **Minor**—when a spouse hides money or other financial goings-on from his or her partner.
    - **Major**—when a spouse makes major (or a series of minor) financial decisions that greatly affect the household without consulting his or her partner.
- **Factual omissions**
    - **Minor**—when a spouse regularly omits minor details of his or her life that, while not significant, still leave the partner wondering why, and how often, information is excluded in this way.
    - **Major**—when a spouse conveniently leaves out important details of information that could have a significant impact on the relationship.
- **Overt dishonesty**
    - **Minor**—when a spouse consistently tells his or her partner unnecessary white lies that leave the other to question his or her partner's day-to-day integrity.

    - **Major**—when a spouse repeatedly insists he or she has stopped a particular behavior (smoking, drinking, gambling, pornography, etc.) even though he or she has not done so.
- **Lack of sharing major life issues**
    - **Minor**—when a spouse fails to share important thoughts or feelings with his or her partner.
    - **Major**—when a spouse fails to share major negative feelings regarding his or her partner or the relationship for long periods of time, only to announce at a later date his or her years of dissatisfaction.
- **Physical infidelity**
    - **Minor**—when a spouse engages in a minor level of physical touching, shares inappropriate photos, engages in sexually charged conversations, or engages in other similar physically intimate activities that don't involve intercourse or other significant sexual acts. (Note: while it's difficult to classify these as minor, they are less serious than the more severe behaviors listed next.)
    - **Major**—when a spouse engages in a sexual relationship of any kind outside of his or her marriage.

If you're in an intimate relationship, it should be clear to you when you read this list that it's all but impossible to avoid experiencing one form of infidelity or another—be they minor or major infractions. We all tell white lies, we are all drawn to others, we all omit information to avoid conflicts, and we all suffer from lapses in judgment as well as brief periods of selfishness. I haven't met a person yet who can say that he or she isn't guilty of engaging in many of these behaviors at some point, even when he or she knew it was wrong.

When it comes to violations in the area of spending time with members of the opposite sex, all couples have a different set of standards. On one end of the spectrum, there are couples who hold the belief that merely driving in a car alone with a member of the opposite sex is inappropriate. In the middle of the spectrum are couples who find Facebook relationships, business lunches, or outings with opposite-sex friends to be threatening, even though others are accepting of such behaviors. And on the other end of the scale are couples who tolerate emotional and physical relationships with others.

Just as in the other areas discussed in this chapter, my wife and I have had to deal with a number of these situations as well. Since, like most couples, we entered our relationship with the naïve belief that neither one of us would ever omit information or lie about anything we did, fantasize about or feel attracted to another person, make any major financial or life decisions without consulting the other, share any form of intimacy with another person, or divulge each other's secrets to others, we often found ourselves extremely offended and hurt when either one of us engaged in one of these behaviors. Although I wish it weren't true, there have been several occasions through the years when both of us, through acts of cowardice, immaturity, or selfishness, violated the trust we have built between us.

While neither of us is proud of these behaviors, our marriage continues on stronger than ever, regardless of how hurtful or out of line both of us have been at one time or another. That's because we both realize that, despite our love for each other and our good intentions, we are both human, which means we will occasionally act badly. Instead of avoiding these hurdles, we have learned to discuss these situations openly and honestly when they occur. When we address them in a mature and loving way, it always brings us closer.

There's no magic to it, but that's the formula that helps other couples as well. If you are reading this chapter with a heavy heart due to a minor or major infidelity in your marriage, take solace in the realization that even these wounds can be healed. Trust that if your marriage is healthy in other ways, and you both are willing to make a commitment to work on mending the damage that was done, you will likely find a way to work through the issue at hand, even if the offense is major. In marital therapy, it's always the case that healthy marriages, because of the overall strength of the relationship, overcome difficult moments like these. It's unhealthy marriages that, because they lack the fundamental strength to weather this additional storm, crumble in the face of these problems. In most cases, infidelity doesn't destroy a relationship; it's just the last, fatal straw.

I recently counseled two couples who dealt with issues like these in vastly different ways, and the way they handled their problems epitomizes why it is so important for couples to address these issues maturely and responsibly when they occur.

Carla and Anthony came to me after many years of arguing over Carla's gambling problems. They had been married for seven years but had been dealing with Carla's repeated empty promises to quit gambling for more than a decade. However, in therapy, it was revealed that their relationship suffered from many more problems than just this issue. They both lied to each other often, and neither one of them ever truly wanted to change his or her behavior. Thus, much of their marriage consisted of each of them trying to keep the other from discovering the bad things they were doing behind the other's back. When problems would come up through the years, instead of discussing the situation honestly and openly and committing to changing their behaviors, they each would just decide to get even with the other through their own secret dealings. By the time Carla's gambling problems brought them in to see me, their relationship was all but over—and it ended soon after they began couples counseling. Even though they believed her latest gambling binge to be the catastrophic event that ended their relationship, it was really just a symptom of a much greater problem and a relationship that was likely doomed from the start.

Spencer and Mia's relationship took a very different course. They came to see me following Spencer's affair. In therapy it became clear that they both loved each other very much and that, despite the great hurt his affair caused for both of them, their relationship was built upon a very solid foundation. As a couple, they agreed to talk with each other honestly and openly about the affair and all the emotions that were associated with it. In time, through a great deal of soul searching, they each agreed to make some changes in how they behaved in the marriage. This allowed them to achieve an even greater intimacy than they previously shared and, consequently, their relationship grew exponentially. By the end of therapy, while they both wished the affair hadn't occurred, they also admitted that it had forced them to deal with issues they never would have addressed otherwise.

Despite conventional wisdom that says infidelity kills a relationship, the story of Spencer and Mia is a common one. Many people find that infidelity, if it's worked through sensitively, can, for many, be an isolated incident that the couple moves beyond. Don't get me wrong; infidelity, especially in its major forms, is incredibly painful and threatening to a relationship. However, all situations and all relationships are different, and with hard work, the relationship can sometimes be repaired.

In order to help you work through any infidelity issues you may face in your relationship, below you will find a list of suggestions for couples to use when confronting such breaches of trust. This list, which I've adapted from the book *After the Affair,* by Janis Abrahms Spring, Ph.D., is specifically designed for couples to use when they have experienced a physical or emotional infidelity. It can, however, be used as a template for coping with any of the forms of infidelity I've identified here. (A more expansive description of how to survive infidelity in your relationship can be found in Dr. Spring's extremely helpful book.)

Six Steps for Overcoming Infidelity

Step 1: Understand that you will experience a wide range of feelings and that all of them are normal. When a spouse discovers that his or her partner has engaged in any type of aberrant behavior, the range of emotion he or she experiences can be tremendous and can include any or all of the following feelings:

1. **A loss of identity:** "Who are you if you do this, and who am I if I am in a relationship with you?"
2. **A loss of feeling special:** "I thought we had something special, but now I feel like we have nothing."
3. **A loss of self-respect:** "I'll grovel or do anything to repair this relationship" or "I've become mean-spirited in order to punish my spouse for this behavior."
4. **Anger at yourself for missing the clues:** "How could I have been so stupid?"
5. **Feeling emotionally out of control:** "How do I stop myself from constantly thinking about this and endlessly worrying about it?"
6. **A fundamental loss of stability:** "I used to believe I had a pretty good handle on the world I live in, but now I feel like I have absolutely no idea what is right, wrong, or even what to do next."
7. **Anger or confusion regarding your religious faith or sense of purpose in life:** "How could God have abandoned me this way?" or "Why would God punish me in this way?"
8. **A profound sense of isolation or loneliness:** "I can't share this with anyone, and even if I did, no one could possibly understand my despair or fix it."
9. **Loss of hope:** "I'll never experience true love again and I'll never trust again."

Step 2: Embrace those feelings and talk with your partner or a therapist about each of them. It is important to explore each of those feelings and to engage your partner in that discussion. Avoiding these feelings or denying them only makes them stronger and puts a further wedge in your relationship. Since the infidelity involved withholding information, in order to fix things everything must now be shared between spouses.

If your spouse refuses to discuss the subject in any meaningful or productive way, it is best to seek counseling to help you identify and work through these feelings. I must point out, however, that if your spouse refuses to discuss the subject, that doesn't bode well for your relationship. As I mentioned above, repairing the damage done in these circumstances usually has to be done together. It's not impossible to do it alone, but your spouse's refusal to join you in the repair process typically only makes matters worse.

Step 3: Give a name to each of those feelings and make a commitment to identifying them and working through them every time they occur. The difference between this step and step two is that in this step you have to commit to digging deeply into those feelings and working through them productively. Since the feelings associated with infidelity are so severe, merely identifying them is not enough. You must explore them and cleanse them from your mind (and heart) in a healthy way or they will continue to invade your psyche and damage you and your relationship. As painful as it may be to discuss these feelings over and over, it is imperative that you and your spouse share a common language about the incident and sew together, one at a time, the frayed ends of your trust.

Step 4: Decide whether to recommit to the relationship or quit. In time, regardless of the infraction, you have to make a conscious decision either to stay in the relationship or get out.

Given the volatile emotions attached to this decision, this can be a difficult step. However, it has to be a conscious, stated choice that you commit to wholeheartedly. Just as you can't be half pregnant, you can't be half committed to your relationship. If you choose to stay, you must remain true to that course. This doesn't mean you have to feel completely content with your decision; it just means that if you pick the recommitment path, you have to stick with it even when you feel frightened or angry. Think of it this way: when you commit to mending the relationship, this commitment becomes the cornerstone of rebuilding the relationship. If you waffle on this decision as you go along, you are, in a way, knocking down the new foundation over and over again. This is especially problematic when you are in the process of attempting to rebuild trust.

Step 5: Commit to rebuilding trust and repairing the relationship in whatever way is necessary. There are two parts to this step:

1. **Agree to specific changes in behavior.** Building trust takes time, but it begins with changes in behavior. The spouse who is responsible for the breach of trust must not only recognize his or her unhealthy behavior, but also actively change that behavior.
2. **Agree to change the interpersonal dynamics of the relationship.** No relationship is perfect and no spouse is without fault. Even if the infidelity that occurred was beyond your control, there are still things you can do to improve the way you behave in the relationship. Dig deep within yourself and consider what behaviors you engage in that undermine the overall health of your relationship. You are still an active participant in your relationship, which means you always have room to grow as well.

Step Six: Forgive your partner. In the end, in order for your relationship to recover fully from this event, you have to find a way to forgive your partner. There are many ways to accomplish this, and everyone has to find his or her own way of getting there. However, in order for the wound to be fully healed, this step has to occur, even if it takes many years.

PART III

Creating Your Ideal Marriage

PREPARING YOUR RELATIONSHIP FOR CHANGE:

Quizzes

If you've gotten to this point in the book, you're probably ready to make some changes. That's great! This section is designed to help you make the most of the time and effort you'll devote to change. I will address ways to identify and overcome the potential roadblocks to your change process later. First, let's talk about your spouse or partner, because I suspect the bigger issue for you right now is how to get your spouse or partner to change with you.

HOW TO DEAL WITH A RELUCTANT SPOUSE

Often, despite the fact that we are unhappy and repeatedly state our desire for change, we are faced with a spouse who is reluctant to change. If both spouses do not agree to make changes together in a relationship, life as a couple can be a constant struggle. When dealing with a reluctant spouse it is imperative that you talk to your spouse in a calm and nonthreatening way about the important role change plays in keeping your relationship healthy and interesting.

Here are five frequently asked questions about dealing with a spouse who is resistant to change:

Q: How do I initiate the conversation?

A: As a first step, make sure you pick the right time and place. Most people only talk about what is bothering them in the heat of the moment. The problem with this is that when tempers flare or hurt predominates, we are unable to communicate effectively. Conversations that occur during emotionally charged interactions thus rarely produce long-lasting resolution. When you want to discuss an important topic with your spouse, make sure to choose a time when you are both calm and in a place that is free of distractions.

You should also make sure to avoid blame. You don't want to start off an important conversation by conveying to your spouse that the troubles in your marriage are his or her fault and his or hers alone. Avoid finger pointing and words that suggest blame. Make sure you are careful to present that both of you have contributed to where you are today and that both of you will need to change.

It is also important to present a win-win scenario if at all possible. When speaking with your spouse, you want him or her to see why making these changes will benefit him or her and the relationship. As harsh as this may sound, many people will only change if they feel they will get something out of it. Most of us need goodies to entice us to take on a difficult challenge.

Be aware of what makes your spouse tick and use this knowledge. Different things motivate different people. What serves as a carrot for one person may be unappealing to another. Ask yourself what motivates your spouse and see if you can connect the changes you want him or her to make with that motivation. For example, if you know your spouse worries a lot about money, try to see if you can frame a proposed change in terms of how it can improve your financial situation. Or if your spouse wants more attention from you, find a way to present the changes in a way that will solve this problem.

Finally, acknowledge the work involved for you as well. When speaking with your spouse make sure you communicate that the changes you are proposing are things you will both be working on and that making those changes will be hard for you as well. It's usually beneficial to have a list of your own changes and be prepared to discuss those first.

Q: What do I do if my partner completely rejects the idea that he or she needs to change?

A: First of all, take the time to evaluate your approach. Review the guidelines above and make sure you have planned and initiated the conversation well. It may be that you have gotten a poor result because of a less-than-tactful approach.

If you feel your approach was good, it will pay you to keep trying. Many people, when faced with rejection, shrug their shoulders and give up. That rarely gets them what they want. It is possible that, for reasons unknown to you, your spouse was unable to hear your previous message but is now open to it. Circumstances like these call for repeated attempts, patience, and clear, assertive discussions on your part that let your partner know unequivocally that you are serious and that a failure to change on either of your parts will likely lead to significant conflict in your relationship. Sometimes people who initially reject change do an about-face when change is thrust upon them in the form of counseling, divorce, or some other unpleasant action. Make sure they know you are serious.

Q: What do I do when the conversations we have regarding change only lead to arguments?

A: Remember that just because these conversations may lead to arguments doesn't mean you shouldn't have them. Arguments happen, and all couples struggle in these situations. Find a way to work through them. One solution is to try having these discussions in a variety of different ways—you could have them in ten- to fifteen-minute intervals, which keeps the arguing to a minimum. Or you could split the time between one person having the floor and then the other. Another idea is to write down and discuss your desired changes first and then do the same with your spouse's. These are also good conversations to have in a therapist's office. Framing your reason for participating in therapy as an opportunity to have a mediator (as opposed to because you are getting a divorce) is a good way to sell your spouse on the process. There are also worksheets in the appendix that may help you and your spouse manage these conversations.

Q: How do I know if my partner is capable of change? When it is time for me to quit and cut my losses?
A: The best indicator of this is past history. If your spouse was reluctant to change in the past, he or she will likely be reluctant to change in the future. Equally, if your partner fails to grasp the importance of change, he or she will likely reject it every time the opportunity presents itself. This is a tough question to answer because the reality is that many people are unwilling or unable to change. Listen to your gut. Most people already know the answer to this question; they just don't like its implications.

It's difficult to say unequivocally when it is time to cut your losses. That particular tipping point is different for everyone. Only you can determine when the time is right to move on. However, it's important to recognize that many spouses appear to change when they really have not. This often happens after divorce papers are served. The reluctant spouse has what many psychologists call "a flight into health" and feverishly comes around to correcting many of his or her complained-about behaviors. When this occurs, I urge my clients to proceed with caution. Most changes that are made quickly under duress are not sustained over the long term.

It's rare for any "now I get it" changes to last because they usually are more motivated by loss than actual insight.

Q: How do I tell my partner that I am leaving him if he doesn't change—and isn't that an ultimatum?

A: It's definitely an ultimatum, but what's wrong with that? Ultimatums are direct communication. It's your life and your marriage. Sometimes you have to be tough. If you're afraid to stand up for what you believe in, even when it causes conflict, you'll rarely get what you want in life. Don't be afraid to make the life and relationship you want and deserve.

If you are concerned about giving an ultimatum, be aware of this: the problem with ultimatums is not giving them; it's following through on them. Once you give an ultimatum and fail to follow through with the promised consequences, you have undermined your own credibility. So make sure you are prepared to back up your statements with action.

EVALUATING YOUR READINESS TO CHANGE

Now that we've addressed how to approach a reluctant spouse, let's get back to you. Before you can begin to change, you have to take an honest look at how truly committed you are to the process. Most people have good intentions and honestly mean to change when they make the commitment to do so. However, actual change takes much more than just good intentions. Therapists' offices all over the country are filled with people with good intentions. These people want to change—and work very hard to achieve it—yet still find the process very difficult.

Drs. James Prochaska, John Norcross, and Carlo DiClemente wonderfully describe this process in their book *Changing for Good*. I highly recommend it for anyone seriously considering making any significant changes in his or her life.

The authors have developed a six-stage model that explains change as a multistep process that occurs over time with the changer transitioning both psychologically and behaviorally through several different stages. As they explain it, lasting change only occurs when people successfully progress through the first five stages and reach the final stage. Therefore, people who want to change have to do more than just desire it; they have to recognize what stage of change they're in and understand what steps they need to take in order to transition into the next stage.

Drs. Prochaska, Norcross, and DiClemente describe six stages of change: Precontemplation, Contemplation, Preparation, Action, Maintenance, and Termination. Each of these stages requires a distinct mindset and specific actions to achieve success.

With that model in mind, I have created five short quizzes that will help you assess your readiness for change in your marriage. Note that I have chosen to skip their final stage, termination, because I do not believe it pertains to the topic at hand. There is no end to changing in a marriage. Our relationships are constantly evolving, even far into our senior years. Your answers will help you identify your readiness to change across the five primary stages of the model Prochaska and his coauthors have developed and will help you determine how prepared you are to make the changes you seek in your life or your marriage.

When taking each quiz, keep in mind that change is situational. There are some areas in life where people are more than willing to change, while in other areas they have no interest in changing at all. Therefore I suggest you take the quizzes several times, each time with a different focus. First, answer the questions based on your thoughts about change in general. Then choose a few very specific areas in life—especially areas where your spouse has requested that you change—and take the quizzes with those as your focus. Compare your results and pay attention to where and why your results vary. Often people find that their belief in the value of change and their commitment to it alters considerably when applied to specific items in their life.

This first quiz was designed to help you determine how well you are embracing the need to change. The beginning stage in any successful change process involves understanding that you need to change. Those who resist change or deny the need for it are in the *precontemplation* stage of change and are, typically, a long way from changing. Your results will identify how far through the precontemplation stage you are and whether or not you are ready to enter the next stage of the change process.

Quiz 1: Your Mental Readiness for Change

1. How often have you used a statement similar to the following in an argument with your spouse: "I am who I am, and people don't change"?	Never	Rarely	Sometimes	Often
2. Before reading this book, how important did you think changing yourself was to the success of a marriage?	Very Important	Important, but not that big a deal	Never thought of it before	I thought it was detrimental
3. How often do you and your spouse have arguments regarding your need to change a particular behavior?	Never	Rarely	Sometimes	Often

4. When your spouse asks you to change a behavior, how often do you argue or disagree with him or her?	Never	Rarely	Sometimes	Almost always
5. When you are pressured to change, how often do you continue your attempts to change when the pressure goes away?	Always	Sometimes	Rarely	Never

Scoring. Give yourself 1 point for every answer in the first column, 2 points for every answer in the second column, 3 for the third, and 4 for the fourth. A score between 5 and 10 means that you are amenable to change and that you encourage change in yourself and your relationship. Typically, people who score in this range are ready to enter the next stage successfully. A score between 10 and 14 suggests that you resist change at some times but not at others. People who score in this range are likely to need some further encouragement and/or explanation before entering the next stage. A score of 15 or above usually indicates that you are resistant to change and that you have very little intention of changing. People who score in this range are not ready to change and are highly likely to fail if change is thrust upon them. These people usually need more education, more encouragement, or more insight into the impact of their behaviors.

Unfortunately, many people never progress any farther than this. In a marriage, this can be problematic. Spouses who fail to even embrace the idea of change are usually very far from ever making changes, and that can lead to many years of marital discord. Many spouses directly reject the notion of change and insist that they don't need to do it, even when that insistence leads to divorce. In couples therapy, it is very important to first identify whether spouses are even interested or invested in changing. This is something you should look at very closely in yourself and your spouse. When one spouse is very resistant to change it rarely bodes well for the future of the marriage because all of the remaining stages of change depend upon the person being intellectually aware of the need to change and emotionally invested in achieving it. Spouses who pursue counseling with a partner who has no interest in changing rarely enjoy their marriage and usually end up divorcing after many years of frustration.

Precontemplators need to be convinced of the need to change before any meaningful change is likely to occur. Typically, these people need either couples or individual therapy to help them recognize the value in changing and the detrimental impact of not changing. Those who resist therapy should be encouraged to read books on the subject, should be spoken to firmly but kindly by influential friends and loved ones, or even (in certain situations) should be strongly confronted regarding their behavior. Nevertheless, keep in mind that you can't force someone to change when he or she absolutely doesn't want to change. Spouses who find themselves in these circumstances should reexamine their relationship and begin considering other options, whatever those may be (just putting up with it, taking a break and revisiting things later, or even, for some, divorce).

Quiz 2: Deciding to Change

The second stage in any successful change process is the *contemplation* stage. It involves understanding what changes you need to make and beginning to think seriously about making them. This second quiz was designed to indicate how well you understand the problem, see what causes it, and can identify solutions. Your results will help determine how far through the contemplation stage you have progressed and whether or not you are ready to enter the next stage of the change process.

1. How well does this describe you: "I want to change, but I struggle with accomplishing it"?	Not at all	Somewhat	Close, but not exactly	Right
2. How long have you been contemplating making a specific change in your behavior?	Just started	A few months	A year or longer	Years
3. How often have you made plans to change a specific behavior but were unable to carry through with them?	Never	Once or twice	Several times	Almost every time
4. When you attempt to change, what stops you from accomplishing your goals?	Finding the right moment	Need more information, preparation, or training	Unsure of myself or fear of failing	Just unable to do it
5. When you decide to change, do you focus more on the problem or the solution?	Solution focused	Mostly the solution	Mostly the problem	Problem focused

Scoring. Give yourself 1 point for every answer in the first column, 2 points for every answer in the second column, 3 for the third, and 4 for the fourth. A score between 5 and 10 means that you identify the problem well, focus on workable solutions, and typically act assertively to make the change occur. People who score in this range are usually ready to enter the next stage successfully. A score between 10 and 15 suggests that you likely want to make changes but that you do more thinking about it than acting upon it. People who score in this range need to focus more on creating specific, workable plans for making change. A score above 15 usually indicates that you are likely a chronic contemplator, more interested in ruminating than in actually doing. People who score in this range are more interested in the idea of change than in actually making changes happen. Even though they may often speak of making changes, they are still far from accomplishing them and are not likely to accomplish any serious changes until they devote more time to action and less to intention.

A common error many people make is mistaking the serious contemplation found in this stage for actual or imminent change. Even though contemplating change sounds good, and may actually indicate progress for an individual, it is still only step two of a six-step process, with the harder steps still to come. I apologize for being a downer here, but it is important to recognize this and understand it. Many people become very excited at this stage, believing that their spouse is changing, only to get extremely disappointed later. Contain your enthusiasm until some more tangible changes have occurred, or you may end up bitter, resentful, or angry if your spouse only makes it this far.

Quiz 3: Preparing to Change

The third stage in any successful change process is the *preparation* stage. It involves developing a detailed, specific, and (where appropriate) public plan with a soon-to-occur start date, as well as several backup plans. People who have progressed well in this stage are on the brink of change and are only making final adjustments to their plans. This third quiz is designed to help you determine how serious you are about making the changes you intend to make. Your results in this third quiz will help identify how far through the preparation stage you are and whether or not you are ready to enter the next stage of the change process.

1. Is your plan to change specific and detailed?	Yes	Very close to that	Plan on having one	Not needed
2. Does your plan involve small changes leading to bigger ones, or do you plan for change to happen immediately and completely?	Small to big	Several stages	Quick, but not immediate	Immediate and complete
3. Do you have a specific, detailed plan for when you are going to change?	Yes	I am making one	It's vague, but that's okay	Not needed
4. Have you made your specific plans public?	Yes, to all the appropriate people	Yes, but only to a few of the appropriate people	Yes, but with vague details	No
5. Have you analyzed potential roadblocks and prepared for how to overcome them?	Yes, absolutely. Ready for anything	A few	Will cross that bridge if we get to it	I won't have any problems

Scoring. Give yourself 1 point for every answer in the first column, 2 points for every answer in the second column, 3 for the third, and 4 for the fourth. A score between 5 and 10 means that you have a strong intention to change and that you have developed a well-thought-out plan. People who score in this range usually perform well in the subsequent stages. A score between 10 and 15 suggests that your plans are somewhat vague and your commitment is not as firm as it could be. People who score in this range usually only experience mild to moderate changes in their behaviors. A score above 15 usually indicates that you have not prepared well for the changes you are planning to make and that you still are experiencing some ambivalence. People who score in this range are less likely to reach their goals than others and need to think their plans through more thoroughly if they intend to succeed.

Quiz 4: Taking Action

The fourth stage in any successful change process is the *action* stage. In this stage, people start seriously—and obviously—engaging in new behavior. This stage is a difficult stage to master because it requires the changer to anticipate opportunities to change and to then actively engage in the change over time. Reaching this stage is a noteworthy accomplishment for most people and should be acknowledged accordingly. However, this stage also carries an inherent danger in that it's easy to believe that taking action is the same as actually changing. Taking action and making real change are very different things. Successful change only occurs once the new behavior is maintained over a relatively long period of time and the previous behavior is extinguished. As a rule of thumb, most behavioral changes have to occur consistently for at least six months before one should begin to believe that any significant change has been established. And even then, keep in mind that six months of change is not an indication that it is successfully completed; it's only an indicator that change is progressing well. Your results in this fourth quiz will determine how likely the actions you are taking will result in permanent change.

1. In the past, how often have you carried through with plans to change and maintained those changes over time?	Always	Usually	Sometimes	Rarely
2. When you typically make changes, how obvious are those changes to others? Do others usually recognize the changes you make?	Very obvious	I receive some comments from others	I have to tell them I made changes	People rarely notice, even when I tell them
3. How much do you equate taking action with making real change?	Not at all	Just a start	Almost the same	Action is change
4. When you make changes, do your plans typically involve just behavior changes, or are psychological and attitudinal adjustments also included?	All are seriously considered and all are included	Somewhat included	Just behavioral	Behavioral is all I need
5. How long do you typically continue with your new behaviors despite the energy it requires and the commitment that is involved?	Once I put my mind to something, I never go back	I'm very good at keeping it going, but I'm not perfect	I fail often, but I keep trying	I eventually revert to my old behaviors completely

Scoring. Give yourself 1 point for every answer in the first column, 2 points for every answer in the second column, 3 for the third, and 4 for the fourth. A score between 5 and 10 means that you are most likely a successful changer and that there is a high probability that the actions you are taking will continue over time. People who score in this range are usually effective changers, and they typically have a strong history of making other changes in their lives. A score between 10 and 14 means that, while you are making good strides, you likely need to make a stronger commitment to this particular change both psychologically and behaviorally. People who score in this range can get over the hump and eventually succeed, but they usually need more external support to help them along (these include things such as personal trainers for those who are trying to lose weight, sticky note reminders on the mirror for those who are changing daily habits, daily e-mails from friends and family to help them stay on course for those who need regular reinforcement, and so on). A score of 15 or above means that, although you are engaging in some new behaviors, your likelihood of continued success is low. People who score in this range are usually more invested in the appearance of change than they are in real change. In other words, they're not emotionally and psychologically invested in their changes enough to maintain the new behavior over time.

Quiz 5: Maintaining Change

The fifth stage in any successful change process is the *maintenance* stage. In this stage people can begin to determine whether or not they have truly been successful at making changes. Many of us view making changes now and then in our lives as proof that we've achieved successful change, but that just isn't the case. True change must stand the test of time. That's why one of the biggest hurdles in any change plan is the continuation of the changes and the prevention of relapses through both stressful and nonstressful life situations. Many people make changes in their life that only last until their next stressful event, when they revert to their old behavior. In most cases, that is indicative of an unsuccessful long-term change. Depending upon the change you're trying to make, and the steps you take to remedy things when you do have relapses, the maintenance phase can be very challenging. For some, struggling to maintain a change can last a lifetime. Your results in this fifth quiz will determine how difficult your maintenance of these changes is likely to be.

1. How often do you relapse or miss an opportunity to change?	Never	Rarely	Often	Very often
2. How often do you need reminders to keep yourself on track?	Don't need any	Need very occasional reminders	Daily	Throughout the day
3. How strongly do your old behaviors tug at you psychologically?	Never	Now and then	Often	Constantly
4. How much lack of success does it take to cause you to stop engaging in the new behavior?	I made my mind up; nothing can change that	It takes several failures to affect me	Failures throw me off track often	Once I fail, it's hard for me to continue
5. How long have you consistently been able to engage in your desired changes?	More than six months	Several months	A few weeks	Just started

Scoring. Give yourself 1 point for every answer in the first column, 2 points for every answer in the second column, 3 for the third, and 4 for the fourth. A score between 5 and 10 means that you will probably have little difficulty maintaining this change. People who score in this range are usually able to maintain their changes with few to no relapses. A score between 10 and 14 means that you will likely struggle with maintaining your changes, but that with good support and a willingness to keep trying, you may become successful over time. People who score in this range have moderate success in maintaining their changes. A score of 15 or above means that your chances for successfully maintaining these changes are low. People who score in this range are often struggling on a regular basis with relapses and with the psychological and physical drain of making these changes. People who score in this range should reevaluate the plan, their dedication, and their motivation and seek a more solid basis for making their changes.

WHAT DO I DO WITH MY RESULTS?

Keep in mind that these quizzes are not the ultimate indicator of how well you will do in making changes in your life. They are just guides and are intended more to make you think than to actually generate change (that comes in the next chapter). My main intentions in providing the quizzes are to help you to understand that change is a process that requires more than just a few simple steps and the willingness to give 110 percent, and also to point to some of the places where your change process might break down, despite your good intentions. Too often people get themselves emotionally geared up to make changes, only to fail because they did not thoroughly understand the full span of the change process. You will no longer be that person.

Now that you've taken these quizzes and have learned about the stages of change, here are some very specific steps you and your spouse can use to develop a plan for positive change.

Making Changes, One Step at a Time

Once couples tune in to the benefits of change, many are so eager to get started that they want to plunge right in. Often my clients ask me for scripts to use in various situations. But those who do this are usually only attempting to memorize lines. The problem with this is that when they run into situations or conversations that don't go according to the script (which happens pretty quickly, given the complexity of life), they either get befuddled and say something that backfires or revert to their old patterns. I want to help you develop *your* method of talking and moving toward change, so you'll feel most comfortable implementing it.

The first step in customizing the change process is to adopt effective communication tools and change strategies. That way, you'll always have the tools you need to cope with arguments, assumptions, and hurt feelings. Best of all, these are tools both of you can use. Remember, the goal is *shared change*. No one should feel shortchanged in the change process. If you both can't use the tools, one of you ends up doing all the work. (If you have yard work, gardening, chores, housecleaning, or fix-it projects to do around the house, you know exactly what I mean!)

You can set yourself up for success by using these five steps:

STEP 1: PREPARE YOURSELF FOR CHANGE

If change were as simple as just deciding to buckle down and change, more of us would successfully complete the weight loss and smoking cessation campaigns that consume our lives. But all too often, we don't. That's because most people concentrate on changing how they *act* instead of how they *think*.

As you learned when you took the quizzes earlier in the chapter, change is actually internal; it requires insight and an altering of perspective, not just behaviors. For example, people who firmly and deliberately decide—with no wavering—that they simply no longer are going to be overweight and out of shape enjoy much more long-term weight loss success than those who simply eat less, count calories, and mark milestones on a scale. Their success is a direct result of deciding that they are going to change *themselves,* not their weight. Otherwise the changes seem forced and artificial and become burdensome because they feel imposed from the outside rather than undertaken from the inside, from a place of commitment and strength. That's a recipe for failed change—and who wants to fail?

The same is true for people who want to change themselves in their marriage. Merely memorizing scripts doesn't work, because they're used in a vacuum. The birthplace of nifty, loving things to say to our spouses doesn't lie in the pages of a book; it lies within each of us and it grows from our internal decision to speak and act lovingly and supportively—which may change from situation to situation. When you work from your mindset and not from a script, you can roll with the changes and not get fazed.

So the first step in a change process is to prepare yourself mentally. Below are some ways to set up your mental game. I suggest that both spouses read these steps and discuss them before attempting any specific changes.

- **Remember that change is healthy, good, and needed—even if it's difficult.** When you're in the middle of a heated battle with your spouse, it's easy to come to the conclusion that "change is not really good for me." But it is. Never let yourself believe, no matter how tough things get, that changing for the better is not a good idea.
- **Remember that change makes life exciting and challenging.** It keeps people active and interesting and it will make you a better person. Even if it means things don't

work out as planned for your marriage, you still have to pursue change for yourself.

- **Remember that change is something you can do.** Change is not reserved for the talented, the wealthy, or the lucky. People of all ages and all walks of life change all the time. Don't buy into the belief that you're not capable or that people don't change. In the time it takes to read this sentence, countless people all over the world are making changes in their lives. The only people who don't change are those who stop trying.
- **Remember that problems don't go away by themselves.** If you avoid changing, your marriage will not grow and it will become stagnant and unfulfilling.
- **Remember that change is your personal responsibility.** If either spouse feels that he or she was coerced into changing, it will likely result in some unpleasant encounters along the way. Teenagers are infamous for taking this line of thinking. Typically mom and dad sit down with their teenager and they all agree that a particular behavior exhibited by the adolescent needs to change. Then, once the family actually begins making those changes, the adolescent angrily accuses the parents of forcing them to do the very thing they agreed to do. You're not a teenager anymore. Thank goodness.
- **Remember to keep an open mind as you move through change.** Changing one area of your life can often open you up to exploring other issues beyond the agreed-upon change (like old family matters or long-forgotten hurts). Even if facing painful history is difficult, remember that keeping it bottled up inside is never a good idea. Be prepared to embrace these things if they occur.
- **Remember that small changes can sometimes be big changes—and vice versa.** Both spouses must under-

stand that not all changes are equal, and not all changes have the magnitude you expect. So don't get too invested in drastic changes having dramatic results. Many couples have told me that after making the commitment to change, they engaged in several positive changes almost immediately and at first felt that nothing came of them. However, after a few days, they began to notice other more subtle interactions that were actually more powerful, like less tension in the home, more loving exchanges, greater intimacy, and more laughter. Remember that these systemic improvements in your marriage are the primary goals of change, not immediate *aha!* moments.

STEP 2: PREPARE YOUR ENVIRONMENT (YOUR RELATIONSHIP) FOR CHANGE

Communication and cooperation are essential for a good working relationship as you move into change. Don't assume that you're both on the same page regarding *why* changes are being made, *who* should make those changes, *how* those changes will unfold, *where* they will be made, and *what* the desired outcome should be. Therefore, before beginning any change process, discuss with your partner how you plan to handle inevitable speed bumps. It's best to sit down and go through the following guidelines for change. Make sure you write down your answers to these questions. A helpful worksheet can be found in the appendix.

Create an Open Dialogue

Ask each other what changes you'd like to see. The main rule here is that each person must listen and seriously consider what is presented. Remember that, at this point, you aren't talking yet about how to do it, when to do it, and so on. This is just a general conversation about things each of you would like to see change in your life or marriage, and why. Also keep in mind that this must be done respectfully and realistically, with each spouse being given the opportunity to bring up proposed changes without interruption, criticism, or expressions of disbelief. Some examples of how to propose changes might be: "I would like you to have a better relationship with my parents" or "I would like you to listen to me better when I am talking."

Outline Specifically What Your Desired Changes Would Look Like

Now talk about the precise ways each of you would like your desired changes to be executed. The following list should be of assistance. Make sure you agree on and write down your conclusions. Again, see the appendix for a worksheet to help you through this process.

- Discuss what the desired outcome will look like and how it will it be measured. Measurement is a very important part of any change process, so it is imperative that couples talk about how the execution of the change will be measured. Many couples have difficulty with this because one spouse measures change based upon their intent, whereas the other measures it based upon an outcome. That's why it's so important to spell out specific measurements of success ahead of time. I know that, in my marriage, I often try to score points for my intent when my execution fails. My wife usually finds this to be a cop-out, and usually she's right. Many needless arguments along these lines can be avoided by predetermining if changes will be measured upon intent, outcome, consistency, the overt responses of others, or any number of other criteria. Make sure you discuss each of the possibilities and agree on specific measurement criteria.

- Discuss how the changes will be made. Who will do what?
- When will he or she do it?
- Where will these changes be made? Are these the sorts of things one should see only at home, or will they also be visible with friends, family, or when socializing? This question is designed to make sure each spouse has the same expectations regarding the execution phase of these changes. Sometimes people agree to make changes at home first and then to adopt those changes later outside their home.
- Discuss what is required of the other spouse to assist in this process. Discussing this aspect is very important; otherwise there's a risk that one spouse will come off as the "good" spouse who is trying to make changes and the other as the "bad" spouse who is angrily leaning on the other to make them, which is not supportive or productive. You're both in this together. Make sure you agree on exactly what assistance is needed to avoid relapse into the same old patterns. I suggest that spouses actually say or write down supportive things that they will do or say, such as, "When I recognize you attempting to make changes, I will offer the following assistance . . ." This strategy is usually very effective in getting spouses to support each other in the change process rather than engaging in behaviors that hinder progress.
- Work out troubleshooting procedures. What will you do when someone drops the ball or slacks off? How will you gently remind each other about getting back in gear? What can be done to avoid anger, accusations, and arguments in these conversations? This step involves working out verbal or physical cues to help each other change. Some couples create a code word (or a double shoulder tap) that alerts the other that this is a change moment

or that they are failing to recognize their own behavior. Another thing some couples do is to create a language or scoring system to use when talking with each other about change. Sometimes a scale of one to ten works well. For example, one partner might say something like, "That was pretty good; I'd give it about a five on the scale: you recognized the time was right to change, you tried to do it, but you just fell a little short. Good job; you are making progress." This sort of language allows the couple to acknowledge levels of progress, even when it's incremental, with specific feedback, instead of just saying things like "Nope, you blew it" or "Not there yet," which fail to take advantage of any good teaching moments.

- Discuss what to do next. What are you going to do if, after a reasonable amount of time, things still aren't working out? What if one of the spouses repeatedly fails to make his or her changes? Do you agree to counseling for one or both of you if this occurs? Make sure you determine these steps ahead of time. You will need that road map to keep you on course.

Once you've completed this process, make copies of your written conclusions for each of you. Agree to review them periodically, individually and together—not in the spirit of competition or criticism, but in the spirit of "Hey, how are we doing?" exploration.

STEP 3: DETERMINE IF YOUR CHANGES WILL HAVE SUFFICIENT IMPACT

Take a few minutes to decide if the changes you want to make are attainable, understandable, and effective. Believe it or not, many people go through all of the above steps only to find that the changes they've chosen are ineffective in addressing their core complaint. Some examples:

- Core Issue: Spouse is critical about many different behaviors.
  - Overly vague goal for change: "I promise I'll do better."
  - Overly specific goal for change: "I won't make fun of your cooking anymore."
  - Unrealistic goal for change: "I'll never say anything negative again."
- Core Issue: Spouses don't spend enough time connecting with each other.
  - Overly vague goal for change: "I'll spend more time with you in the evenings."
  - Overly specific goal for change: "Every night I'll ask you about your day, your friends, your mother, and your job."
  - Unrealistic goal for change: "When we come home from work, we'll spend the entire evening together."
- Core Issue: Spouse spends too much money.
  - Overly vague goal for change: "I'll get rid of some of my credit cards."
  - Overly specific goal for change: "I'll stop going out to lunch on Wednesday."
  - Unrealistic goal for change: "I'll never buy anything without checking with you first."

Changes also have to be actual changes: drinking less beer but more wine is not really making a change; changing from overspending at Saks to overspending at Walmart is not really progress;

spending less time at the office is not a real change if you're sitting in front of the computer in the den rather than at the one in the office.

STEP 4: MAKE THE CHANGES

If you're anything like my clients and me, you will fall short at first in making the changes you intend, despite your best preparation. This is normal! Let me repeat: This is normal! It occurs for two reasons.

First, we typically get caught up in what we're doing and don't realize we're in a change moment, so we forget to implement the change. This is where the feedback we agreed upon with our partner comes in. It reminds us of the times and places where we forgot to make the change. When we internalize that correction, we can put it into play in the moment, rather than remember it after the fact.

The second reason people typically fail is that they wait for the opportunity to present itself instead of making change moments happen. Sometimes you have to take active steps to force yourself to execute the plan, rather than passively wait for an occasion to arise. Those who honestly pursue change find many more opportunities to change than those who resist it. Believe me, your proactive efforts will not be lost on your partner. You'll get big points for taking the bull by the horns.

One example of being proactive is to anticipate change moment opportunities with your in-laws, your family, or friends before they happen. Most of the time we are good predictors of how our friends or family are going to act in a given situation. Anticipating events and discussing a strategy beforehand for how to respond is usually more effective than just responding on the fly. Here are some tips to help the process go smoothly:

1. **Practice and have patience.** Our real-time execution can fall short despite our best intentions. Take correction, keep moving, and create opportunities to practice new skills. This is a case where practice can—and does—make perfect.

2. **Realize that there are times when a worst-case scenario can happen.** I would like to tell you that all change produces positive results, but that's not always the case. Unfortunately, there are times when adopting change produces a different result than intended (like when a spouse decides he or she really doesn't want to change and fights the process). Understand that this is always a possibility, but also remember that if you don't make changes, your marriage is likely to be difficult anyway. Most of the time it is better to make your best attempts at changing, even if it takes you down an unpleasant road. Those who don't usually end up bitter, resentful, and disconnected from their spouse, whereas those who continue to pursue change, even when they don't always succeed, usually end up feeling much better about themselves and their marriage than those who gave up.

3. **Remember that all marriages—and all people—are different.** Every couple must determine what matters to them. Often, this has absolutely nothing in common with other couples or other marriages. A woman with six kids typically needs her husband to be someone very different than a woman with no children. But that doesn't mean that all wives with six children have the same needs. Some wives need their husbands to be very involved in the day-to-day upbringing of the children, while others wish their husbands would just get out of the way. Everyone's marriage needs something different, and the people in that

marriage dictate what those things should be. In short, the secret is not being the "right" husband or wife—it's being the right husband or wife, at the right time, in your particular marriage.

4. **Surround yourselves with people who support and encourage change.** There are many negative messages about change. Naysayers are not helpful or welcome. When we surround ourselves with positive people, positive things happen. And when we surround ourselves with negative people, negative things happen. So even if it means distancing yourself from some friends who are bad influences or taking a temporary break from relatives, remember that your ability to change is definitely affected by those around you.

5. **Revisit your commitment.** Sometimes repeated failure despite feedback and patience can be an indication that there's still resistance, perhaps operating under the radar. Use the next step to take a constructive, yet unflinching, look at your commitment.

STEP 5: EVALUATE YOURSELF

Incorporating an effective system of checks and balances is the best way for couples to get a clear sense of their progress. Sometimes people feel they're making great progress, only to find that no one else sees it happening at all. Others find that they're making great progress, yet it's having no impact. That's why this step is vital to understanding how changes are being received and whether any of the goals need tweaking or revising. Evaluating yourselves, either casually or by creating a scale of one to ten, is an essential part of the change process—and one that is often overlooked. The following steps should be agreed upon and followed by each spouse, even if some are uncomfortable or awkward.

1. **Conduct regular check-ins.** Spouses must evaluate both themselves and each other on a regular basis, asking questions like "Is change really occurring—or do I just want to believe it's happening?" and "What specific improvements are happening in our relationship as a result of the changes?"

2. **Solicit external evaluation.** Enlist the support and help of mature, experienced people outside your marriage who are objective and insightful—but make sure your supporters are restricted to your inner circle, such as close friends, parents, counselors, and the like, not people like the poker buddies and the lonely wives club. Couples should agree upon who fits this description and make it a habit to check with these trusted, unbiased others to ask whether they notice changes happening in the couple's marriage. It should be an understood rule that unsolicited input from biased, uninsightful people will be viewed as suspect unless both spouses agree on the validity of the observation or comment.

3. **Keep trying/keep experimenting.** Remember, change doesn't happen overnight, so don't have unrealistic expectations, don't set a rigid timetable, and above all, keep trying. Most people are always working on it.

4. **Reward yourself/your spouse.** Build in rewards for each other. It really helps keep the process positive and makes it easier to stay on track. Have fun making a rewards list and checking off items. Your list might include taking your spouse out to his or her favorite restaurant specifi-

cally to acknowledge and reward him or her for making a particular change or treating yourself to a manicure (or a double latte) specifically because you're making progress on some tough personal changes. Spouses who encourage and reward each other and themselves through verbal and experiential rewards are far more successful at making successful, lasting changes.

One Last Thing

When you began this book, you were already ahead of the game: you wanted to make a positive difference in your relationship. "Difference" is the operative word here, because in order to make a difference, one has to be willing and able to change. While love is powerful and beautiful to behold in a couple, it's the ability to change that enables a couple to mature together through constant attention to synchronized growth, fostering mutual trust, intimacy, and respect. Those couples are the ones who are best able to navigate life's inevitable ups and downs together and to fall in love more and more deeply as the years go by. Love and the ability to change go hand in hand in making a marriage that nourishes and inspires not only the couple, but all who know them.

At this point you've probably learned a lot about yourself and relationships, and I hope you take that knowledge and use it to create a fabulous marriage. There is, however, one last thing I'd like to leave you with as you move on.

When I got married, like most other couples, we vowed to love and cherish each other. I took those vows very seriously, because in many ways, they form the foundation of the relationship, the first step in a long journey together. But as I look back, I think we left out a very important part. That's why, if I could redo my vows, I would make sure I said something I didn't think about at the time, yet it is the single most important part of a successful marriage: the commitment to change.

I would say:

> *I promise to share my life with you for as long as I live.*
>
> *To accomplish that, I promise to change when my marriage needs me to change and to grow when my marriage needs me to grow.*
>
> *I promise to be more than the husband you need me to be today. I promise to be the husband you need me to be today, tomorrow, and in the future.*
>
> *Life is about change, and I promise to change.*

ACKNOWLEDGMENTS

It's been quite an adventure writing this book, and it would not have been possible without the insight, support, and kindness of many people. I would like to formally acknowledge those without whom this book would still be merely an idea.

First, I would like to thank Laney Katz Becker deeply for her initial faith in me as a first-time author, and for her seemingly unlimited insight and wisdom. She always had an answer when I needed one, and, as a literary agent and champion of this book, she was an advocate who always exceeded my expectations. Without her dedication and resolve, there is no way I would have gotten this far.

I also have to acknowledge the wonderful work of Toni Sciarra Poynter. Her unending encouragement and uncanny ability to help me hone my words and fine-tune my thoughts brought my ideas into focus in a way that regularly amazed me. Working with Toni was a pleasure and an experience I truly cherished.

Thanks especially to the wonderful team at Simon & Schuster, which included Amanda Murray and later Trish Todd. Both women showed a real commitment to this project and offered wonderful advice, guidance, and a keen editorial eye.

Special thanks also go to psychologist Dr. Sonya Friedman. Her ardent support for me as both a practitioner and an author has encouraged me to tackle challenges I would have thought were beyond me.

There is also a long list of friends and supporters who offered their time, resources, and encouragement in a variety of ways. Although there isn't space to acknowledge them all, I'd like specifically to thank Nicole and Tim Ryan for their eagerness to help and for their gracious offer of their cabin whenever I needed a place to hide away and write; my in-laws Deane and Barry Safir for their limitless support and encouragement; my father, Jim Craig, for always believing in me; my father-in-law, Ronny Smith, for being a loyal fan; Judy and Larry Pazol for the use of their northern Michigan cottage; Karen Lewis, my longtime assistant, who kept me organized and kept the ship afloat when things got overwhelming; Chris Andrews, for eagerly offering his assistance in any way possible; and, last but not least, my very good friend Scott Schuck, who always finds a way to make me laugh and feel grounded when I need it.

There is also no way this book would have seen the light of day without the tremendous love and support I receive on a daily basis from my mother, Christa Craig. I hope she's beginning to figure out that I am the man I am because of her.

Finally, I thank my wife, Ronna, and our sons, Cameron and Jeremy, for allowing me the time to sequester myself away from them to work on this book. I missed them terribly during those times, and I know they missed me, but they never complained, and they never made me feel like the bad dad I felt I was being. I know that my intense work on this book made my wife feel like a single mom at times, but she never mentioned it, and she was always happy to have me home. It's hard to be away from those you love, but they made it tolerable. I cannot thank them enough for that.

APPENDIX: WORKSHEETS

Change Worksheet

The following pages contain a worksheet designed to help you identify the changes you want to make and create a detailed, written plan for accomplishing them. The worksheet is based upon the change model from *Changing for Good* by James Prochaska, John Norcross, and Carlo DiClemente that I mentioned earlier, and it provides users with guided prompts to assist them in working their way through this model regarding any change they choose to make. A copy is provided (along with a completed sample), but I suggest you photocopy these pages so you'll always have a fresh copy as you develop new goals and changes you want to achieve in your marriage. You can also download a copy of the worksheet from my website, drstevencraig.com.

I suggest that spouses fill out these sheets together. Remember that this is not just a solo exercise; it is designed to create conversation between spouses. So take your time, talk things out, and customize this process for the two of you.

Preparing Yourself for Change

Completed Sample Worksheet

Identify the behavior you want to change and explain specifically what that behavior looks like, when it typically occurs, and what situations bring it about:

When we are out with other couples, I criticize my spouse repeatedly. I get impatient when she gets details wrong, so I jump in and correct her, even when it embarrasses her or derails the conversation.

Section 1—
Thinking About Change

1. Discuss what impact the behavior you want to change has on your marriage, your spouse, yourself, your family, your career, etc. and how your change will affect them:

When I do this, my wife gets angry, feels embarrassed, and we get in a big fight later. She also stops having a good time and sometimes things become very tense between us for the rest of the night. My change will allow us to have a better time out together and keep her from feeling embarrassed.

2. Explain why you want to make this change:

I want to stop embarrassing my wife and I want to be a better husband. I also need to stop doing this because it makes me look bad and it affects some of my other relationships.

3. Describe the change you plan to make (be specific):

I will stop criticizing her and I will let her speak without interruption.

4. Whose idea is it to make this change and why?

She has told me many times that I need to change this behavior, but I have finally decided to really do something about it.

5. Explain why it is your responsibility to make these changes:

I am responsible for what I choose to say—no one else. I can no longer blame her for my choices.

Section 2—
Getting Ready to Change

1. Describe when and where this change will occur (be specific):

I will do this in all of our social interactions and when we are alone discussing things together.

2. Describe what the change will look like (be specific):

She will be able to continue talking without feeling like I am going to interrupt, criticize, or embarrass her.

3. What is your spouse expected to do to aid in this process (be specific)?

She needs to have some patience, as I may struggle. Also, she should let me know when I am doing it by tapping me twice on the shoulder or saying our agreed-upon code phrase "Isn't that what you learned from your uncle Bob?"

4. How will this change be measured (by intent, outcome, reaction of others, lack of reaction by others)?

My wife will feel less tense, our conversations will flow better, we will fight less about my interrupting.

5. Explain how you plan to discuss failed attempts and how you expect to reduce these failures:

I will ask for feedback from my wife and we will discuss why I forgot to do it or didn't recognize I was doing it.

Section 3—
Taking Action

1. Explain the specific date and time when this change will begin (estimate if a specific date and time cannot be determined):

Now, when we are done finishing this sheet, and during our night out this weekend with friends.

2. Who are you going to make aware of this change, and what are you going to tell them?

My spouse and our best friends (Scott and Juliet), whom we spend most of our time with.

3. Explain how this action will translate into change over time:

The more I do this correctly, the less I will feel compelled to do it, and we will have a better time when we're together.

4. Explain the mental, emotional, and attitudinal adjustments you will also be making when executing this change:

I will have to realize that getting the facts and details right is not as important as her feelings. I have to remember that shaming her is not loving, kind, or productive. I have to start putting her feelings above mine.

Section 4—
Keeping the Change Going

1. How long will this change have to occur on a consistent basis until you and your spouse can label it a successful change?

Give me six months and let's talk about my progress along the way.

2. What reminders will you need to keep you from relapsing?

I will need to anticipate events where this can happen and prepare myself, and I will need her to give me signals when I am interrupting and/or correcting, to forgive me when I mess up, and to even pull me aside if I am missing the cues.

3. Explain how you will keep from letting failures stop your progress:

I will not give up. If I am failing, I will try harder, and if I continue to fail I will explore why I can't seem to correct this, even if it means I get some therapy.

Section 5—
Grading Yourself

On a scale from 1 to 10, where 1 indicates a poor performance and 10 indicates an excellent performance, measure your success below (circle one):

1 2 3 4 5 6 7 8 9 10

Preparing Yourself for Change

Worksheet

Identify the behavior you want to change and explain specifically what that behavior looks like, when it typically occurs, and what situations bring it about:

____

____

____

____

____

____

Section 1—
Thinking About Change

1. Discuss what impact the behavior you want to change has on your marriage, your spouse, yourself, your family, your career, etc. and how your change will affect them:

____

____

____

____

____

____

____

2. Explain why you want to make this change:

____

____

____

____

____

3. Describe the change you plan to make (be specific):

____

____

____

____

____

4. Whose idea is it to make this change and why?

____

____

____

5. Explain why it is your responsibility to make these changes:

____

____

____

____

____

Section 2—
Getting Ready to Change

1. Describe when and where this change will occur (be specific):

____

____

____

____

____

____

2. Describe what the change will look like (be specific):

____

____

____

____

____

____

3. What is your spouse expected to do to aid in this process (be specific)?

____

____

____

____

____

4. How will this change be measured (by intent, outcome, reaction of others, lack of reaction by others)?

____

____

____

____

____

5. Explain how you plan to discuss failed attempts and how you expect to reduce these failures:

____

____

____

____

____

Section 3—
Taking Action

1. Explain the specific date and time when this change will begin (estimate if a specific date and time cannot be determined):

____

____

2. Who are you going to make aware of this change, and what are you going to tell them?

3. Explain how this action will translate into change over time:

4. Explain the mental, emotional, and attitudinal adjustments you will also be making when executing this change:

Section 4—
Keeping the Change Going

1. How long will this change have to occur on a consistent basis until you and your spouse can label it a successful change?

2. What reminders will you need to keep you from relapsing?

3. Explain how you will keep from letting failures stop your progress:

Section 5—
Grading Yourself

On a scale from 1 to 10, where 1 indicates a poor performance and 10 indicates an excellent performance, measure your success below (circle one):

1 2 3 4 5 6 7 8 9 10

INDEX